D1025418

# The Gypsy in Me

## From
## Germany to Romania
## in Search of Youth,
## Truth, and Dad

# Ted Simon

Random House    New York

Copyright © 1997 by Ted Simon
Map copyright © 1997 by David Lindroth

All rights reserved under International and Pan-American Copyright
Conventions. Published in the United States by Random House, Inc.,
New York, and simultaneously in Canada by Random House
of Canada Limited, Toronto.

Library of Congress Cataloging-in-Publication Data
Simon, Ted.
The Gypsy in me: from Germany to Romania in search of youth,
truth, and Dad / Ted Simon.
p.   cm.
ISBN 0-679-44138-7
1. Europe, Eastern—Description and travel.   2. Simon, Ted—
Journeys—Europe, Eastern.   I. Title.
DJK19.S56   1997
947—dc21            97-15595

Random House website address: http://www.randomhouse.com/
Printed in the United States of America on acid-free paper
24689753
First Edition

# Acknowledgments

May I first say how grateful I am for the tolerance and goodwill of all those whom I embroiled in my adventure. As usual, the members of my family had a lot to put up with, and my friend Ginny, though she shared some of the journey's rewards, undoubtedly had to suffer much disappointment on my account.

In particular I want to express regret to my friend Manfred that our hopes were not fulfilled this time, and to congratulate him on his marriage and the birth of a lovely daughter.

Profuse thanks, also, to my editor, Enrica Gadler, who has enriched the book immeasurably with her enthusiasm, lucidity, and unstinting energy. Whatever the faults of this book, they appear in spite of her best efforts, and would have been much more numerous without her concern.

I need hardly add how grateful I am to the many who shared their homes and their time with me as I stumbled across Europe. Most of them, I suppose, will never read these words, but perhaps, by virtue of the inscrutable rule that what goes around comes around, they will benefit in some mysterious way.

Finally, I would like to dedicate this book to the memory of the thousands who were killed in the former Yugoslavia as I was struggling helplessly to comprehend the reasons for their fate.

# THE
# *1500-Mile Journey*

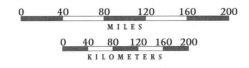

RUSSIA

ingrad
eyo Medovoje
Bagrationovsk

Bartoszyce
Reszel
Święta
Mrągowo
Piecki
Babięta
Szczytno
Chorzele

Przasnysz
Ciechanów

N     D

Warsaw

Przeworsk

Przemyśl

Lvov
Bibrka

Rohatyn

U  K  R  A  I  N  E

Ivano-Frankivs'k
Kolomyia
Yaryemcha

A R P A T H I A N   M O U N T A I N S

B U K O V I N A

Suceava
Ilişişte
Gura
Humorului

Botosani

Iaşi

M O L D O V A

R  O  M  A  N  I  A

Sighişoara

Sibiu

Brăila

Black Sea

N
W        E
S

# The Gypsy in Me

# Chapter 1

*I* sat on a willow bough with my boots off, dangling my legs, letting the breeze cool my suffering feet. Before me lay a village pond ringed with tall green rushes, then a sandy country road, picket fences, and small cottages set back in large and fruitful gardens. On one of the cottage chimneys stood a white stork, absurdly large, pasted against the milky blue sky. It was how I had always imagined Russia to be: the unchanging backdrop to the long drama of czarist rule, Bolshevik revolution, triumph, paranoia, and collapse.

It was my first day alone on a journey I had contemplated for so long, and I was feeling joyfully rewarded. How could it have taken me most of a lifetime to arrive in this land, where half my family originated? My grandmother, for all I knew, might have come from this very village of Medovoje, fifteen miles south of Kaliningrad, the same fifteen miles that I was now feeling in the soles of my feet.

But in her day Kaliningrad was Königsberg, she was Prussian, not Russian, and fifty years ago this most Russian-seeming village was in Germany. Such a wild and unruly fate had blown across Europe, scattering people and cultures like leaves, and yet even the thought of violent change was inconceivable today as the warmth of a summer afternoon wrapped the village in permanence.

There were men fishing in the pond. I had seen them arrive, two younger men in shirtsleeves. They were concealed among the reeds, only the tips of their rods visible, but I could hear fragments of their conversation. I thought if they were to emerge now in embroidered smocks and cloth boots, I would be the anachronism, not they. Soon they were joined by an older, noisier man in a jacket and a flat, peaked cap like the one Lenin used to wear. Their words came a little faster and louder. The word *Demokrati* was spoken, with scorn I thought. The stork had begun to patrol back and forth along the ridge of the rooftop opposite. Then, in a movement that was quite strange to me, it bent its neck backward, far back so that the beak was pointing directly up into the sky, and made a startling series of staccato noises, like slow machine-gun fire. DE-MO-KRA-TI.

Resting against the tree trunk with my shirt open in the humid warmth, I let the murmured words of the anglers drift past me, catching only cadences and inflections as they mingled with birdsong and the fluttering of leaves. It was the threat of rain that made me move. Clouds were massing to the south, darkening with intent, raising ramparts, battlements, and banners in the sky. Reluctantly, I pulled on my boots and rose to walk back to my tent.

The shop at the edge of the village had come to life. Hoping to find something to drink, I entered a large, airy room with a wooden floor and a smell of dried apples. It was like a child's drawing of a shop; you could count the different objects for sale on your fingers. There was a counter at one end. The shelves along the walls were for the most part bare. An aproned woman waited behind the counter, and across from her three older women in headscarves, with shopping bags, stood in attitudes of decisive inaction and regarded me with indifference.

I was spared the problem of making choices in a language I couldn't speak. There was only one choice. Many identical bottles of some kind of orange drink were ranged along a shelf. I pointed at them, mumbled something, and pushed a one-thousand-ruble note across the counter. Studiously impassive, like a mechanical doll set in motion, the shopkeeper passed over a bottle, gave change, and resumed her previous position.

The bottle contained a colored chemical fruit concoction made in Belgium, and I sucked at its synthetic flavors as I went up the hill. Far away to my right a procession of black-and-white holstein dairy cows was winding out onto the scrumptious green meadows from a long, low milking shed. Peace enfolded the landscape, as tangible as the faintly aromatic mist that floated in the air. It was impossible to feel anything but contentment. If I had any concern at all, it was only an automatic nervousness about my tent and belongings until they actually came in sight.

Hours earlier I had been sure they would be safe. A journey is a series of gambles, and after a while you get to be good at it. They are part of what makes traveling worthwhile. The automatic assumptions of ordinary life don't apply, so awareness and intuition take their place. The more risks you can afford, the more freedom and spontaneity you win. Every traveler chooses differently, every choice is a test of fate, and every fortunate outcome strengthens confidence in the next decision. But sometimes, alas, through ignorance one makes choices without even knowing that a choice has been made, as I was soon to find out.

My tent was the lightest I had been able to find. It weighed less than four pounds, and was necessarily small. It was cleverly designed to make the most of the fly sheet—in fact, the fly sheet really *was* the tent. Beneath it was a colorless cellular material sewn to a groundsheet to make a cocoon supported by two flexible hoops. The construction made it self-supporting, and to that feature, possibly, I owe my life.

The tent was about three feet wide and just high enough at the taller end for me to sit up without my hair brushing against the fabric. Soon after I returned to it, the clouds broke open, the storm gathered strength, and the rain beat down hard. I comforted myself with supper and thought it was time to try the fish. Three smoked herrings in a plastic bag had come to me as an unexpected gift the day before in Kaliningrad, and I had them hanging under the fly sheet outside the arch-shaped entrance to the tent. I brought them in and cut fillets from one of the three herrings. The fish was raw-smoked and hard, with a strong, pungent taste like the one I had learned to like as a child in my aunt's fish shop. I washed it down with the chemical brew from Belgium. The storm reached a climax of thunder and cloudbursts. I wondered for a moment whether this was one of those parts of the world where people were often struck by lightning, but it was no more than a passing twitch. Carefully, I wrapped the remaining fish with the stripped skeleton and put the strong-smelling package back outside the zippered entrance. Then I sampled my supply of bread, sausage, and cheese.

It had been raining and blowing furiously for half an hour when I was startled by a loud, resonant voice, very close to the tent, saying something in Russian. I unzipped the two flaps to see a man of middle age and medium height standing directly in front of me. He had a plastic cape over his head. Rainwater gushed over him and splashed off him so that he seemed to be looking out from behind a waterfall. His left hand was clasped around a thick white-painted stick as tall as he was. Two things were immediately clear to me: first, that he must be herding the cows I had seen, although the probable existence of a cowherd had never crossed my mind; and second, that I liked him.

He had a square, open face with well-proportioned features; a man without guile, wearing a quizzical but friendly expression. To set him at ease, I pronounced the words *angelski* and *tourist*. He smiled and said more things I couldn't understand, but they were said in a pleasant, conversational tone. I smiled back reassuringly. Laughing, he raised his hands above his ears, lifting the stick to do so, and pointed his index fingers up to indicate horns. I poked my head out of the tent and saw that we were indeed surrounded by cows. I laughed with him and said, in English of course, that cows would not worry me.

"No problem," I said. *"Nyet problema."* I still didn't get it.

He laughed once more—*"Dobra, dobra"*—and with a slight shrug moved away into the rain. I went back to the remains of my supper, and then occupied myself with my notebook and my feet for an hour, until the skies had finally drained themselves dry. Daylight was still lingering on, and I was eager to stretch my legs for a minute before trying to sleep. Also, the rain had loosened the guys of the fly sheet, and I thought I would tighten them up. I pulled on shoes, unzipped the tent flaps, and emerged into the last rays of the setting sun.

The scene was as lush and peaceful as any I had ever seen. Under a sky still bearing wisps of cloud away to the west, the green hills shone with the most intense color, and the air was like cool wine. The cowherd stood leaning on his staff about a hundred yards from me at the top of a slight rise, looking rather majestic. Around him in small groups were the black-and-white holsteins, surely the most cowlike of cows. I waved to him and began to walk around the tent, stooping to pull on the guy lines. A loud bellowing protest interrupted me. Still serene, I looked up to see what had disturbed these placid creatures. One of the animals in a group between me and the cowherd was facing me with its head raised, and in that same instant it detached itself from the others and began to move my way. Several things registered simultaneously in the following moments. The animal, now clearly outlined against the horizon, was enormous, and was evidently not a cow but a huge bull. It was coming my way, had already accelerated to a trot, and was gathering speed. Its horns were prominent and ugly. Most chilling of all, the bull was making a noise so threatening that it curdled my insides.

Nothing could stop it from reaching me. Obviously, it was bent on my destruction. I had a few seconds to do something or nothing. All around me was open pasture. Flight was impossible. The nearest tree was half a mile off, and I could not hope to outrun the animal. The idea of engaging barehanded in a bullfight was so absurd I didn't even consider it. In a fraction of a second I passed from alarm through fear to sheer terror, and then on the other side of terror I reasoned that since the bull had not objected to the tent before I appeared, I would restore the status quo. If I disappeared, I thought, perhaps the beast would be mollified. Because there was nothing else to do, when the bull was still fifty feet or so away, I dived back into the tent and crouched there, quaking with fright.

It was a desperate gamble. I knew that if it failed, I would be utterly helpless. If the bull attacked the tent, I could not hope to disentangle myself in time even to run. I felt sure I would be killed, or at least terribly gored. There was no way to see out of the tent. All I could do was listen, and what I heard was horrible in the extreme. No living thing has ever made such a terrifying noise in my presence. Not even the trumpeting of elephants came close. More awful than the volume, which became deafening as it approached, was the unmistakable ferocity in the sound.

Then it arrived. I should have been grateful that it did not instantly rip the tent to pieces, but by now I was past feelings or expectations. The bull was right up against the tent. Although I could not see it, I knew it towered over my pitiful refuge. Its head was inches away from mine, separated from me by only the flimsiest of fabrics, and it was howling, literally in my ear. This was anger on an Olympian scale. It was all-enveloping, paralyzing fury. Even in my state of terror, I had room for astonishment. It occurred to me as I waited for my doom that the minotaur itself could not have filled the earth and the heavens with more noise than this creature was making.

It was determined to seek me out. It knew something. Far from being mollified by my disappearance, it was baffled and frustrated. It screamed with rage. It tramped around the tent beating against the cloth with its head but not, thank God, with its horns. I heard one guy rope give way. If it had been a conventional tent on poles, that would have been the end of me. The noise did not diminish one decibel. If anything it got louder. I was as still as a mouse, and as petrified, waiting to be torn to shreds at any moment.

Out of my darkest fears, as the seconds ticked by and the bull inexplicably failed to find me, a faint hope emerged that the cowherd would get to the bull before the bull got to me. Thinking about him as my only hope for salvation, the grotesque humor of my case did not escape me. Viewed through any other eyes, my predicament must have been hilarious. "What the Cowherd Saw" would be as funny a sequence as Charlie Chaplin or Jacques Tati ever made. The innocent ignoramus from the city, with his fancy clothes and equipment, prancing around in front of a jealous bull and diving ignominiously into a tiny tent. What a gas! But laughter was beyond me at that moment. I wanted only to know what the cowherd was doing out there. Was he rushing over to save me, or was he shaking with mirth at the spectacle?

The ordeal may have lasted no more than a minute, but every second felt like my last, and I died sixty deaths waiting to be rescued. Then I heard the cowherd's voice outside the tent. There was a sharp command and what sounded like a stick striking the animal. The horrifying bellowing ceased immediately. I was limp with relief and could not believe my good fortune. My impulse was to scramble out of the tent and embrace the man, but the trauma of those awful moments had left me terrified. I was deeply afraid of showing myself to the bull again. Presumably, if I were standing next to the cowherd, the bull would not attack me. Should I have leaped straight out when I knew he was there? But how was I to know what effect that might have? How would the bull behave if it saw me or heard me again? Was the cowherd really in complete control? I had no idea, and I did not dare put it to the test. The moment passed, and with it my opportunity, because I had no way of knowing who was closer, the man or the bull.

Never have I felt so bereft of speech as I did then. I would have given anything to be able to talk with him. There was the obvious, practical problem that sooner or later I would have to emerge from my ludicrous little lair. Would I have to wait until the herd was gone? That might not be until the morning milking session. Traumatized as I was by this murderous animal's rage, I dared not take the chance of provoking it again. At the same time I could not help imagining the laughter of the cowherd if he had been able to listen in to my thoughts. Overwhelmed by my own ignorance, I longed to learn something more from this experience. What I had already learned was how little I knew about an animal that has fascinated and awed mankind for thousands of years. My story was a parable for our time. A literate, sophisticated, well-traveled (and, I had always believed, intelligent) gentleman finds himself humiliated and terrorized by an animal that any village bumpkin could presumably control. What did this cowherd have that I didn't have? Familiarity—and a stick.

Well, I thought, I had given them plenty to talk about around the fishpond. My story might well enter into the folklore of the village. Perhaps my fame would spread throughout the province and my great-great-grandparents would chuckle in their graves. In the blessed relief of my reprieve I was only too happy to be made a fool of, but I did wish heartily that I could converse with the cowherd. Instead, with the better part of valor, I resigned myself to hiding away until the morning, when I hoped my tormentor would be grazing in some other field.

The day seemed endless. It was nine o'clock, the light was bright as ever, and it was getting cold. I put on everything I could wear and spent some time going through all the scraps of paper I had accumulated along the way—bus and train tickets, restaurant bills, newspaper fragments, and scribbled addresses. Soon I felt drowsy, lay down and thought of sleeping, even though it was still light.

Then the bull returned. With a sudden ear-splitting howl, the bull announced that it was right there outside my tent and ready to finish me off. The shock was stupefying. Oh my God, I thought, the cowherd's attention must have wandered. Will he get over here in time? The animal's rage was unabated. It was behaving as though there had been no interruption at all. The horror mounted, the fearful noise and the thrashing against the tent continued and continued, and I began to realize that this time I was being inexplicably abandoned to my fate.

To be confronted by such a mortal threat twice in so short a time was bad enough. To know that the best and only thing I could do was to remain utterly still made it worse, but to be robbed even of the last resort of resignation was worst of all. With this tornado incarnate whirling furiously around me, drowning my thoughts in tempestuous screams of rage, I reached in vain for the quiet place inside me where I had taken shelter in the past. I had been threatened with death before, but now began the most prolonged and intense period of terror I had ever known, and all my mind could do was to reiterate desperate, ridiculous questions. Why had the bull remembered me? Where was the cowherd? What did the bull know that made it so determined? Could it smell me in there? Did it smell the fish? Did bulls hate fish? When would it rip through the tent? When would its legs tangle in the lines and pull it down?

Now, between the howls, I heard something else just as frightening. It was the sound of huge drafts of hot breath blasting from its nostrils, a sound so violent that it suggested jets of smoke and flame issuing from fiery caverns. For every moment of that interminable ordeal I was aware of the bull's immense size, of its unrestrained fury, of its terrifying proximity, its unpredictability and its lethal stupidity, which, I had to admit, was matched only by my own. I was on all fours, like a sprinter on his marks, waiting for the moment of truth. I had calculated every movement I would make to escape if I was given the slightest chance—which hand would pull which zipper, which foot would propel me through the opening—but I had no real hope of success. The thing went on and on and there seemed to be only one possible end to it.

It may have been ten minutes, it may have been much longer, before the bull relented. While I was crouching there, quivering, it didn't occur to me to look at my watch and fix the time of my extinction. As suddenly as they had started, the howls stopped, and for that I was ineffably grateful, but a new danger presented itself immediately. As soon as the bull had judged the tent to be harmless, the wives came to investigate. Now I was surrounded not by one large animal but many, and their curiosity was extreme. First they licked the rainwater off the fly sheet, driving their heads into it dangerously far. Then they pushed their noses under the tent flaps, convinced that the hidden grass would be more succulent, or possibly intrigued by the fishy odors. Vying with one another for the best position, they began tripping over the lines, skittering away in fright, crowding back again, and I felt just as much in danger of being exposed to the bull as I was before.

And the cowherd? He had either fallen asleep or gone home to dinner or . . . but I could not bring myself to face the possibility that he had been watching the whole thing, unconcerned. Because somewhere in the corner of my mind was the quite unacceptable notion, also born out of my ignorance, that I had been a victim of unreasonable fear—that for reasons I could not imagine, there had never been any danger and that the bull was all sound and fury, signifying nothing. It was only several weeks later—having after all survived to tell the tale—that I learned more about the truth of my situation, and it provided some solace, though it would not have helped me at the time. I discovered that of all bulls, the most jealous, ferocious, and destructive is a dairy bull in the company of its wives in mating season. And by chance, reading an English newspaper in Budapest, I came across a warning issued by the British Ministry of Agriculture. To go anywhere near such a bull without a stick and a dog, it said, is sheer insanity.

# Chapter 2

*H*air-raising as the episode was, my escape from the bull does not, in retrospect, surprise me now as much as it did. At the time I thought myself extremely lucky to have survived. But then I have to ask myself, What about the other times I have emerged unscathed from life-threatening situations? Was it just luck? If so, I should think of myself as one of the luckiest people alive, yet somehow the idea doesn't sit right, other than in the most general sense that applies to all of us who are fortunate enough to have some time on this earth.

I have read or heard about people who died doing things I've done—falling through a roof, being caught in the wrong place at the wrong time in some third world dictatorship, losing my way at night in high mountains, having a throttle stick at a nasty moment on a motorcycle, or even something as silly and mundane as stepping off a curb without looking. The car whistles by six inches from my nose, and I feel the breath of death on my cheek. I step back, shuddering, as I contemplate what almost happened to me. How stupid I was! How lucky to survive! But actually, on reflection, I realize I was misled by a very rare set of circumstances. Certainly stupidity played a part, but I would have been *unlucky* to have died that day.

And so it was with all my other narrow escapes. Perhaps they were not so narrow. Perhaps the odds are on our side.

We hear so much about death and misfortune. As our societies become ever more populous and connected, there are always more harrowing tales to be told and more channels for them to reach us by. Those who don't travel very far from familiar territory must get the impression that ours is a dangerous world, where one is lucky to survive, but that impression is wrong. For every account of a tragedy, there are hundreds, maybe thousands, of untold stories of tragedy averted. My own experience convinces me that on the whole, given a decent attitude, the world will be lenient.

Attitude is important. My friends will probably agree when I say that I am not an especially intrepid type. I mean, I don't go looking for trouble. At school I only once challenged anyone to a fight, and never landed a blow. It just happens that some of the things I have wanted to do—going around the world on a motorcycle, for example—involved some danger. I used to put a tremendous amount of effort into minimizing the risk, until it finally came home to me that most of my efforts were wasted. The problems I anticipated hardly ever materialized, and the dangers, when they came, were usually unpredictable, and sometimes bizarre. For the most part I attribute my survival to having a good attitude—and a prime ingredient of that, in my view, is not being afraid to be afraid.

So I don't seek to confront death, but several times I have known how it feels to survive when I expected to die, and there is no feeling like it. Everything begins at that moment. I would compare it with coming out of a tunnel into a sunlit landscape of unlimited possibility. It is like being born again, although not, I hasten to add, as one of the zealots who claim that distinction.

I try not to tempt fate too flagrantly, but I was pushing my luck with that Russian bull. I think perhaps I should take the episode as a gypsy's warning. Bulls and I go back a long way—right back to my birth on the first of May, which makes me a Taurus and no doubt explains why bulls have figured more frequently in my life than one would expect. On reflection, I see that our encounters have become increasingly threatening.

On the first occasion I was too young to count my blessings. I was seven years old, and during the summer holidays, my mother had lodged me with a farmer outside London to give me a rare whiff of country air. One day I was found alone in a field with a bull, happily seated on top of the animal.

Apparently, I had climbed up there with the help of a small ladder and I was quite annoyed at being rescued.

My second encounter was more traditional. It came thirty years later, when my life in London went into crisis. I said, "To hell with it," and left for Spain with some friends who enjoyed being around bullfights. Hemingway had been dead only four years, it was the time of the fiesta in Pamplona, so we went there first, and after a night spent carousing, I ran in front of the bulls. I was not as deeply immersed in bullfighting lore as my friends, so I can only report what they told me. Normally, they said, it took the bulls about fourteen minutes to get from the station to the bullring. On this occasion, they broke the record and made it in three.

I was running with the mob, thinking I was well ahead of any four-legged animals, when I heard an unusual sound and at the same time glimpsed a horned head coming up behind me to the right. Exactly what I did or what the animal did I cannot say. I know I tried to dodge, was knocked down on the cobblestones, got up, and staggered to one of the many barriers erected to keep the bulls on track. Excited spectators hauled me up and over, and pointed at my suede jacket, which had a ragged rip right across the side under the right armpit.

I was sure I must have sustained a mortal wound and prepared to swoon gracefully to the ground like Nelson on the *Victory*, but there wasn't a scratch on me. The effect of this reprieve was electric and liberating. For the first time in my life I felt blessed independently of my deserving it. I threw caution to the winds (until then an act as inconceivable as the cliché is predictable), forgot the few plans I had made, and simply took every opportunity that came along. For many weeks I wandered around the Mediterranean, intoxicated by the wonderful adventures that arranged themselves for my benefit.

Eventually, with other friends, I found myself in Yugoslavia, where we stumbled on the town of Cetinje, in Bosnia. It had once been the capital of the kingdom of Montenegro, and I was astonished by it. I could not believe that so exotic a culture could exist so close to the heart of Europe: rows of long, low whitewashed stone buildings, women in brilliant costume, savagely handsome men in homespun clothing, donkey carts everywhere—I had never thought to see such sights this side of Yemen or Mongolia.

It was there that I came across a hilarious faux pas, a prank frozen in stone. It was on a relatively grand edifice, three floors high, one of the few that were built in the Western style. Inexplicably, the facade at ground-floor level had been decorated with engravings of pyramids, camels, sphinxes, and various other symbols of Arabia. I went inside to inquire—the building was being used as a cultural center—and I was told that it had once been the French embassy to Montenegro. When it was built, they said, all French embassies were designed by architects in Paris. The Quai d'Orsay had made a mistake and accidentally sent the plans for their embassy in Cairo to Montenegro. I thought the Montenegran stonemasons must have had a great sense of humor to let the mistake go through unremarked.

There was other evidence of this sly tongue-in-cheek behavior. Needing milk and not speaking Serbo-Croat, I walked into a village shop, mimed the milking of a cow, and went "M-o-o-o." After a moment of surprise, light-bulbs lit up, smiles of comprehension spread over peasant faces, a babushka scurried into a back room, and I was presented, triumphantly, with a bottle of mineral water. This has puzzled me ever since.

We saw a fair bit of Yugoslavia, and could have gone anywhere. We saw the treasures of Dubrovnik and a nightmarish industrial town invented by Tito, named Titograd. We also saw Belgrade and Budapest before going back to France and to the rest of my life there, which is not a part of this story. What really amazes me is that having wandered so far into the Balkans, I made no effort to go just a little farther.

Ten years later I was returning through the same region from a four-year journey around the world on a motorcycle, the extravagant culmination, I suppose, of all my earlier adventures, and the one that gave birth to my book *Jupiter's Travels.* Although curiosity had taken me to the edges of four continents, I was still not curious about the other Balkan countries. I came back from India through Istanbul and Macedonia, and went straight as an arrow along the road from Skopje to Belgrade. I remember that two-lane highway very clearly. It was the one from hell. An unbroken stream of impatient German vacationers surged south to Greece in one lane, sometimes only inches away from huge trucks, going north, loaded with merchandise from Iran and Turkey. There were many close shaves, some horrifying collisions, and the wreckage from past accidents was strewn along the edges. I had time, and a little money. I could and should have taken any other route. I could have crossed the mountains to the Adriatic . . . or I could have swung east through Bulgaria and into Romania. Now *that* would have been an intelligent, creative thing to do. I would have stayed clear of that horrendous traffic and added a couple more countries to the forty-five I had already visited, but most promising of all, I could have come to the end of that enormous journey by delving into the enigmas of my father and the country where he was born.

It would have been difficult. I could not have known where to begin. At the time, I knew virtually nothing about my father's background other than that he had been Jewish and Romanian. Even his name, which he changed when he settled in England, was only vaguely known to me. And yet, given the unrelenting curiosity that had kept me on the road for four years exploring so much of the world, why did it not carry me those few extra miles? It was as though I had obliterated all thought of my father and his origins from my mind.

I was tired, of course. I had already done too much. In any event, the thought never occurred to me. I clung to that homicidal Yugoslav highway as though I were on rails, and could think of nothing but getting home. Looking back now at the way I deliberately ignored several opportunities to explore a full half of my heritage, I can't help but conclude that I was strenuously avoiding a painful issue, that some unseen and unsuspected force from my childhood was steering me away from any confrontation with that side of my family. Of course, there *was* a conflict. It was the same conflict that had blown my parents' marriage apart. It appears that I have gone through most of my life determined to make myself invulnerable to the force of that explosion, as though I had pulled on a psychic flak jacket that would shield me from the flying shards of guilt and anger and shame. More recently I have begun to wonder whether that flak jacket was more of a straitjacket, and to ask whether its effect was less to protect me than to imprison me. Meanwhile, much has changed.

Thirty years after I got news of my father's death in 1962, my mother died, very close to the place of her birth, in Hamburg. Touching as the thought might be, it is improbable that my parents were reunited in heaven. My mother, though quite saintly in her way, was not conventional heaven material. She was raised in a God-fearing Lutheran family, under the imperious eye of her Prussian mother, but she rebelled early, became a convinced atheist, and was always fairly contemptuous of religion and people who consoled themselves with prospects of an afterlife. My father, as a Jew, and a Romanian to boot, was presumably destined to occupy a different compartment of heaven anyway.

Nevertheless, my mother's death did, curiously, have the effect of bringing them together in my thoughts. Perhaps with her disappearance some sort of involuntary self-censorship was lifted, allowing new impulses to squirm to the surface of my emotions. For the first time—appallingly late, really—I began to contemplate their life together, to speculate on what had driven them apart, and to wonder just what kind of man my father was and what kind of world he had come from.

In England, where I grew up, we took a rather supercilious view of the Balkans. They were the banana republics of Europe—comic, backward principalities, only suitable as locations for Dracula movies and dumping grounds for surplus goods. When I thought about the population at all, it was a mental roundup of the usual suspects—men of sinister mien throwing round black bombs at absurdly overdressed aristocrats, peasant girls twirling in hand-embroidered dresses, tin-pot dictators rattling sabres. A world of Gypsies, gigolos, and cosmopolitan con artists. I could not have told you which countries bordered on which.

Most of these attitudes lingered on by default as the Balkan countries disappeared behind the Iron Curtain and lost even their picaresque interest. The picture did not change for me until 1989, when Europe underwent its profound transformation. The dramatic collapse of the Communist regimes in the East produced a flood of images, and some of the most lurid and fascinating came out of Romania. I remember all the pictures as if they were taken at night. It was winter, and swirling crowds struggled and demonstrated in the streets of Timişoara and Bucharest. There was the hunting down and killing of the Ceauşescus, then the increasingly awful revelations of what the population had suffered under their perverted rule, the ghastliness of the orphanages, hospitals, and asylums, and the havoc they had wreaked throughout the country.

Dreadful as the picture of Romania was, I recognized it at last as a real country, rescued from the cartoon image of corny legends and third-rate monarchies. And *this* was where my father came from!

Living on the west coast of America, feeling excluded on the sidelines of history, I soaked up all I could see and hear about those tumultuous changes happening from Berlin to the Black Sea, and inevitably they encouraged my thoughts to dwell more and more on my own origins. In the end, the conjunction of these processes, public and private, generated an irresistible desire to make up for lost time and opportunity, to go there, see for myself and discover what I could about that buried half of my life.

I was helped by a stroke of good luck. Several years earlier I had become friendly with a high-ranking police officer who revealed to me, quite by chance, that papers would still exist in the British Home Office archives recording my father's naturalization process. I was able to get copies, and at last learned a few precious details. I found out how he came to England and the name of the town where he was born, in the north of Romania. So I had a natural goal for any journey I might make.

From what I could remember being told, at some time in his youth my father must have decided that being Jewish in Romania was not a promising start to life. He made his way, rather mysteriously via the Sudan, to England, where he attempted to slough off all the last remnants of his childhood faith and origins. He changed his name from Haim Sin Simha to Henry Simon, assimilated a bowler hat, an umbrella, and the *Daily Telegraph*, and went to work in the City of London. In July 1930 he bought a house outside London for eight hundred pounds, and a month later, to drive the message home, he married a stunning blond, blue-eyed Aryan of Prussian extraction—my mother. Exactly nine months after that, I was born.

I deduce that things must have been sticky from the start, because I was born in Germany, my mother having gone home to *her* mother for the confinement. She stayed three months, but came back to London, and for five years my parents tried to live a respectable English suburban life free of all foreign attachments. They couldn't carry it off. In the sixth year, my father left us and became what is now called a deadbeat dad.

In his absence, with the encouragement of my mother, I carried on the mission that he had abandoned. I banished all thought of my racial origins. Soon after the divorce, in 1937, my mother joined the Communist party, and religion followed race into the trash can. This effort by all concerned to define me as a paragon of modern secular citizenship, devoid of race, color, or creed, had some curious consequences, some of them quite comical in retrospect. When I was five years old and my parents were bringing their particular ethnic squabbles to the boil, they sent me back to Germany again. Not knowing why I was traveling, I had an absolutely wonderful time. I crossed the Channel on the S.S. *Deutschland*, a huge transatlantic liner on the last leg of its scheduled voyage from New York to Hamburg. I was taken on board at night by ship's tender, and to my unprejudiced child's eye it looked like a fairy castle and Aladdin's cave rolled into one. The memory has never left me of seeing this vast object, lit up like a department store at Christmas, floating out there on the dark waters. It is the source, I'm sure, of much of my later fascination with travel.

My grandmother and my four aunts, Hanne, Mimi, Emmi, and Marta, lavished affection on me, and I stayed for three months. Since they spoke no English, I learned German very quickly and joined in the general neighborhood fun in the square. I played with my friends in the Hitler Youth, and envied their knives and belts inordinately. I threw my arm out in salute and shouted "Heil Hitler" at every passing soldier. I particularly admired the very glamorous peaked caps of the SS. I watched the stormtroopers hold their torchlight processions in the square at night from our second-floor window and wished I were old enough to be part of it all.

A confusion of thoughts must have passed through the minds of my family. The worst assaults on the Jews in Germany were yet to come, but they had seen plenty already, and the signs were clear. They knew my father was Jewish, but they were not naturally anti-Semitic. The people of Hamburg, living by one of the world's great seaports, prided themselves on their openness to people of all kinds. My aunt Hanne, the oldest, was the one I recall best. She had a shop where I often played, a heavenly place with tanks of live eels and barrels of sauerkraut. Her main line of business was smoked fish, and the aroma so intoxicated and impregnated me that I have been a slave to it ever since.

Aunt Marta, the youngest and most beautiful of them all, was married to a ranking Nazi and simply adored Hitler. There must have been some awkward moments between her and my mother. Divided loyalties may account for the fact that I don't remember her being around much at that time. I think Hanne and the other two must really have believed that the whole Hitler thing would blow over. Not until much later, when Germany lay in ruins around them, could they allow themselves to believe the worst of what had happened, and then only when my mother insisted on rubbing their noses in it.

I was, naturally, in blissful ignorance, and I suppose it gives me yet another occasion for celebrating my good fortune. Like those happy few who arrived at the dock too late to catch the *Titanic*, I am left with a mixture of dread and euphoria at thinking how lucky I was to be there in 1937 and not later, when those dashing black uniforms would have had a different significance.

So I returned safely to London and the rather rigorous existence of an only child with an impoverished, hardworking, politically passionate single mother through the second war to end all wars. My mother did a lot for refugees from Germany, most of whom were Jews (and some of whom were Communists). I was evacuated (the indelicate term for being moved out of harm's way) to the north of England with a school that was almost entirely peopled by the children of refugees. I can remember being taught Hebrew for a while, and have a few memories of Jewish ceremonies, but the Jewish culture made no lasting impression on me.

I was never given any reason to think of myself as even half a Jew, and I didn't qualify for the Jewish faith anyway, since my mother was Aryan. I longed to go home to London and join the war, which seemed terribly exciting to me. When I did, my Jewishness was never mentioned, and my father hardly ever, and I sang Church of England hymns at school along with everyone else.

It is obvious to me now that I was in hiding. I wanted to have straight blond hair, blue eyes, and a square chin and be thought of as a good, solid British chap—with none of that Jewish or Romanian stuff. I didn't understand that a mysterious foreign connection could have been a much bigger hit with the girls, so I squandered my adolescence, as so many do, attempting to be what I was not. Like most of us then, I was infected with anti-Semitism and racial snobbery, but being unaware of it, I was unable to see how ill these prejudices fit me. On a conscious level, of course, I was devoted to the brotherhood of man, and my admiration for artistic and intellectual achievements embraced all races and creeds. In fact I was quite happy to have Jews as my best friends, just so long as they didn't try to get Jewish around me.

All the same, as people age, certain physical characteristics become more dominant than others. My nose was merely cute when I sailed to Germany (I have the passport picture of a sweet, soulful young boy with shadows under his huge dark eyes, indicating that perhaps he did know something was up). The nose must have become more prominent when I was at school in London. An Irish schoolmaster, Mr. Murphy, who himself had a distinguished nose of a more rosy and spudlike variety, came up to me one day and told me my nose was just fine and I shouldn't let anyone tell me other-wise. I was quite astonished by this because nobody ever *had* remarked on my nose before. It took me several years to deduce that he was kindly com-pensating for a prejudice that I had never known or felt.

Indeed, it seems that merely by thinking of myself as having nothing to do with Jews or Jewishness—or rather, by not thinking about the subject at all—I deflected the prejudice that was so common and pervasive even dur-ing the war years in England. How well this strategy worked was proved to me on several occasions. There is no doubt that since Mr. Murphy singled my nose out for praise it has flourished even more, and though I would not call it extravagantly large, I suppose that some people, the sort of people who think about such things, might look at it and wonder whether I was one of the chosen people. Or, to stop pussyfooting around, maybe I do look Jewish. And then again maybe I don't. I have sat across a table with people who, treating me as a kindred spirit, invited me to join them in trashing the Jews. I did not oblige them, but at the same time I did not take their insults personally, either. Without realizing it, I have had a lifelong investment in the idea that *I am not Jewish*. Only since my mother's death have I been will-ing to deal with the subject.

Naturally, this played a big part in my thinking about some kind of ad-venture that would expose me to the realities of a new Europe. Then came the mounting tragedy of Bosnia. Having so newly come to realize that the Balkans were my world, too, the outbreak of civil war in Yugoslavia hit me with particular intensity. Terrible atrocities, unthinkable, monstrous per-versions of human behavior, were being retailed, fresh and dripping like newly slaughtered carcasses, from the killing fields of Bosnia and Croatia. For onlookers like myself, those months in early 1993 when I first conceived my journey were, I think, the worst period of the conflict—worst because it took most of us until then to understand just how gruesome and consistent the tortures and massacres were and how powerless we were to affect them.

At that time it did still seem as though these awful events, and the fear and hatred that provoked them, had arisen spontaneously. Although it was known that the Serb aggressors had the support of figures like Karadzic and Milosevic, it was not clear—at least not to me—that the mayhem had been orchestrated. Nor did I realize how organized and professional were the armies involved. What made it so sickening was the thought that ordinary men and women who had lived peacefully alongside their victims for years should suddenly turn into such vindictive killers. I remembered the people I had met on my trips through Yugoslavia, and the thought of them engaging in these obscene acts was intolerable. I was ashamed that nothing had been done to stop the senseless bloodshed. To the extent that this was a Balkan tragedy, I came to terms, very late in my life, with the fact that this was *my* story—that this other half of me, whom I had harbored but tried to ignore all my life, was actually involved. Even then, I think, I was wondering what an individual like myself could possibly do about it.

Along with the horrors of ethnic cleansing in the East, the wealthier West was suffering a rash of obscene crimes against immigrant workers and Jews. In France there were outbreaks of neo-fascism, with attacks on synagogues and Jewish cemeteries. From Germany came reports that gangs of skinheads were roaming the streets at night, cracking the skulls of dark-skinned foreigners, mostly Turks. There had been a particularly nasty event near Hamburg, in a charming little village called Möln, where young nationalists had set fire to the home of a Turkish woman who had been living there peacefully for thirty years. She, her niece, and her small granddaughter were all burned to death.

From this welter of information I formed the idea of walking through Europe, connecting those two incompatible halves of me—the northern Aryan and the southern Jew. I would start in Prussia and finish up in Romania. And, perhaps, if I deliberately dwelt on the Jewish half of myself instead of avoiding the issue, I might gain some useful insights. I could not help but think that I might be offering myself up as a target along the way, and hoped my lessons would not come at too high a price.

Quite aside from such fancied perils, I wanted to travel in a way that would test me. I am convinced that unless the body is forced to adapt to physical demands, it is too easy for the mind to rest on old assumptions. Walking was the most challenging form of locomotion I could think of, and the one I had never tried. It was difficult at first to reject the idea of doing it by motorcycle. The machine had served me so well before, but I saw that while a bike had made me usefully vulnerable to the natural hazards of huge, undeveloped continents like Africa and South America, here it would have the reverse effect. It would shield me from trouble, and move me too quickly.

I thought the walking itself would be easy. After all, everyone can put one foot in front of the other. I supposed that the true challenge would be mental, keeping focus, controlling impatience, and using the slow rhythm to bring my thoughts down to earth and away from the kinds of easy generalization that seem to flourish with rapid transit.

Having made that decision, I was immediately confronted with another. How much could I really accomplish on foot, even in three months? Without reference to anybody, I decided I ought to be able to walk four miles an hour for at least seven hours a day. Simple arithmetic told me that if I walked six days a week, in three months I could go a staggering two thousand miles. Even in my naive state I thought that unlikely. In any case, I wasn't out to break any records. It wasn't the distance I walked that mattered, it was the time I spent doing it.

I looked at the map and thought maybe I should start in Hamburg, where my mother was born. Then I could cross northern Europe to Königsberg in East Prussia, where *her* mother had come from. This would be all the more interesting because Königsberg was now in Russia, renamed Kaliningrad. Then I would go south to where my father and his father had come from, in the Carpathian mountain province of Bukovina, Romania. Symbolically, it would be like running my father's life backward. Maybe I would get a feeling for what he had left, and why. Then there was always the wild, outside chance that some trace, some scent or fragment of his life, might have survived those seventy-four years since he left his homeland and that I might find it.

All told, the distance was about fifteen hundred miles. Could I walk it all? Why not? I thought. Anyway, I'd be able to walk enough of it to serve my purpose. And there would be local buses and trains if I needed them.

# Chapter 3

*T*he question I did not at first ask was the one people usually have at the top of their lists when they go on journeys.

"Who's going with me?"

I have almost never traveled in company, and usually maintained that taking someone else along was a pretty dumb thing to do. Why? Well, however compatible, resourceful, intelligent, and wise your companion may be, he or she will always speak your language, share something about your background, and have expectations of your behavior. You will always be taking a part of your environment with you. Some people like to travel that way. If they could, they would take with them everything they own, including the kitchen sink and enough water to fill it twice a day. I have seen recreational vehicles surrounded by AstroTurf, picket fences, garden gnomes, and cute little street signs set out on the Mojave Desert or on Mexican beaches, their generators humming with satisfaction, their TV screens flickering through the windows, and it was clear that the owners were getting exactly the experience they wanted. It's not what I want.

My idea of travel is to plunge into foreign lands and cultures with the least amount of support I need to survive. To come with even one other person speaking my own language creates a barrier of sorts between me and strangers. I have always taken this rather for granted, and it appears to me that I came across this way of traveling by accident. That was how I first escaped from a dismal postwar Britain in 1948, when I took my bicycle on a ferry across the English Channel and rode it to the Mediterranean. Now I wonder, for the first time, why I went alone. Did I even consider looking for a friend to go with me? I don't think so. Was that not, at the age of seventeen, unusual? How could I have been so confident, with my schoolboy French and hardly any money, going through a country that had only recently been ravaged by war? At any rate, the journey was a colossal success. I slept in a field infested with vipers (they told me later), and a prison cell (as a visitor), and a ruined château, and a former Gestapo headquarters. And when I first saw the Mediterranean and confirmed that it really was blue, ecstasy took my breath away.

So, except when I was more interested in romance than adventure, I have always traveled alone. Now, all of a sudden, I wondered whether the habit of solitude was somehow a part of this protective wall that I imagined I might have built around myself. Maybe, if there was a pattern or mold to be broken, it would help if I broke with other habits too. My girlfriend, Ginny, was keen to go along and not at all daunted by the prospect. She was a devoted walker, and I had no doubt she could handle it physically. With all my new doubts in mind, my reasons for wanting to travel alone began to seem too precious and restrictive. I made a feeble attempt to cover myself by pointing out the difficulties.

"For one thing," I said, "you're vegetarian, you think pigs are cute, and you're not specially fond of alcohol."

"So what," she replied.

"Because it's well known that once you get east of Berlin, there is nothing to eat but pork and nothing to drink but beer."

She insisted that she could take care of herself perfectly well, and if she had to starve, well she was a lot better at starving than I was, hinting at the extra weight I had acquired recently sitting in front of my computer.

"What about the pollution?" I exclaimed. "You hate pollution. You're convinced that the slightest hint of it will do you in. You read every food label, including the bar code, you never peel your potatoes, and you drink gallons of water. It's well known that all of Eastern Europe swelters in pollution, there are no labels, they always peel their potatoes when they have any, and the water is a stew of heavy metals.

"And just suppose," I went on, pressing the point, rather, "that I wanted to visit a sausage factory in the deepest, dirtiest part of polluted Poland. What would you do?"

"Maybe I'd take off into the Carpathians. I don't know. You needn't worry. You can visit all the sausage factories you want. I'll manage."

At about that same time I mentioned the idea to a friend in Germany, a filmmaker and editor, who also became very enthusiastic, until he heard that there might be three of us.

"My experience of traveling with more than one partner is not very encouraging," he wrote. I knew it was true, but what was the point of always following the safe, predictable pattern? The more I thought of the three of us traveling together, the more I warmed to the idea. Maybe it would loosen things up even more, I thought. Three is not always a crowd. Take the musketeers and the three men in a boat, not to mention the Holy Trinity. We would all have quite different responses to contribute to a common pool. As a painter and musician, and an unashamed believer in emotion above all things, Ginny would be a counterpoise to the rather cerebral and ascetic Manfred, while I would hold the middle ground with my own more sensual enjoyment of the earthy nature of things and people. Of course, I had the advantage of knowing them both, while they did not know each other and would not even meet until the adventure began. Even so, I loved them both and never thought they would not get along. I told Manfred how I felt, and although he sounded naturally a little cautious, he said, "Okay. If you think so, then we will try it."

That was in February. We made a date to meet in Frankfurt at the end of June. I was in the middle of writing a book, the most difficult I had ever attempted, which was causing me all kinds of trouble. It had to be finished before I could leave, and so for the next three months I chained myself to the computer and became a fat, dyspeptic misanthrope with a loud ringing noise in my ears. I arranged to get a visa for Romania and an airline ticket. At my local bank I got a stack of one-dollar bills to use as tips, bribes, and gifts, and another stack of twenties. They were all old, creased, and filthy notes, and the clerk apologized, saying it was all she had. At the time I wasn't too worried, thinking that brand-new notes might look suspiciously like forgeries. As it turned out, the opposite was true. Also, at the last minute, I lost my nerve and bought a bunch of traveler's checks, and that turned out badly too. They have always been a serious nuisance. Every time I have traveled with them, I have regretted it and sworn never to do it again, and then when I am back in America or England, that paranoia peculiar to the affluent West overcomes me again.

Apart from these necessary preparations, I scarcely gave the journey another thought until four days before my plane was due to take off. Then the day arrived when the FedEx lady came and took my finished manuscript away. I felt as though a sack of cement had been removed from my head, and I almost floated off the deck of our little wooden house on the Pacific coast. For my twelve-year-old son, too, it was a time of great relief and opportunity. He had been suffering with me all through this ordeal, and as a reward I granted him one of his dearest wishes. It was a symbolic act of great importance to both of us. I let him cut my hair.

Knowing that I would be traveling through the land of skinheads, I said he could cut it as short as he liked provided he didn't leave me bald. He was very proud of the haircutting gizmo he had been given for Christmas. It had a myriad of strange attachments, and he used them all. He lingered over the job for hours, reveling in his complete authority over bossy old Dad, and it was one of the most peaceful times I have had with him.

At the end of it all, when he had cropped me within a centimeter of my scalp, I looked in the mirror and congratulated him. It was really a very good haircut—or would have been for a lean, tough young quarterback. William had stripped away all pretense. I saw that my overabundant hair had somehow compensated for the overabundance lower down, and I was revealed, rather shockingly, as a pretty funny-looking fellow with nothing on top and too much around the middle. This journey, I said to myself, has come just in the nick of time.

I had a day, before leaving, to think seriously about what I would need to take. I gathered the few things I wanted to carry on my back—sleeping bag, underwear, socks, shirts, a pair of light shoes, maps, and notes, and stuffed everything into a large suitcase. The next day I left my son with his mother and drove my rusty brown Honda down to the San Francisco Bay. Peculiar circumstances dictated that Ginny and I fly on different airlines. My flight took off the day before hers, and because of that, and other commitments, I went to San Francisco two days before she did.

The two most joyful recollections I have from childhood are of going on holiday and being given money to spend as I liked. Nothing has changed. Shopping for a journey is still just about the best fun there is—all the joy of anticipation, without actually having to face the challenges. Of course, this was nothing to compare with planning a motorcycle journey around the world. That pleasure was exquisitely prolonged for several months, but what this lacked in duration it made up in spontaneity. There was something wonderfully extravagant about walking into a store and buying so much exotic gear in such a short time. I had hundreds of dollars to spend and only a day to spend them in, so I went to the most comprehensive store of its kind in the San Francisco area, REI in Berkeley.

My list of necessities was very short indeed. The sleeping bag I already had. Boots, pack, and tent were the essentials, and of these, the boots seemed to demand the most consideration. I had heard dire warnings about boots, and I went for the best. There were three pairs to choose from, and all of them, to my surprise, were much lighter than I had imagined, remembering the nailed boots I had clumped around in when I did my military service. The ones I chose were made in Switzerland by Raichle, and they had long brown laces that fastened through eyes and a series of hooks in the upper part. They were a soft brown color, with no exaggerated features, and I thought they would be the least noticeable, but there was a subliminal reason for choosing them, too. They brought back suddenly a memory of those childhood months in prewar Germany when I had been made to wear similar boots with lace-up hooks, and also, I later recalled with some mirth, long brown stockings suspended from a garter belt. There was a little wooden "hillside" in the store, and you are supposed to stand on it and make sure the ends of your toes don't hit the boot, so I did that and bought the smallest size that fit the description. There was some mention of socks being important too, and Ginny had bought us both some special socks meant for hiking, but I didn't have them with me. I believed that I had left room for them.

If I had been able to find it, I would have taken the same tent I carried around the world fifteen years earlier, a Swedish design in forest-green nylon with telescopic aluminum poles that weighed only four pounds, but it had disappeared among all the junk I had stored in different places, and so, mercifully as it turned out, I chose the even lighter Sierra model. The pack was a lucky find, and might have been made with me in mind. It was an almost invisible grayish color, with two metal bars that slipped through inside pockets to act as a frame, straps that could be hidden away, and a handle on the side that allowed it to be used as an ordinary suitcase.

The boots and the tent cost about the same, the pack was rather less, and it all came to about four hundred dollars. I caught sight of a white cotton vest made in China, with zillions of pockets of all shapes and sizes, some open, some zipped, some concealed. It seemed the perfect thing to use as a walking filing cabinet, and I bought it. Together with a few little items like oil for the boots, a small flashlight, and a water bottle, the bill amounted to about five hundred dollars. I took my booty back to my hotel room near the San Francisco airport, oiled my boots, and played at packing.

Then I picked up *Time of Gifts*, by Patrick Leigh Fermor. In 1933 this upper-class rebel decided to walk across Europe from London to Constantinople. He was not quite nineteen years old. In the thirties, you will recall, there was a marked absence of things we take for granted. Plastic, for one thing. There were no lightweight waterproofs, only heavy oilskin. Windbreakers were made of leather. Tents were canvas. And there were no fancy Vibram soles on your boots. If you wanted them to last, you doubled the leather and stuck hobnails through them. Two of his choices I was already familiar with from my own military service. He took an army greatcoat, a monstrous, heavy, woolen thing weighing about thirty pounds, but good for keeping warm and shedding water for a while. He wore army boots, a leather jacket, and puttees around the bottoms of his corduroy breeches. He stuffed his clothing in a prehistoric canvas rucksack and carried a big stick. The only fairly weight-effective item was a sleeping bag, which he "lost within a month and neither missed nor replaced." My guess is he was carrying about twice the weight I had. And on top of that, he had the effrontery to set off, in northern Europe, in midwinter.

Just reading about it left me ashamed, and wondering how I would have done had I been in his boots. In a few ways, things might have been better for vagabonds in those days. Poverty was more general, so there were recognized sanctuaries for the honest destitute that he could, and did, take advantage of. The poor were everywhere, and not herded into ghettos as they are now, so if you had even the least of means, which Fermor did, there were always cheap meals and lodgings to be found. Things were undoubtedly rough, but he would have been, as it were, in good company. It was the same company I kept in Paris in the early fifties, when the city was still black—by which I mean that the buildings were still covered with soot. You could live in a tiny hotel room for next to nothing, and almost survive on the bread and oil that they put on the table with the knives and forks for a cover charge of thirty centimes. It was still honorable to be poor, and there were enough of us to constitute a sort of mutual aid society.

Another advantage he and I shared was that of being well educated, acceptable in polite society, and therefore welcomed along the way as eccentric entertainment. Europe was still liberally sprinkled with aristocracy. Leigh Fermor was very well connected and could come across as an English milord, so he was guaranteed at least the occasional relief of baths, banquets, and four-poster beds.

But I just don't know if I could have handled the weight, and I don't much care for snow and ice! As for the books he wrote about that journey more than forty years later, they are beyond comparison.

On that same Sunday, as I was learning how to fill my backpack, the U.S. Army in Kuwait sent a barrage of Tomahawk missiles into Baghdad. It was a strange echo of my departure twenty years earlier, when the Yom Kippur War broke out in the Middle East, and although I could hardly be glad to think of terror and destruction raining down on anyone's city, I could not repress a superstitious flicker of optimism thinking that this trip might also be somehow singled out by the fates.

Other echoes resonated from that earlier trip. My long stint at the computer had really left me in awful physical shape, and for two days I had suffered from an unusual and unpleasant headache, as though my brains were sloshing around in my head. On the day I climbed into the plane an even more ridiculous affliction struck. My right foot developed a strange, nerve-racking pain around the ankle so bad I could hardly walk. What a cruel joke. I cheered myself up by recalling how I had suffered from rashes and various other aches and pains before leaving London in 1973 and how they had all dissipated in the excitement of the journey. I was sure that once we got going, the physical effort and its reward would banish all these problems—assuming that I would be able to walk at all. As for the headaches, I discovered that a couple of beers chased them away. Great, I thought, now I'm an alcoholic, too. After a drink I feel better.

My airliner was one of too many monsters rumbling around on the tarmac getting in one another's way, like so many dinosaurs in *Jurassic Park,* which had just then been released. We waited in line endlessly, and I longed to be free of the ground. Freedom felt more and more like just having the space to move in an increasingly gridlocked world. Well, freedom was near. As we rushed forward at last into the wind, I felt it coming.

# Chapter 4

*T*he "peculiar circumstance" that caused Ginny and me to fly separately to Europe was the quite unexpected gift, to me, of a first-class upgrade to Frankfurt. I know a number of people with unusual attributes. One of them rides unicycles. One once achieved the extraordinary feat of being in two places at once, thanks to astral projection. Another writes limericks in Sanskrit. And one has a ticket that allows him to fly first-class anywhere, anytime, on American Airlines, and to take a friend along. He thought it would be fun to take me to Frankfurt, and I flew to Dallas to meet him but, to our mutual distress, something came up and I had to fly on alone.

Even after all these years, after flying the Atlantic so many times, I still feel, deep inside me, that there is base trickery at work. The actual flying is an experience like any other, but to be spirited from one side of the ocean to the other at unnatural speeds encourages delusions, I am sure, and I am always very careful not to take it for granted. The time differences themselves are the least of it. More important is the sense of being ripped out of one culture and dropped naked and unprepared into another. People, I think, do not end at the outer surface of their skin. They carry with them, and around them, an interactive space. It may, for all I know, correspond to the auras that some say they can see. I don't see them, but I can certainly feel the quality of a presence. At any rate, I depend a great deal, in my judgments and actions, on what happens between me and others in that space. My theory is that since this space is shared with whatever emanations the life, the culture, and the sticks and stones around me are producing, it is severely degraded by rapid movement and needs time to be restored. It's a cranky theory, compounded of metaphors for things I don't understand, but there is solid evidence in my own experience to support it, and I am inclined to blame rapid transit for much cultural impoverishment and a certain bleakness of spirit that overemphasizes material things.

Ironically, it was easier to dwell on these matters in the comfort of a first-class cabin. Perhaps because we were at the front of the aircraft and I had a sense of the skin of the thing curving in toward the nose, I felt as though we were in a sumptuous cave, being prepared for some kind of religious experience. Through a grainy twilight I saw an altar in front of me decked out with silver chalices of caviar and buckets of champagne, all softly gleaming under discreet lights, while temple servants attended to our every whim, preparing us for . . . what? Well, sleep, mostly. But there was a waking dreaming period, too, when I did my best to defend my integrity against this deceitful dash across the ocean.

The very notion of traveling is so personal—subjective and unreal. At any given moment the "traveler" is among people—or at any rate among phenomena—that are strange only to him. Take me, here, now. I have never been in a situation like this before, flying at thirty thousand feet in the executive version of Tutankhamen's tomb. It is strange to me, and so are the people. I look around. A huge amount of money has been spent to put them here—five times more than the people in the rest of the plane have paid. If money talks, that ought to make them pretty special. I have a choice. I can sink into this thing, pretend to be one of them, concentrate on our similarities. Hell, I've lunched with presidents and maharajas. I can pull it off if I want to.

Or I can really get into the differences between us. When I think that to someone it is worth four thousand dollars to make each one of these people comfortable for ten hours, I have to wonder what crazy world they live in. I mean, these are not prima donnas resting their throats between La Scala and the Met. How come these people have so much small change? I have to say, casting my eye on them, that they don't look so special, just pampered. But to them this is nothing strange. This is normal. And for me the choice is how far to allow myself to become part of this strangeness, how much familiarity to permit.

There are some people, with the innocence of a Schweik or a Candide, who find all human behavior normal. Since they always feel at home, they can hardly be travelers. Nor can those others, the tourists who feel forever threatened and move in bubbles of comfort and protection from which everything they see is as lifeless and incomprehensible as images on a television screen.

So what distinguishes travelers from the rest? I'm inclined to think they are magic realists in action, for whom travel is a perpetual challenge to their powers of invention. There are some who project such powerful fantasies on the world around them that their account of it would be unrecognizable to any other person following in their footsteps. Some are romantics who, like Don Quixote, see grandeur everywhere; some are curmudgeons like Dr. Johnson, viewing the world with lofty disdain through dung-colored glasses. If I qualify, I suppose I tend more to the Quixotic variety.

And if traveling is a matter of perception and interpretation, then it has as much to do with time as with space. Whatever is about to happen to me on this trip—whether I am crowned king of Romania or have my head cracked by a neo-Nazi boot—will only be truly interesting in the light of my past connections with these instruments of fate. What happened to me during those earlier violent and catastrophic decades of European history, already darkened and curling at the edges, is a necessary part of the story of what is going to happen to me now. I am flying to my past as well as my future. By comparison, losing nine hours is a trifle.

When Manfred and I met at the airport in the morning we both laughed. He had cut most of his long blond hair off, too (although he looked a good deal better than I did without it). Then, in the evening, we met Ginny and went back to Manfred's house in the little Rhineland village of Schornsheim, where he had been born. I couldn't help a twinge of anxiety. Now that we were committed to this journey together, I saw that I had taken a considerable gamble, in a rather high-handed fashion. Suppose that Ginny and Manfred took an instant dislike to each other? Such things happen, and I really hadn't taken account of the possible consequences.

Mercifully, they seemed to tolerate each other well enough, though I noticed that there was no spontaneous outbreak of warmth between them. We talked awhile about our ideas for the journey, wondering just how many contingencies we wanted to prepare for. I had brought a neat little Optimus stove—another round-the-world relic, which weighed only a pound—thinking it would be nice to be able to make tea or even heat food sometimes, but then there would have to be fuel and utensils and provisions, so we gave it up. With just our sleeping bags, the minimum of clothes, two light tents between us, and a few books, maps, and toilet articles, we still could not bring the weight down to less than forty pounds each.

I cheated by putting an extraordinary number of little objects, from Band-Aids to zlotys, in the many pockets of my Chinese vest, where they seemed to weigh nothing at all. The two bundles of small-denomination dollar bills were hidden in the inside front pockets. The big bills and my passport I put in the back, where they were even better concealed. Although I once wore a money belt under my clothes for a year or two, it was more as a tribute to the woman who made it than for the good it did, and I am not inclined now to think it a precaution worth taking. Anyone who has the power to search my other pockets would be able to find that, too. It seems to me better to put my effort into anticipating or disarming such threats before they are carried out.

When we had finished weighing ourselves and our packs, we looked at maps. The special nature of the area we planned to cross began to come clear. We were going to walk through a belt of low-lying country along the southern shore of the Baltic Sea, full of lakes and rivers, stretching from Germany across Poland to Russia. We would begin just below the point where Denmark, jutting out toward Sweden, causes the bottleneck that divides the Baltic Sea from the North Sea. We would finish that leg of the journey at Kaliningrad, where the Baltic shore makes a sharp turn north toward Lithuania, Latvia, and Estonia.

In Germany this area is known as the Landseenplatte, or "Land-lake-table," and so pervasive are the waterways that it was possible, Manfred said, to travel from Hamburg to Berlin by small boat—a pleasant thought that we reluctantly rejected. Even so, there would be opportunities, perhaps, to take short ferry rides, and we would be able to camp beside lakes most of the way. Manfred had a map that showed the trails, for there were many, and we were certainly not the first to think of walking this route. I saw that both Ginny and Manfred took great pleasure at the prospect of being in such lovely country, and it reminded me that my focus was different from theirs. They were excited by the prospect of walking through fields and forests, while I imagined myself more among people, but I was glad that they had a common interest to bring them together. They seemed to be treating each other with undue caution.

It was Manfred's idea that we should start walking from Möln, the scene of that awful tragedy—partly for symbolic reasons, but also because it was more or less where the countryside outside Hamburg began. So it was decided that Ginny and I would go to Hamburg on Friday and stay for a day with my cousin. Manfred would come up later and meet us at the *Hauptbahnhof*, the main railway station, early Sunday morning, and we would take the short train ride to our starting point.

We spent much of the next day in the medieval city of Mainz, and I marveled at the miraculous reconstruction of a city that had been all but destroyed by bombing in the war. Ginny found, in a bookshop, pictures of the roofless, gutted, and crumbling shells of those same buildings we were walking among, and was astounded. I don't think anyone who has not seen European cities in ruins after the war, or at least seen pictures of the destruction, can have any idea of the effort and will that have been put into restoring them. It goes so far beyond what mere buildings could be worth that I am inclined to explain it as an effort to obliterate some memories by resurrecting others and giving history an invisible mend.

Manfred's father, sadly, had been seriously ill in a hospital in Mainz for a long time. On many occasions he had seemed to be on the point of death, and yet had survived. Manfred, preparing for the possibility that the end would come while he was away, spent some time at his bedside. It reminded me that I had my own farewells to make at my mother's grave.

My grandmother—the only grandmother I had known—used to live not in Hamburg itself but in a smaller twin city across the Elbe, called Harburg. She had arrived there as a girl late in the nineteenth century, traveling with her family from the farthest reaches of the Prussian empire, sitting on a wicker basket in the luggage compartment of the train to save money. She grew into a sturdy young woman with good, regular features and a look of great determination, which she displays to effect in the only portrait I have of her from that time, her wedding picture. They lived in a row house, and her husband worked at the Phoenix rubber factory. He had been brought up as a peasant farmer, and had the habit of chewing on a straw. One day the straw pierced his gum and caused an abscess to form, but he could not afford to take time off from work to see a dentist. The abscess poisoned his blood and he died.

She had six young children, five daughters and a son. The municipality gave her a job as caretaker of the school. With the help of her daughters, she cleaned the building every day, did the laundry, lit and stoked the coal fires in the classrooms every morning, and did a thousand and one other small jobs. It was pure drudgery, and my mother resented it. To help out, she and her younger sisters also had the job of delivering a monthly newspaper put out by the evangelical church. They did it on foot throughout Hamburg and Harburg, often in bitter winter weather, when a moment's warmth or a hot drink would have been a godsend. She often told me that the un-Christian way in which the pious subscribers shut her out in the cold gave the first revolutionary impulse to her life.

When my mother's oldest sister, Hanne, was able to work, things got materially better and they moved into a small flat, but my mother now felt tyrannized by both Hanne and her mother, and as soon as she could, she took off for London on one of the many ferries that shuttled between the two cities, to make a new life for herself.

My mother, the Communist (known affectionately in the family as Guschi—for Augusta), and my aunt Marta, the Nazi, might have seemed rather like mirror images of each other. Both were blond, blue-eyed, tall, and slender; both had one son; both were left to manage on their own; and both finally had their belief systems shattered. There were other opposite characteristics, which were still symmetrical. My mother was older, and the rebel of the family. Marta, the youngest, was the conformist. My mother was convinced, by her own bitter experience, that socialism was the only decent objective to aim for and that the Communists were the only people with a credible plan to bring it about. She threw herself wholeheartedly into the movement, and worked with Prussian determination to bring it about sooner. Marta came to her convictions more by osmosis. She fell in love with a man who had joined the Nazis early and reached a respectable rank (if that's the phrase) in the *Schutzstaffel*, or SS. She was swept away by what she saw as a glamorous proximity to power, and for a while they did live the high life in Berlin—a grotesque thought that has always fascinated me. According to my mother, who tried hard to be objective but surely was not, Marta was something of an airhead, whose proudest moment was the night she danced with Heydrich—of all people, it would have to be Heydrich, Himmler's right-hand man and scourge of the Jews. I took my mother's opinions with a grain of salt because, by her own admission, Marta outshone her in the looks department. My aunt may not actually have been the closest the Third Reich ever came to producing a bimbo.

Curiously, on one of my mother's visits to Hamburg in the thirties, Marta's husband confided to her that he had become disgusted with the Nazi movement and would quit if it were possible, but he was by then too highly placed to defect with impunity—and punity, I guess, did not appeal. He later got out of the SS by moving to the Sicherheitsdienst, or SD, a security and intelligence service, and I heard that he was sent to America—North or South, I'm not sure which—to spy for Germany. At the end of the war he escaped from Germany to Peru. My cousin Henning, a war baby, lived there with him for a while, before returning to Germany, and while he knew nothing much of the war and only a little of its aftermath, he seemed to be subdued by the weight of what he did not know, as if some dreadful apparition might at any moment roar up and breathe fire and brimstone in his face.

It was with this most gentle, peaceful person and his very private, meticulous, and loving wife, Erika, that we were going to stay for a day before leaving. And it was with their daughter, Christine, that I crossed the river to plant freesias in the cemetery where my grandmother, my mother, and my aunts were buried, before beginning this odd pilgrimage.

# Chapter 5

*E*arly on Sunday morning Ginny and I have arrived at the station with a rental car to dispose of, because that was the cheapest way to get from Frankfurt to Hamburg. Now I have to drop off the key and the papers, but the rental office is shut, and a note on the door says: "Leave key at luggage counter." Behind the luggage counter is a large male body topped by a huge, flaming red drinker's face, like an angry lighthouse, a bizarre sight before breakfast. He treats me with undisguised hostility, for no apparent reason, and I am taken aback. What is he angry at? The world? His job? Me? Already I am playing with this image of myself as an "undesirable." As a rule I scarcely ever think of my appearance and how it might be interpreted, but I am made aware of it now by the very purpose of my journey. This will take some getting used to.

The man, with his unbridled temper, belongs to another era, to the station as I remember it from almost half a century ago, when I first reentered the smashed-up world of my mother's family. In 1949, on a train that ran for two days and two nights from Ostend to Stockholm, I traveled, again alone, past barbed wire and gun emplacements, through ruined cities, military control posts, and customs sheds piled to the roof with confiscated coffee and cigarettes. The train paused at Cologne, where the station was damaged but functioning. I walked around for fifteen minutes in a bleak dawn. All I could see of the city was bombed, literally, to rubble. The destruction was so conclusive it was eerie, as though someone had gone around afterward making sure that nothing was left intact—except for the incomparable twin spires of the cathedral, which were miraculously untouched and loomed over the devastation with a somewhat ambiguous message.

At early evening the train eased into this same Hamburg *Hauptbahnhof.* In those days of steam locomotives, the high roof of glass and steel vaulted over a grimy world of snorting, howling, hissing, and throbbing machines. The great railway stations were circuses for mechanical monsters with fire in their bellies, celebrated for their incredible feats of strength. I remember the juddering and grinding of their wheels on the track and the deep bass thumping of their hearts as they strained to bring hundreds of tons into motion. The air was rent with the whistles and shouts of the guards and the stuttering clamor of the loudspeakers. The atmosphere had a pungent, masculine odor related to tobacco smoke and the fish in my aunt's shop. Far, far above the platforms, the flying glass canopy captured a chiaroscuro half-world like a scene from Valhalla, of roiling smoke and clouds of steam, shot through by rays of sunlight. Below, at platform level and alongside the upper walkways, buried in smoke-blackened recesses, were ticket counters, bars, barbershops, cafés, kiosks, and the offices of the British occupation army. To my mind, this was a world where extremes of human behavior might be appropriate. Prostitution flourished. Misery and deformity were commonplace. I could see anger, drunkenness, poverty, and violence playing their parts in an extravagant display of the human condition.

Today, although the station's skeleton is the same, its character and meaning are completely changed. Now it is a huge shopping complex with trains attached. The air is clean; the paintwork, bright. Shops flaunt fabrics and materials that would have been ruined in a day by the corrosive fumes of the steam age. The floors are colorful and spotless, delectable food is openly displayed, and this big, angry German with the alcoholic face is out of his period. Whom does he vote for? What does he think of Turks and Jews? In what kind of world does he long to be?

Enough of him. It's breakfast time, and I'm more interested in food. We find Manfred at the ticket office, buy our tickets, and get breakfast. I am overwhelmed by the variety and quality of food laid out for me on the counters of the delicatessen—the hot soups and sausages, the bratwurst, knockwurst, metwurst, leberwurst, and all the other wursts; the cold meats, hams, salamis, and cheeses; the mixtures of egg with chopped vegetables and mayonnaises; the herrings, smoked and pickled and fried; the smoked eel and pieces of fried cod; the fresh, creamy butter; and above all, the wonderfully tasty, crisp, satisfying rolls sprinkled with poppy seeds or sesame, which anybody anywhere ought to be able to bake, and nobody else can.

On the train—clean, airy, and modern—we talk about many things, from local politics to child prostitution in Thailand. A scandal is brewing in Germany. A supposed terrorist was shot dead on a railroad track, and some say that the shooting was expedient rather than necessary. A German politician was recently exposed as a liar, and Manfred is shocked and appalled. I am not. Of course they lie, I say. How can they hope to be elected if they don't? Ginny, no friend to politicians, is with me in this, but Manfred sincerely believes that postwar German politics, until this moment, have been conducted with integrity. He defends his position with less humor than I expect of him, and we change the subject without resolving it. Then, for reasons I cannot remember, we find ourselves in Thailand, arguing about the horrible Thai custom of putting schoolgirls in brothels. Now it is Manfred and I, searching for reasons and connections, who are scoffing at Ginny for her uncompromising stance as anger and contempt flare from her expressive face. We are all a little tense, but with such a big adventure before us, I'm not unduly perturbed. "Two's company, three's Yugoslavia," I joke in my notebook just before we arrive at our destination.

If Möln were in America, it would attract tourists by the millions, but here it is just one of thousands of pretty villages with roots in the past, jealously guarding its rural character with strict rules—some written, but most simply understood. Möln is particularly desirable because it is so close to Hamburg, an easy commute for affluent businessmen. The standard of living here is high. If there were a German Dream, it might look rather like Möln. What makes that particularly interesting is that we are only ten miles from the old Iron Curtain, the defunct border between West and East, between the home of the free and the land of the deprived. As we walk through its tidy streets, the notions of foul prejudice, murder, fire, and burning flesh are inconceivable, yet it was from these same neat, expensive homes that the youngsters came who scandalized Europe with their brutality, and the people here still shake their heads in bewilderment and shame. Needless to say, there is not a skinhead in sight.

Manfred leads us past the last trim front gardens and out of town along forest paths that skirt our first lake, the Pinnsee. We come out of the woods to walk between brilliant yellow fields of flowering rape. The hedgerows are full of diverse plant life and wildflowers, and every now and again we come across neat little enamel signs for hikers—FREDEBURG 5 1/2 KM; BRUNSMARCK 8 KM—with arrows. Ginny is most impressed.

For the first few miles I have felt very fit and capable, and we seem to be making good progress. In the distance now, I see a group of tall, narrow banners, held aloft on poles, with bold red-and-white symbols fluttering in the wind. Obviously they denote a detachment of samurai warriors pausing before the charge. As we draw nearer, the Quixotic vision resolves into mundanity. They turn out to be advertisements for a roadside fruit stand, less romantic but more welcome.

The pack is already beginning to weigh on my shoulders, which are not, I must say, those of an ox. I try to relieve the weight with my hands under the straps, but this is not a long-term solution. Without giving away my concern, I ask Ginny idly how her pack feels, and she tells me some cock-and-bull story she says she got from the salesman when she bought it. He explained to her that when you tighten the strap around your waist, it takes the pressure off your shoulders. This is such obvious nonsense that I snort in disbelief, and tighten my waist belt just to prove her wrong.

Actually, it proves her right. Raising more of the weight onto my hips provides amazing relief, and rather grudgingly, I share my discovery with her. However, it also has the effect of pushing the base of the spine forward, so my whole walking action is changed and I have to kick my legs out in an unfamiliar motion. And now other internal events are occupying my attention. A tickling sensation, as well as a kind of intermittent numbness, is attacking parts of my right leg. After a while I think it is caused by the waistband's being too tight and crimping a nerve, a depressing thought. It is at this point that my physical deterioration begins and, once started, proceeds with alarming speed. At first there are just twinges, then in no time the twinges become pains, then torments. Although the pain I had in my foot when I left San Francisco has gone, a new rheumatic pain has enveloped my ankle a little higher up. My left hip has begun to hurt, and that peculiar headache continues to come and go. In other words, I am a walking illustration of neuralgic disorders. During the course of covering that half mile to the fruit stand, all these discomforts make their presence felt, each one pressing its claim to be first for attention. But even before we arrive, they are displaced by even more demanding messages from the soles of my feet.

A dramatic change has overtaken me during this short distance. When we emerged from the woods I was in fine fettle, seeing myself striding confidently across the continent like Jack in his seven-league boots. I envisaged myself at the end of each day, tired but exultant, losing weight, regaining my youth and elasticity, feeling the staleness of my sedentary life purged by the rejuvenating combination of physical labor and happy mental activity. I imagined this cumbersome baggage on my back becoming like a part of me, a featherweight that I would scarcely be aware of.

Now, as I feel all these different parts of me giving way, each weak link connected to an even weaker one, I wonder whether this whole enterprise was a terrible mistake. How could I have been so confident? Younger men than I had asked me, "How much walking have you done?" and "How are you preparing for this?" and I would laugh and talk about "on-the-job-training," but in my heart I believed my body would rise to the occasion, as it always had in the past. Far from rising it seems to be collapsing, and now the worst news is announced. While I can go on walking somehow with these other aches and pains, the soles of my feet are telling me a different story. Something bad is going on down there. Major pain is on the way.

As these grim thoughts course through my mind, I cannot help being aware of the carefree way Manfred is handling his burden. With a pack at least as heavy as mine, he seems to be dancing. Occasionally he will turn around and skip backward as he talks, or dash out into the field and look at a plant. He has an incredible eye for four-leaf clovers, keeps spotting them on the verge of the path, crouching down and rising up with the annoying ease of an acrobat and handing them out for good luck. An uneasy thought forms in my mind that there is something about Manfred I don't know, and as we talk I realize I must have assumed, with no justification at all, that he was as much of a novice as I am. It is intensely embarrassing to discover that I have never asked him how much walking he has done before. If I had, I would have learned that he has been walking the way some people climb mountains—in fact, he has been walking up mountains quite recently, in the Alps. What we are planning to do is, to him, like an extended Sunday stroll.

In fact, Manfred has brought walking to the point of being in part a religious devotion and in part an instrument of revolution. He talks of a man he has come to admire, named Don Johnson, whom he describes as a "body worker." According to Johnson's credo, "My body is what I use to experience the world and to construct relationships with others. It is on those relationships that larger social structures are based. If I change the way my body behaves, all the rest changes too."

I have to admit to myself that one of my hopes for this journey was that it might, in some way, change how my body behaves. Not because I was dissatisfied with its behavior in any particular way, but because any change at this stage in my life would be an exciting event. I am well aware that fundamental change usually hurts, and I hope the pain I'm experiencing now won't be for nothing. All of this gives me a lot to think about as I totter up to the fruit stand, where they are selling strawberries.

The strawberries, when we eat them, are extraordinarily ripe and sweet, with an intensity of flavor that makes a mockery of the fruit I am used to eating in California. For years I have been boring people with my story of how strawberries were eaten in nineteenth-century England. It is one of the ways in which I discharge my missionary duties in the New World. As a boy long ago I read, in a little magazine called *Lilliput,* that Victorian households had silver platters with depressions in them that could support up to forty different varieties of strawberry. I have no idea whether this was true or a wild exaggeration, but as a city kid in wartime, I hadn't seen a strawberry in years, and the extravagance of the idea stuck in my mind. So I am accustomed to pouring scorn on the miserable choices now available at the supermarket, with their tough, tasteless texture made to last on the shelf.

Despite this, my critical faculties have obviously been corrupted. I have forgotten what a good strawberry is like, and the thrill of it distances me from the discomfort of my feet. But only for a while. The fruit stand, naturally, is beside a road, and from here we have to walk on hard asphalt. The throbbing pain grows until I resent every step I take. It does not help that Ginny seems to be relatively at ease, while Manfred's bouncy nonchalance is a positive affront. After a short time he becomes fed up with following the road and decides to cut across some fields and along a canal, which he thinks will take him to the same destination, but I am hurting too much to take a chance on prolonging the route by even an extra yard. He disappears into the bushes. Ginny cruises far ahead of me, and I plod on, feeling as though my feet are being roasted on a fire.

The sensation brings to mind another piece of bizarre information I learned, from a handbook issued to motorists during the first decade of the century. It concerned the origin of the word *chauffeur*. Apparently thieves, with steam-powered automobiles, drove up to farmhouses in the middle of the night, seized the occupants, and forced them to reveal where they had hidden their gold by holding their feet in the fire. These sadistic villains quickly became known as *les chauffeurs*. Now I am learning the effectiveness of their methods. I would gladly give gold to stop the torment. Is it pure coincidence that our lunchtime destination is the village of Salem?

Even though the village is in sight, I am forced to stop. My feet feel as though something quite terrible and irreversible has happened to them. I cannot bear to keep the boots on a minute longer, and sit down on the shoulder of the road to take them off, frightened of what kind of raw or liquefied horrors I might find when I do. Inside are two very hot, wet things, shapeless and shocking pink, that radiate pain. As I sit there lamenting, Ginny walks back and Manfred bursts into view through a thicket, like Puck. The three of us examine my feet sorrowfully, and then, since there is nothing else to do, I change my socks, put my feet back in their boots, and hobble on as though on glowing coals.

The first building at the entrance to Salem is an inn. Sighs of relief give way to cruel disappointment. It is closed for renovations. A little way down the street is a café. By now I am measuring my ordeal by the number of doors we pass and—oh my God, the café's a dud. It sells no food. Somehow I reach the other end of town (was it really only half a mile?), where there's an expensive establishment ringed with BMWs. They remind me that we are scarcely an hour's drive from Hamburg, and for a moment my faith in this enterprise weakens. As I stagger into the driveway, a 750iL rolls up and discharges another batch of economic miracle-workers, here to take brunch by the lake. I look up, hoping for admiration from those shiny, overfed faces, but see only worried disdain. They wonder whether they've come to the right place.

At a table on the terrace, as far from fastidious noses as possible, I am finally able to pull off my boots and socks. On one foot, the entire heel is a blister. On the other, the heel is the only part that is not a blister. I can imagine a way of walking on the toe of one foot and the heel of the other that reminds me of Dustin Hoffman's Ratso Rizzo character in *Midnight Cowboy*—hardly a practical way to cross Europe. Ginny examines her feet, too, but finds only one blister under a toe. Manfred is disgustingly unscarred. I am clearly the critical case, the broken reed, and I feel seriously depressed, wondering how I can continue like this. Surely it will take weeks for this damage to repair itself. Manfred offers words of sympathy and encouragement.

"Don't worry, Ted," he says. "It will not take so long, and you can walk on blisters. I have done it. But it will be best to pierce the big ones and drain them. Perhaps we should not go any farther today?"

How could he even ask? Ginny fetches an unfamiliar packet from her bag. It's a blister-prevention outfit, another item on which, she says, I previously showered my scorn and derision. It consists of pieces of a colorless jellylike material that is supposed to cushion the skin, but surely it was never intended to deal with massive traumas like mine. The concept strikes me as a pure gimmick—the sort of product a yuppie might buy when planning to ascend a rather low hill, but I am far from the feisty fellow I once was. I'll try anything that will help me keep going, and I promise to give it a go tomorrow. I can see from the carefully neutral expression on Manfred's face that he thinks this is a supreme folly, and probably immoral.

Manfred orders something called *Apfel Schorle*. Big, cold goblets of sparkling mineral water and apple juice materialize at the table, which helps me to see life differently. Delicious food follows. Now that I am sitting down, with the weight off my feet and a soft breeze playing over my pinkies, things seem a lot better. It's my turn to view those BMW people with pity and contempt. What a dull life they lead. If they only knew the challenges, the excitement, the ineffable sense of fulfillment that comes from fearlessly confronting the wild world and, with muscle power alone, forging a path across the Continent, they would shove their limousines into the lake. Why, while they have been pampering their stale bodies in sinful luxury I have hiked a full—how far have we come? Eight miles? Oh, dear!

That, effectively, was the end of the first day of my heroic adventure. I vowed to do better soon. Below the hotel terrace, along the shore of the lake, was the campground where we planned to pitch our tents. With lunch over, we rose from our seats to choose a site. That is, some of us rose. I made the attempt and failed. To my surprise, my body had set solid in a sitting position. It had grown used to sitting, it could see no reason to get up, and it told me so. I tried to take charge, and eventually I found a way to move, with my body permanently bent in a sitting position, remembering of course to keep on the toes of my left foot and the heel of my right. So, looking like an aged Ricky Henderson at bat, I shuffled past the BMW crowd and down the steps to the lake, a grand advertisement for the outdoor life.

As soon as possible, I went into the lake and swam a bit. Gradually, my muscles loosened and straightened out. Ginny helped me perform surgery on my feet, and I experimented with her curious blister kit, but this time my prejudice proved right. My macho blisters were just too damn big for her prissy pads of jelly.

It is, in fact, possible to walk on blisters, as I found out when we left the next morning, but it is not fun. At Manfred's suggestion (I seemed to be singularly short of ideas at this time), I left off the boots and wore my shoes for a change, and it did help somewhat, but I was still what might be called a conservative walker. In other words, I begrudged every step I had to take. Manfred had the map and thought we might be able to follow the lakeshore around to where we were headed, but the path was cut off by a fence and woods, and we had to climb back up the escarpment.

Not understanding his idea, and thinking he had caused me to walk several yards further than necessary, I began to meddle ungraciously with his plan, and insisted on taking us back to the path that he had actually intended to avoid. There was some resentment, and talk about failures of communication. Manfred had assumed, since he had the map and it was his country, that we had tacitly agreed to let him be pathfinder. Ginny, being an independent female artist, was amazed that anybody would dream of leading anyone anywhere without discussing it first. She put this point of view in her usual positive manner, which didn't go down well with Manfred. So my clumsiness served to set them further apart, and my feet hurt too much for me to care.

We were hoping to find a restaurant in Kittlitz, a village five miles away and just this side of the old Iron Curtain. Privately, I was even hoping there might be a bed. As we got closer, the land seemed to get wilder. The fields were more often fallow and carpeted with wildflowers, the hedgerows were overgrown but gorgeous, and birds everywhere sang their hearts out. The significance of this change became clearer when we got to the village. Unlike most villages in western Germany it had no *Gasthaus*, no restaurant or café, not even a shop that we could find, though we were lucky enough to intercept a passing baker's van and buy *brötchen*, and at a farmhouse with a small dairy we found some milk and cheese. The next village, Kneese, was across the old border, only four miles farther on. A telephone repairman passed by in his service van, and we asked him what we might find at Kneese. He had no idea. We got the impression that he had never even been there. Gradually, in conversation, it became clear that life continued as though the Curtain were still up. His service area stopped at the border. Local bus routes didn't cross it. Delivery routes still operated as though they were at the edge of the known world. And so, of course, since there was no through traffic, the village had nothing to offer people going through. Would Kneese be any better? Who could say? All we could do was "follow the yellow brick road" east of the border and see.

The old East-West border, when we came to it, was defined by a stream running in a deep ditch. Some men were working to build a bridge and they were far enough along for us to cross on it. "What a perfect metaphor," Manfred said, and of course it was, but I was struck by the apparent *unimportance* of it, the absence of flags, bells and whistles—there was not even a prosaic sign, like the one at Dachau concentration camp informing visitors that "the ovens are open from 10 to 4."

It was a letdown. In California, you get so used to all that jazz on the roads—the lollipops and roadside banners, and the burly guys and gals in orange vests and hard hats bucketing around on gaily painted equipment. There, road work is a show, a celebration. Here, everything was drab, dour, darkly serious. I had the entirely unjustified thought that they could have been building anything—a bridge, a prison, a cathedral, a gas chamber— with the same uncritical thoroughness.

The thought had more to say about me than about them. Germany can still give me the horrors. The revelations of what had taken place here during the war hit me at a time when my imagination was at its most active and impressionable, at the age of fourteen. The news and the photographs came back from our occupying army shortly before V-E Day. Although everyone, or almost everyone, was shocked and outraged by the pictures of walking skeletons taken at Belsen and Buchenwald, the adults were better prepared for atrocities of some kind. For me it was sudden overkill, and in addition I had to cope with the complication of a personal involvement, a familiarity, and a living connection with the society that had produced these perverse images. I had to build a bridge, in my own mind, between my aunt's fish shop, with its delicious smoky aromas, and that camp at Belsen a few miles down the road which produced the nasty-smelling smoke that nobody had wanted to question.

Strangely enough, all the outpourings of indignation and disgust that filled the air in London in 1945 rather put me off. It seemed to me that the phenomenon was too extreme to be dealt with by words and gestures, and it made me curiously sympathetic to the eccentric behavior of my mathematics teacher at school. In his misguided allegiance to objectivity and truth, remembering the false propaganda of the First World War, he had the notion that the pictures might have been faked. He was a gaunt, gangling man who stood before us one day, sucked in his cheeks, and said: "See, I can look like a Belsen victim. Don't believe everything they tell you."

It was, I suppose, a valuable lesson. I would rather have learned it in a less gruesome context, but perhaps there was something comforting for me in this retreat into rationality. Growing up amid death and destruction, albeit on the winning side, it was hard for me to be immediately and passionately alive to human suffering, and I must have grown somewhat detached from my feelings. From the bus I took to school in the mornings, the 31 bus from Notting Hill Gate to Chelsea, I passed freshly bombed buildings where people had been slaughtered in the night. Coming home one afternoon I saw the ruins of the Lyons tea shop at the top of Earl's Court Road. It had been hit by a rocket, together with its lunchtime crowd. We had to live with these things somehow. There was not much point in shouting about it. Better get on with the geography homework and read up about the latest fighter planes. Eventually, we became known as the silent generation.

In the fifties and sixties I visited Germany often, sang around the Christmas tree with my jolly aunts, who all had fine, melodious voices, made friends with students and joined with them in a summer work camp, ate and drank well, and marveled at the beauty of the Rhine valley on my way to Italy. Gradually, I allowed the meaning of the torture and degradation of millions to expand in my imagination. Whenever I crossed a railroad track, my imagination was haunted by sealed boxcars moving through the night. I had a particular vision I could not dispel, in which I saw the victims in the boxcars rolling to their doom at the same time as I saw the burghers, comfortable in their bedrooms alongside the railway lines, unnaturally close as in a dream, pretending not to hear them go by.

Manfred took pictures of the bridge, and we crossed to the other side. There was no yellow brick road. It was made from slabs of old, gray, pebbly concrete—the same stuff that Hitler's transport minister had used to create the autobahn network, much of it by slave labor. Walking over it, eyes to the ground, I noticed that the slabs were numbered consecutively, with figures crudely drawn by hand into the cement at one corner of each slab. I was reminded of that grotesque Nazi obsession with accountancy and record keeping, and of numbers tattooed on wrists, and I began to wonder whose hand had drawn these numbers. The pain in my feet gave me no respite, the concrete made it worse, and it was hard to turn my mind to more pleasant subjects.

The previous day's miserable trauma had completely altered my attitude. From joyful anticipation I was cast into dread concern. I had made, I realized, a huge investment in this journey. Although my insouciant plan to march fifteen hundred miles was always a dream, I did intend to walk a long way. Now I saw that it might take weeks to bring my feet through to a usable state, and training them to do the job was my top priority. I was quite prepared for the pain and effort that would require, but I feared that too much too soon might ruin them. On that day, at any rate, I felt that nine miles were quite enough, and I longed to find some relief soon.

By the time we came to Kneese, the concrete road was miles behind us but I was still under its spell. It had seemed like a road to the past, and the village fit that vision. It was as though a selective filter had fallen over everything made by man. The grass, trees, flowers, and birds were as brilliant and vital as before, but the structures were dimmed and drained of color, with a greenish tinge, as if a flood of chlorophyl from the exuberant vegetation had seeped into their bricks and plaster. An uncanny quietness lay over the single street as we stood and looked about us. There was a public building of some sort, dating back to prewar days, perhaps a school, perhaps a town hall or community center, but closed and seemingly unused. Beside it was an open area of grass and trees, where house martins swooped about between the eves of the building and the branches of the oaks. The road was lined with careworn houses but empty of people or traffic. We rested for a while on the grass, and as we sprawled under the trees, leaning on our packs, only one Opel car passed. It was clear that in these few miles between Kittlitz and Kneese we had passed into another existence.

Not since childhood had I known such a quiet neighborhood, and in the absence of traffic there might have been a pleasing innocence. I was reminded of Sidewood Road, the suburban street outside London where I lived my first five years, with its horse-drawn dairy carts and Walls' ice cream barrows and a car every ten minutes, maybe. As I remember it, that was a brighter, more hopeful place than this, and tinged with rose rather than mildew, but my mind's eye is, after all, only the eye of a child. I often wish our streets were not choked with traffic, and our lives less burdened with trivial choices, but would I prefer the jaded stagnation I sensed here? Of course it was too soon to judge, but nonetheless it seemed extraordinary that in three years the West's vitality had not managed to reach across those four miles from Kittlitz to Kneese, not even with so little as a coat of paint.

How could such an intangible border remain so potent? Thinking about this crude slash across the face of Europe that had defined the world for me throughout my adult life, I realize how rare it is for countries to lock their people in. Frontiers are meant to keep people out. It is institutions, rather than nations, that like to hold on to their own—prisons and asylums, of course, but also clubs, churches, extended families, professions, any kind of culture. A Communist society is much more an institution than a nation, but then we are probably all in some sense institutionalized, inhibited by borders that were once real but are now maintained only for fear of what lies beyond them. Is it possible to belong to one culture without having some degree of antagonism for others?

Even though Kneese was bigger than Kittlitz, it offered nothing to the traveler at all—not even the smallest grocery shop. Manfred asked a rare passerby whether there might be a private room we could rent, but the response was depressing. We were told that even if such a thing could be found, there would be no food for our dinner, so if we wanted to eat we had better go on to Roggendorf. That was only another three and a half miles, on the main road from Ratzeburg to Gadebusch. There would surely be something there.

The rest had eased my feet slightly and in any case there was no alternative, so I hobbled on, still dragging along behind the others. Manfred began to show signs of impatience and, saying it was easier for him to walk faster, he soon left us behind. We passed between open fields, some fallow, some of grain (*Roggen* is German for "rye"). I began to get used to the discomfort and was able to take my mind off it, encouraged again by a profusion of wildflowers and birds in joyous song. The big bird population struck me as very significant. I thought it a good sign. So much had been said about the abuse of the land with pesticides and other chemicals, yet there seemed to be more birds here than were usually heard in the West.

Through a straggle of houses we arrived in the center of Roggendorf, where our smaller road met the main road. For the first time we saw a little traffic passing through, which made the village seem busier than Kneese, but it was pervaded by the same aqueous tint that again seemed to be leaking from an open grassy area on our right. In the middle of it was a tree, and I saw Manfred sitting under it with two shabby-looking men. They were passing a bottle around among them. Manfred, who was never much of a drinker, had told us in Salem that he had given up alcohol, the better to sharpen his perceptions, so I was rather amused by the spectacle.

"Drunk in the shade again," I yelled. Manfred waved and smiled unconvincingly, and as I came nearer I saw that both his companions were in fact drunk. They were in their thirties or forties, unshaven and run-down, but they did not strike me as habitual drunkards. It was mid-afternoon on a Monday. I had heard that for those who would not, or could not, move to the West there was little work.

Manfred repaid me for my insult with the news that there was nowhere to stay in Roggendorf, either. We would have to go on to Gadebusch, which was another four miles away. I gave up pretending nonchalance. It was no use trying to kid myself any longer. My feet were killing me, and my legs buckled at the thought of it.

"But," he added slowly, "there is a bus."

"Where?" I burst out, as though my life depended on it. "When? Are you sure?"

He pointed to a bus stop about a hundred feet away and said the bus was coming soon, "if it has not already gone."

"Jesus," I exclaimed, and began to jog uncomfortably to the stop. I was not going to miss that bus even if I was the only one to get on it.

"Don't panic," Manfred called out in a chiding voice, only to see the bus come around the corner at that instant, so that we all ended up running to get it.

The bus was shockingly modern, and covered in bright advertising. It swept through the dog-eared dilapidation of Roggendorf like a relief mission from the cathedrals of capitalism. I sank back into a seat and spread my legs, with a huge sense of gratitude for my rescue. After walking on rawness and flaps of skin for twelve and a half miles, I felt I had done my bit. The word *bastinado* kept springing to mind, an unpleasant habit Spaniards had in the seventeenth century of beating people on the soles of their feet. I suppose dwelling on the exquisite pain that I had so narrowly escaped helped me savor my relief.

Gadebusch was a small town with shops. There were a few people in the narrow, cobbled street, and we heard that some way down was a *Gaststätte*, or pub. As we passed along the narrow sidewalk under windows with tiny wrought-iron balconies, Ginny was bemused by what to her were strange metal fixtures attached to the stone walls. I explained that they were intended to support flagpoles, three at a time, and she immediately visualized all the blackened stones bedecked with bloodred Nazi banners and flags, and Adolf himself, arm raised in a trance, moving like a phantom down the street in his open Mercedes.

We ate well at the *Gaststätte*, and the only disturbing note was the growing discordancy between my two companions, emanating mainly from Manfred, who seemed to have become strangely alienated. I began to have serious doubts about the viability of our threesome. He and I exchanged good conversation. She and I got along fine. But when she spoke to him, there was only polite indifference, and I could see no way to break the impasse.

From the barman Manfred obtained a list of people in the area who rented to visitors, and soon we had a room with the Wiener family. They were a couple with two children and two energetic dachshunds, both called Lumpi. The father was a sadly poetic man of small stature and graying locks, who had been a truck driver but was now seriously, if not terminally, ill with cancer in the marrow of his bones. He lay on a narrow bed in a smaller room watching television. A metal plate, connected to a tube, had been inserted in his chest, and through this he received a constant infusion of some kind of medication. Manfred spent some time with him and heard his story.

Herr Wiener first became aware of his sickness a year after the Berlin Wall came down, and it had the effect of anchoring his family in the defeated culture of East Germany. Although we were only one short day's journey from the former border, it was plain that prosperity would not flower spontaneously anytime soon among these drab buildings. In keeping with the victorious ethic of the West, to profit from the change demanded energetic individual initiative, and usually meant crossing over. Many younger "Ossies" were going West, either permanently or for work, but the Wieners were going nowhere.

Yet, even given Herr Wiener's parlous state, they did very clearly have a life. Frau Wiener, a dry blond, seemed to have the energy and good humor to keep things going. They had good food. Until a little while back they had raised pigs, and Wiener, tapping on his metal plate for emphasis, said you could buy nothing in the shops to compare with it for taste. Their home, which they had built themselves, was comfortable. Their large living room was crammed with furniture. Most of it was convertible, with chairs and sofas that could be taken apart or folded out in a bewildering variety of ways. There were two more black-and-white television sets stacked one upon the other, and a number of cabinets stuffed with memorabilia. You could say they lived in style, but a style that was forty years out of date, and again reminded me of England after the war.

In the fifties we had become used to the idea that the war was over and life was getting a bit more comfortable. Many people still lived in a honeycomb of "bed-sitting rooms" that filled the cavernous interiors of Victorian houses and apartments. Their furniture had to be versatile, like the Wieners', but the pressure on space was easing. That was when I got my first flat in London, shared with a friend, on the ground floor of a five-story building in Kensington that had once housed a single middle-class Victorian family and its servants. Most of the debris of war had been swept away. The bombed sites had been cleared and fenced, or tarred as parking lots. The air raid shelters in the streets were dismantled, and the post office pillar boxes were painted red on top again, instead of the sickly yellow paint that was supposed to change color in a gas attack. Things were tidy but drab. Above all, we still lived in the age of coal.

Our houses were heated by coke and coal, with an open grate in almost every room. We cooked on coal gas, factories ran on coal, power stations and trains burned coal, smoke was a permanent presence in our lives, and there were some wintry days when London's notorious "pea-soupers" immersed the city in a greenish, sulfurous fog so thick that I remember being literally unable to see my hand held out in front of my face. Bricks were black; stucco was sooty and stained. Outside, the houses had hardly been touched in over twenty years. But rationing was over, food was getting better, cheap wine was coming over from Algeria, coffeehouses were opening . . .

I don't think any of the families we knew then were in better material circumstances than the Wieners, but they had expectations, or at least they had hopes. Rationing provided us with all the necessities of life and protected us from decadent luxuries, but things had been worse and were getting better. For the Wieners, however, things had been better and looked as if they were getting worse. We got only a glimpse of two teenage children, a boy and a girl, but the mother was friendly and solicitous, and told us something of the sad circumstances in which her family was placed by the collapse of the Eastern regime and her husband's illness. I got the impression that they were satisfied with the medical attention the state was providing, but nothing could dispel the sense of loss and despondency. Only the two Lumpis, charging around the room, were immune to it.

# Chapter 6

*T*o my embarrassment, my feet were now the controlling factor in our expedition. Ten miles a day just would not do. On Tuesday morning in Gadebusch, a foot conference was convened to consider the offending extremities. They were discussed with the solemnity usually accorded to the Balkan question or the doctrine of transubstantiation. First, delegates heard testimony from the owner of the feet. In his opinion, it was the burden on his back that did the most damage (the delegates tactfully avoided discussing the excess weight of the owner, which almost equaled that of the pack). He thought a day of light duties would best promote the rehabilitation of the pedal support mechanisms, and it was resolved that rather than walk the fifteen miles to Schwerin, our next planned stop, we would take the bus, find a place to stay, and walk around the city instead. After that I should walk as much as I could just to get my feet in shape.

Actually, in shoes and without the pack, my feet were not too uncomfortable, and I began to feel some optimism that they might recover and toughen up quite quickly. Meanwhile, we would have to make more short hops on buses and trains, otherwise getting through Germany and Poland would take far too long. It felt like cheating, even though I couldn't figure out who was being robbed.

I spent the half hour on the bus looking for signs of revival in the small communities we passed. Until now, everything seemed to have been neglected for decades. Tiles were missing from roofs, stucco crumbled and fell off facades, weeds had cracked and shifted the paving, gates and fences sagged and bellied out, gardens were unkempt, windows went unrepaired, and paint peeled off the woodwork. For the most part things looked the same from the bus, but now and again we passed a house, a barn, or a shop that had been completely renovated, replastered, brilliantly painted, with a new roof, and maybe a whole shop front remade in the latest Western style. There was no sense of the community as a whole rising up, just isolated examples of gaudy affluence, which seemed to be flaunted in a rather offensive manner. The first symptoms of transformation, perhaps, but such an extreme leap across so many decades that it was disconcerting. I wondered what would become of a society that had to accept such drastic changes after such a long hibernation.

Like most people in the West, I had not sufficiently questioned the idea that the East Germans were all prisoners counting the days to their release, when they would bound out into the open air and become like us. Just one night with the Wieners brought me to my senses. The majority of these people, I knew, would have found ways to live with this system. They would even have found advantages in it that we did not recognize, and would have invented ways to be content with it. People could survive and manage in far more oppressive circumstances, as I knew well from my passages through Latin America and Asia. Already I felt there might be many here who would resent the changes being imposed on them by their rich cousins across the border.

Schwerin was the provincial capital, an old city complete with a castle on a lake, picturesque squares, cobbled streets, and trams. Coming so abruptly from the west coast of America, I saw with fresh eyes the drastic difference age makes to the shape of a city. Beyond the obvious architectural differences, there is the complexity of the street pattern. For centuries peasants and farmers from a multitude of villages in the neighborhood had been bringing goods in and out of town, all making their own way along paths, which had become roads, so that Schwerin now was like the hub of a cartwheel, with roads to Crivitz, Ludwigslust, Hagenow, Grambow, Wittenburg, Lübeck, Wismer, Brüel, and no doubt many other lesser satellites. A crazy cartwheel at that, with crooked spokes that crossed and meshed and separated again, swelling at times to accommodate a market square or a church.

The bus took us to the railroad station, placed on one side of a square, as is customary in Europe. This square was twice the size of a football field, large enough to accommodate the horse-drawn traffic of the nineteenth century and the regiments of troops that were regularly shunted between garrisons and off to one war or another. The square, too, had had a partial face-lift. Facing the station, the old five-story facades, packed side by side with common walls, included an enticing hotel, but at a hundred dollars a night the rooms were priced for "Wessies" and not for ten-dollar-a-night tramps like us.

Although the traffic was thin compared with the suffocating density of cars normal in Western cities, nonetheless there was a good deal of bustling business in the streets. The pastel-colored "Trabis" were still running around like mobile chicken coops, but there were many modern cars, and Wessie money had clearly gained a foothold here. It was in the station foyer, where I was hoping to find lodging information, that this intrusive new culture—mine, that is—hit me hardest. Several magazine racks stood squarely in the middle of the stream of departing passengers, thrusting a very explicit tit-and-pussy show in their faces. It was the incongruity rather than the vulgarity that shocked me. Most of those passing by were conservatively if not downright shoddily dressed people who, judging by their appearance and expressions, were far from adjusting to the wonderful freedoms these magazine covers promised. Having this pulp pulchritude shoved in their faces while they were dealing with matters of laundry and what fish to take home had to be as obscenely irrelevant as offering blow jobs to flood victims.

Peering out from under the inflated breasts of a Miami topless dancer was Prince Andrew's cheery grin as he made the best of his newly announced decision to divorce his duchess, who appeared across the page uncomfortably close to the bushy bifurcation of a self-styled Balinese princess pursuing a modeling career. The effect was more an insult than a titillation. Look, it was saying, this is what's coming. You want freedom? Well, here it is, the right stuff, right up your nose. Out of the long dead and putrefying corpse of Communism (was that the source of the bilious tinge I detected everywhere?) arose this virulent, mocking strain of capitalism. And it is supported by well-meaning people, as misguided as my Communist mother, who believe that capitalism is synonymous with democracy.

Having seen the world from both sides, I know that each social extreme has its well-meaning adherents and that they are always betrayed. Although my mother was a Communist from nineteen thirty-something up to the Hungarian uprising, I know very well what kind of society she had in mind. It was nothing like Stalin's or Honecker's or Mao's, and it was a lot nicer than anything either President Johnson or Reagan dreamed of. Her big mistake was to believe that people could be better than they are.

When the Wall came down, it was sickening to hear the hawks of capitalism screeching about their victory. There was no victory. The enemy collapsed under the weight of its own excrement. Communism, as my mother believed in it, had never existed except as an ideal in the minds of people who, often enough, were purged for it or who, like my mother, never got close enough to the brutal truth.

Churchill is credited with the just observation that democracy is a lousy form of government that just happens to be better than any other. My mother experienced a good deal more of the seamy side of democracy than Churchill ever did, and without the advantage of his lofty perspective, she wrote it off at first. Ironically, through years of very hard work, she did well enough under it and was reconciled to it in the end, but the exploitative nature of capitalism always angered her. That anger lives on in me, and is directed at the corporate minds who feel they have a manifest destiny to ransack the post-Communist globe. They are an expression of democracy at its worst, and I'd like to see them improved out of existence before they do away with all of us.

While I was indulging these subversive thoughts, Manfred had divined that the city had a tourism office on the central square where people with rooms to let were registered, and we found accommodation about ten minutes from the center. We followed Wittenburgerstrasse, where the trams run between tall, dark commercial buildings, to Friedenstrasse, a narrower and calmer street, and from there into Steinstrasse, a quiet, residential street with smaller houses and apartment buildings. The house to which we had been directed had a semi-basement floor, a common form of construction, and the threshold of the front door was well below ground level. We entered a long, musty hallway like a tunnel, from which steps rose up to the first floor. The smell threw me back instantly to the forties with almost physical brusqueness.

Really, I thought, this time travel is *exhausting*. Here I am, a kid again, carrying the copper scuttle down six flights of stairs to fetch the coal. It was the odor of coal dust and mold, and mingled with it were fragments of "Moonlight Becomes You" and the moment that I nearly blew my head off sticking live wires into a beaker of water to investigate the mysteries of electrolysis. The feeling of being in a cellar intensified the connection. Much of our time in London was spent below ground. Sheltering from bomb blasts was the colorful part of it, but more often we were down there for more prosaic reasons. There was the London Underground itself, of course, which is much more of a below-ground experience than any other subway system I know. Beyond that, a good proportion of London's people lived below the surface, in the basements of Victorian houses. Even if one didn't live in one of those converted kitchen-and-scullery warrens—as we didn't—the coal stores for the flats above were down there, little oubliettes, each with its own coal-hole, capped by an ornately molded cast-iron disk set into the paving stones outside, where the coal men, wearing leather hoods and long flaps to protect their necks and backs, tipped the glistening black hundredweight sacks of "Welsh nuts" or "anthracite" off the horse-drawn drays that came from Charrington's coal yards down by the railway line.

All of these assorted motifs—like the municipal horse troughs of granite with brass fittings, the real paving stones, the thickly painted iron railings with fleur-de-lis points—are joined up in a web of poignant episodes peopled by the dead, and I want to tell stories, endlessly, hoping in some way to resurrect them so that I can ask what was *really* going on—what *was* it all about for me, the war, the fear, the deprivation, the unhealthy excitement, the unrealistic hopes and dreams.

These vivid transports to my adolescent past were having a profound effect on me, as though I were being vouchsafed a glimpse of something precious, a tantalizing sense of having it almost within my power to redeem squandered opportunities. Quite what it was I had failed to grasp in those days I could not say. It was like looking for meaning in a dream. Perhaps I was simply reliving the perplexity which engulfed me at that time because I know that at some level—maybe at many levels—I was lost. Superficially, I was blessed with the prerequisites for success—intelligence, motivation, a passionate interest in a marketable discipline (chemistry), and a good work ethic. Yet somehow I was quite unable, in those days, to visualize myself as the "successful" person, with a university degree and a career, that I was supposedly destined to become. Relationships were a mystery, and even my own identity was a secret I could not fathom.

The hole in my personal fabric was most probably the consequence of divorce and separation, and it seemed appropriate that I should be reliving those emotions now in a society that had, in a sense, also suffered through a divorce and was experiencing somewhat the same dislocations.

There were some other, much more practical, connections between then and now. The boy I was revisiting had learned that far away, across the Atlantic Ocean, was a land he knew of from Hollywood. It was a place where heavenly things he could only dream about were a commonplace. Chocolate powder, for example, in tins, that you could eat by the spoonful. An intriguing brown substance that was oily and dry at the same time, called peanut butter. Mysterious stuff called shakes, malteds, and sodas. The sodas, in particular, confused me. We used soda to wash the dishes and to give cooked cabbage a ghastly viridescent color. How anyone could want to drink it was a test of the imagination.

When the profligate Yanks turned up in person, I and my friends became quite sophisticated about nylon stockings, whole cartons of cigarettes (an unheard-of quantity in England at that time), and even liquor in monstrous bottles that could be procured by certain persons from the PX. To get any of these things you had to know an American, from the land of booze and money. At the time, none of us could have explained why Americans had all this stuff, and we didn't. Now I was here in East Germany, with my credit cards and my clever lightweight tent and a grasp of the ways of the West that gave me immense material superiority, and there was no rhyme or reason to that, either.

A very tall, slender, and courtly young man showed us to our rooms. Manfred took a smaller one to himself. Ours was a large, airy room with a bow window and high ceilings plastered and molded in rosettes and chevrons. The furniture, another fold-out bed with wicker chairs and tables, was again incongruously flimsy but quite functional. Ginny, feeling out of sorts and needing rest, went to sleep.

Manfred and I wandered back to town, to a lunch counter I remembered having passed earlier. It was loaded with delicious food that could have put any American fast-food joint out of business in one afternoon, and had some quite wonderful fishy things. The food was only a little cheaper than it had been in the West, but it was certainly as good, and the principal difference to us was its scarcity. In the bigger towns there would obviously be no problem finding whatever we wanted, as long as we were willing to stay near Western prices. For the general population, however, these prices would clearly be punishing, and in the smaller villages there would be little opportunity to pay them.

Manfred had many personal experiences to relate of the effect of the change—*"die Wende,"* as Germans call it—on the two populations. He was very concerned with the way reunification had diverted Germans from what he thought were the essential moral and political problems of the West. Like me, he was skeptical of the claims that everything Eastern had been bad and everything Western good, and I knew already that many younger Germans were afraid that a greater Germany would be drawn irresistibly into playing for power again.

From a traveler's point of view, the great advantage in the East was the cheap lodging, and as long as employment and the economy remained depressed, that would no doubt continue. Our host on Steinstrasse was a teacher—the young man we had met was his son, a student of aeronautics—and his salary was tied to a hopelessly inadequate scale for the changing times. They, the Wieners, and millions of others like them with fixed salaries and pensions would depend heavily on extra income from travelers like us. If I hadn't already discounted all these bargains ahead of time— simply in order to be able to afford the whole three-month trip for two people—it would have been fine. But actually, we were still spending more than I could afford to spend on an average day.

"Don't worry," said Manfred. "When you get to Poland it will all be much cheaper."

I wasn't paying attention at the time, but he didn't say "we."

Bearing a few morsels for Ginny, we returned to Steinstrasse, and later Ginny and I went out again together to look at the castle. Manfred excused himself politely, saying he wanted to get his notes up-to-date. The June weather had turned blustery. It was not so much unpleasant as inconvenient, and viewing the castle in this way from across the lake, dodging occasional showers and feeling the bite of chill wind, was preferable to seeing it as a picture postcard under a clear blue sky. In truth, it would have made a poor postcard anyway. It had obviously been tampered with a great deal in recent centuries. Ungainly Victorian additions were stuck on the back of it, and the facade was being worked on. The rain slanting across the high stone walls under an unsettled sky restored some of its dignity and lent it at least a touch of the threatening aspect that gives old castles their authenticity.

We had noticed in passing that a concert was being presented in the castle that evening, and after Ginny had spent enough time admiring the ducks on the lake, we went back to investigate. In our rough hiking gear we were hardly dressed for a sophisticated affair, but a rather unctuous woman, looking like an inverted tulip in her chic white gown, rushed across as though we were the Rothschilds and beamed us over to the ticket table. The program—part of a "youth in music" promotion—was conventional but ambitious and very satisfying, consisting of Brahms, Beethoven, Hindemith, Popper, and Fauré, performed by two young women on cello and piano. I was concerned for them at first. The massive proportions of the castle entrance, the echoing halls leading off in all directions, the grand staircase, and finally the pomposity of the throne room, where the concert was to take place, might have been overwhelming. We entered through massive carved doors to sit on rows of plush chairs. All four walls around us displayed dozens of heavily gilded and encrusted baronial arms, most of which emphasized the importance of hunting. At one point I had to stifle my laughter, when it occurred to me to compare these posh quarters with the diner of the hotel in my Western ranching valley, where all four walls are similarly hung with cedar shingles bearing the brands of the Diamond H, the Bar B, and every other local cattle operation. How I wished that Keith Hurt, John Rohrbough, Elmer Bauer, and the other ranchers could, just for a day, be made to change places with the Junker barons of Schwerin and swap their baseball hats for plumed *Pickelhaube* helmets, monocles, frogged, brocaded, starched, and bemedaled uniforms, and polished thigh-high boots!

I need not have worried for the musicians. They rose to the occasion and acquitted themselves extremely well. Ginny, being a violinist, remarked that the cellist, Veronika Wilhelm, seemed to be held back somewhat by an inadequate instrument. The pianist, Sibylle Penkert, had the advantage of playing on a Steinway. Their beautiful music stayed with us on the walk back through the town as we searched for a congenial place to eat supper.

The deserted streets, black and glistening after rain, soaked away the light from the street lamps. We could find nothing open. Finally, before turning up Wittenburgerstrasse from the tram terminus, we glimpsed a tavern farther along Lübeckstrasse and, leaving the bleak darkness outside, found ourselves settled in a bright corner among a crowd of workers sitting at tables and drinking around a bar. It has always seemed to me that civilization at its best is expressed by an easy acceptance of foreigners, however odd their appearance and speech, and in that sense these ordinary people of Schwerin scored very high. It was late, but the hosts prepared food for us gladly. We were clearly strangers, yet nobody paid more than ordinary attention to us, and still we both felt warmly included.

I made a note of this later because of what followed when we left. As we moved along the pavement on one side of the dark street, a group came toward us on the other side. They and we were the only people in sight. I paid no attention until they were fairly close, and then, diverted by the loud and harsh quality of the sounds they were making, I looked over. At that same moment some particularly strident guffaws came our way. I saw pallid faces turned toward us and a number of closely shaved male heads shining in the lamplight. A jolt of fright shot through me.

"Don't look at them," I said, and pretending not to notice them, we walked on, heads turned to each other.

"Skinheads," said Ginny nervously, probably infected by my fear. Almost immediately, I heard girls' laughter coming from the group as they passed by and felt ashamed and angry with myself, but there was no undoing that first, unbidden response. I saw that I had thought my way only too well into the part of the pariah, and yet only a few moments before I had felt so differently. I worried for my future, since experience has taught me that it is not only dogs that are excited by the scent of fear.

# Chapter 7

*A*fter an extravagant breakfast, included in the thirteen dollars we each paid for our rooms, we took a tram to Zippendorf and started walking again. I was back in my boots and feeling a lot better, although I was a long way from being able to forget what my feet were doing. We passed through a beech forest full of enchantment. Tall, slender, effeminate trunks dressed in a smooth, powdery green rose up like columns to support the canopy above. The floor was inches deep in the chocolate-colored shells of beechnuts, soft and silent underfoot, and the absence of undergrowth lent the forest an unusual spaciousness, like a mansion of many rooms. It was not difficult to imagine it, by moonlight maybe, draped in silver and gold, the underground forest where the soldier with the tinderbox followed the princesses on their nocturnal escapades. It reminded me of the woods of Shropshire where I had played as a child.

We walked around the Pinnower See and ended the day at Demen, a village with one *Gaststätte,* where we got a rather expensive meal and permission to sleep in the back garden. The next day's journey took us over wide expanses of grain fields between small peasant villages, often with names ending in *ow.* In former days these had all been the property of the Junker nobility, who made up the Prussian officer corps and whose family arms we had sat beneath in the Schwerin throne room. Bulow, I thought, might have been the seat of von Bülow, a Prussian reformer who made an unsuccessful effort to persuade Kaiser Friedrich Wilhelm to adopt constitutional rule. The *Schloss* stood in the middle of the village, a large and unattractive ochre building, and I munched my sandwiches in front of it in a spirit of uncouth defiance.

All around us the wheat, rye, barley, and oats were ripening in the fields. We knew the land had all been incorporated into a large collective farm since the war, and wondered what was to become of it now, but on the streets of the first two villages we saw nobody to ask. If farmers were doing anything in these lazy summer days they would be in their shady barns, fixing their machinery for the hectic harvest time ahead. At the third village, Gross Niendorf, a woman in her sixties confirmed that her collective, like so many others, had not been able to survive the change. This would be its last year, she said, and just the other day they had made the decision to sell all twenty of their horses. She held herself primly, seeming to begrudge the information, yet at the same time was impelled to share it. The reason, it transpired, was that she could not contain her sense of outrage. That very night, she told us, someone had broken into the stables and stolen all the tackle. This anarchic act clearly symbolized for her the unpredictable horrors that lay ahead. She had spent her adult life under the Communists, and whatever the faults of the system, it had fed, clothed, and cared for all her community, good and bad, lazy and industrious. The puckering of her mouth made it plain that she was not looking forward to the future.

We walked as far as Mestlin, about fifteen miles altogether, and while waiting for a bus, I stood in front of a haberdasher's shop window, admiring an ancient-seeming corset of marvelously intricate construction. My feet were aching but not insupportably, and I had some hope that the worst was really over. Our campground for the night was again by a lake, at Goldberg, and the following morning we tried once more to follow a path around the lake and were foiled as before. This time the obstacle was an immense dump of obsolete military equipment. Among the more recognizable trucks and troop transports were many contraptions that challenged the imagination, devices that more closely resembled the toys known as Transformers that my son had played with years before. I could have spent the day speculating on how these strangely segmented steel puzzles would unfold and what would be revealed. Rocket launchers, helicopter pads, hospitals, canteens—who knew what was there, disappearing into the vegetation, as immovable and inscrutable as a Mayan ruin.

And the military continued to get in our way. Our map showed a path through a lightly wooded area that would have taken us very pleasantly toward our destination, but a brightly painted pole barred the route and a sign announced it as a MILITÄRGEBIET. Manfred asked a passerby if we could go through, and was warned off it, but our own instincts were to disregard these stories as old-fashioned nonsense, and we decided to walk through and take our chances. After half a mile, though, it seemed that we had taken the wrong path and would have to go back almost to the gate. When we got there, another local told us even more extravagant stories of shooting ranges and minefields, and of people being arrested, grilled, and deprived of their papers. To me these stories sounded like paranoid ravings from the past, but even if they had substance (I discounted the minefields altogether), I would have accepted the risk for myself. Quite possibly any one of us, traveling alone, would have done so, but none of us dared to assume responsibility for the others.

It was a good example of how group dynamics can confuse things when there is no deep mutual understanding to fall back on. Probably, we all had distorted perceptions of how the others felt. In this instance it made us more timid than we should have been, but in other circumstances it could just as well have led us into unwisely rash behavior. In my own solitary journeys around the world I had come to rely heavily on my intuition, but would never normally feel justified in imposing it on others. That is, of course, what is meant by the quality of leadership, and I have struggled with it all my life. I have little desire to lead and a great antipathy to being led. My ideal for society is a group of people sufficiently in agreement on their values and choices that they don't need leaders. Just how utopian that ideal is was demonstrated that afternoon.

Reluctantly, we took the long way around on a busy, hot road. Once again Manfred moved far ahead of us, while both Ginny and I found the going hard. We toiled on, mainly uphill, for several miles, and came to a bus stop with a shelter. Rather reluctantly we decided to take the bus, but found that the schedule made no sense, neither to us nor to anyone we asked. Having sacrificed our principles to no benefit, the walking was made to seem even harder, and we were extremely glad when a driver stopped to offer us a lift.

He was a short, energetic man with a ginger mustache, a no-nonsense manner, and strong opinions. He was probably the first person we had met who was heartily glad of the changes that had taken place. As a man of strong religious belief, he said, he had been completely out of sympathy with the regime and had had to content himself with doing relief work connected to the church. Now he was a bustling businessman with a new hotel and some other building projects in hand. When we told him about our disappointment at not being able to walk through the woods, he snorted with derision. He lived, he said, in Sandberg, exactly where the barrier was, and he knew for certain that it was entirely safe to cross unless warning flags were actually raised.

"Those people," he said scornfully, "are just full of bitterness, and like to take it out on the Wessies whenever they can."

Before long he overtook Manfred, picked him up as well, and then took all three of us to within walking distance of a campground he had recommended. Compared to the two other places we had been at, both rather makeshift affairs run by bedraggled optimists, this could have been a socialist workers' paradise in action. We signed in at a real office, staffed by severe ladies with brochures and forms to fill out. There were actual facilities, including a small shop stocked with junk food, and even boats to sail on the inevitable lake.

On a circular patch of balding grass laid out like a dartboard we were given two segments for our tents. Every space around us seemed to be taken, and the campground was packed with tiny cars, tiny caravans, tiny tents, and comparatively large people, but in spite of the crowds of families I thought the place was remarkably calm. No radios blared, no generators hummed; there were no angry shouts or boisterous brawls. There was no high-tech equipment, the clothing was dull to the point of dowdiness, and scarcely an item there would have fetched a dollar at an American flea market. Feeling rather old-fashioned in my appreciation, I thought how pleasant it was that people here seemed to take a naive pleasure in the environment and to draw satisfaction from each other's company without having to compete. An elderly gentleman in ancient khaki shorts limped by, drawn along by a small dog on a yellow leash. A matron in a frock pedaled past on a bicycle with only three gears. A small family sat on metal chairs beside a peach-colored caravan small enough to park in a garage, waiting for a kettle to boil on a Primus stove.

To my mind the most remarkable feature was a collapsible pub that had a curious resemblance to one of those abandoned Warsaw Pact contrivances we had passed in the morning. It was amazingly intricate and thorough in its design and execution, and although it must be a familiar sight at German fairs and outdoor events, I had never seen one before. It took me a few puzzled moments to figure out how both sides of a quite big panel truck had unfolded to create a substantial circular bar with room for a dozen or more drinkers. In gleaming white plastic, the counter came complete with all the fittings, including polished brass taps, and drains for the overflow. At the center of this giant Frisbee, among racks of bottles and glasses, stood the barman, dispensing liquid joy by the foaming steinful.

By the side of the lake, at the end of our fourth day, I returned to the subject that still dominated my thoughts—the mystery of my feet. The huge and alarming blisters of my first day had been almost worn away, and new, tougher skin had grown beneath them. My troubles now were smaller but more numerous, and drew me into a kind of meditation. On each of my feet, I noted, there were five toes. This profoundly significant information had been lost to me for nearly sixty years.

As a small child I was introduced to them by my mother, who counted them off, singing: "This little piggy goes to market, this little piggy stayed home . . ." Once I knew those ten toes intimately, well enough even to suck on them, an activity that today would be both unachievable and offensive. But when I started walking on them, it seems, I lost interest. Since then each foot had been composed of a big toe and a clump of digits with no more individuality than a bunch of bananas. Actually, bananas did have a place in the story of my feet. Two elderly ladies on the verge of retiring from a custom-shoe business in London once traced my right foot into a book that already recorded the shape of many famous feet. In fact mine followed closely on the footprint of Sir Edmund Hillary, conqueror of Everest, who was only a few pages away. The ladies were kind enough to say that they had never seen a foot like mine. They pronounced it banana-shaped, and this distinguishing feature (I would certainly not call it a deformity) was pushing my right big toe up against the side of my boot.

But that was only a minor problem at this point. All my toes were rebelling against anonymity, and thrusting their personalities at me. One had an awkward nail that was attacking its neighbor. Several had unusual second-generation blisters. Others were raw at the tips, particularly the middle toe on the left, and peculiar things were happening between them. While the soles of my feet now carried me without too much discomfort, these smaller outbreaks of hostility had to be treated with plasters and unguents, and I lavished care and affection on them.

If I hadn't been so absorbed in my own recovery I might have noticed that Manfred had now detached himself almost entirely from our group, and yet a sense of unease did affect my perceptions. The lake we were camped by was the largest we had visited so far, one of an interconnected series that stretched eastward for many miles. I woke unusually early the next morning and made my way at first light past silent tents to a small sandy beach. There I sat on a log and looked out across the lake to wait for the sunrise.

Framed by rushes, the lake reached almost to the horizon. The water itself seemed still to be sleeping, and every object on it was stained by the receding darkness. Ducks and geese drifted by, waiting for the sun to release them from the night. The sky was an unclouded dome, pink at the horizon, rising up into the palest blue above, with the texture of painted eggshell. Two portentous swans emerged from the tall reeds on my left and floated majestically, but meaninglessly, to the right. For some reason this display, which should have seemed so tranquil, frustrated me. It was like a stage set for a drama that failed to occur, as I projected onto it the anxiety ruffling my own thoughts.

The sun struggled up. Layers of mist sliced it into strips and then obliterated it with cloud. I moved to a metal table next to the junk-food kiosk, ordered a coffee, and sat sipping it. A very busy, confident crow, wearing a gray vest with black tails, landed nearby and bustled about eyeing everything, like a typical Wessie entrepreneur. The old man with the stiff leg, now wearing a running suit, walked past me with his dog and acknowledged me with a curt nod. I noticed that he had a military air about him, and I cast him fancifully as a veteran of the Russian front. Gusts of wind were beginning to play across the campsite as the weather deteriorated. I went over to the tents. Ginny was just emerging from her sleeping bag. Manfred was in the washroom.

The first drops of rain fell as we began to take down the tents, and we packed frenziedly in a shower. As soon as we had all the wet things rolled up and packed, the shower stopped abruptly, leaving me, at least, with that slightly foolish feeling of being out of step with events. This, I thought to myself, could be one of those days. We set off to the town of Plau, a couple of miles away, to get some breakfast and maybe even catch a ferry to Malchow or beyond. Plau was small and rather Dutch in appearance, consisting mainly of a few houses alongside a canal. We walked over a hump-backed bridge and, looking down, saw several boats tied up below us. On the other side of the canal was an unkempt garden with chairs and a table, served by a kiosk.

Some older men, relaxed and unshaven, were sitting under the trees drinking beer and schnapps, and a very frisky little dog was running from one to the other. The kiosk offered bad coffee and prepackaged snacks, not what I had been hoping for. Manfred talked to the men and discovered that the ferry had gone. Ginny was disappointed and was determined to get on a boat somehow.

"Maybe we can hitch a ride on one of those boats out there," she said. The boats did not look as though they were going anywhere, and I said so. My supine attitude annoyed her, and she walked off down the quayside to find out for herself. Manfred took advantage of her absence to tell me that he was going to leave us. He had been thinking about it a lot, trying to explain it to himself as well as to me. I was taken by surprise, and yet, as soon as it was said, it appeared inevitable, something I had subconsciously foreseen. We could not have continued as we were.

Although he did not say so, I had clearly let him down. In order to join me, he had made time in a busy life. The original idea had appealed to him as a rather heroic endeavor, but by introducing a third person I had, in a sense, trivialized it for him. The dynamics of the group, as he had feared, distracted from the adventure. "Too much energy goes into the relationships," he said, "but in any case, traveling with a couple doesn't work for me."

It was awkward being in the middle. I could sympathize with him intellectually, and yet it had seemed to me that Ginny had been remarkably undemanding. In fact, I was the one who was causing all the problems and delays, but there seemed no point in looking for ways to prolong what was obviously an unsatisfactory arrangement. I could only be grateful to Manfred for taking the initiative, and he was rather pleased with himself for the same reason.

"Usually I hang on too long. It's good to stop when you know things aren't right. I will walk with you as far as Alt Schwerin, and there I will take a train on to Malchow. Perhaps I will walk alone for a few days. Afterward I will be at home if you want to call me."

So we walked together, partly in sunshine, partly through heavy rain, for the rest of that day.

Alt Schwerin, as its name implies, has made a feature of its age. It accommodates a museum of social history, and several of its buildings have been converted into exhibits of peasant life in earlier times. At its center, where a fine *Gasthaus* shares a building with one of the museums, we found a small souvenir kiosk with sheltered benches. The railway line ran nearby, past an old windmill. Ginny and I waited on the benches while Manfred went to the station to check on the train. He returned to say that the train, like the ferry, had gone.

We had come a long way, my feet were hurting again, and I had taken off my boots. Across the road facing us was a long row of agricultural cottages. Manfred thought it likely that they would rent rooms, and I asked him if he would mind asking them. While he was gone, I told Ginny of Manfred's decision. She said nothing. I thought she must be relieved, but she kept her feelings to herself. I took my shoes from my pack and tried, ineffectually, to fit my boots in their place. Only one would fit, so I casually stuck the other in a string bag we used to carry food. Ginny objected loudly. I was angered by her fussiness, and for a moment we traded accusations. Then she said what was really on her mind.

"Do you want me to go home so that you can go on with Manfred?" she asked hotly. I thought for a moment, to be quite sure.

"No," I said. "But let's stay here for a day or two and give ourselves a break—and figure out what what we're doing."

Manfred returned to say he had found a place for us, and pointed to the house very close by.

"It's only thirty marks, and you have a little kitchen for yourself. So I will go on now to Malchow. Good-bye, Ted. I hope to hear from you." He smiled at me and gave me a hug. With a polite farewell to Ginny, he turned around and walked off down the road.

# Chapter 8

*I*t was the end of the beginning—not an end I would have chosen, but you work with what you get. Every adventure, I imagine, goes through a reality check of some kind when aspirations and expectations have to be measured against experience. We spent a day and two nights in Alt Schwerin, sitting out the bad weather, learning our lessons, and absorbing Prussian history as we wandered around the various museums. After that, I thought the important thing was to get to Poland soon. Our feet seemed to be recovering well—mine had suffered the worst traumas, but Ginny had had her problems, too—and we planned our course, which went through Waren, the next big city, then to Neubrandenburg, and from there to the border. We gave ourselves four days, feasible but hard enough to stretch and toughen us.

Every lake we came across was more impressive than the last. Waren stood by the Müritzsee, and when we arrived there, in the mid-afternoon, the lake seemed merely beautiful. The weather was still unsettled, with wind gusting among the trees, raising waves and throwing smatterings of rainfall around, but it settled down toward dusk, and the water grew calmer. Clouds scattered around the fading sky, caught the light and redistributed it, aided by reflection from the surface of the lake itself, so that every object, from foreground to horizon, was evenly illuminated. The effect, transcending mere beauty, was to give trees, buildings, people, no matter how near or far, a clarity and solidity that was supernatural. It is at times like this that one seems to penetrate into the very essence of things, to feel a magical clairvoyance that lends fairy stories their credibility and can even make you feel you are taking part in one.

In the whole of this Baltic region, air, earth, and water seem to be most closely intermingled. The earth is sand, loam, and clay. You need only add the fourth element, fire, and you have brick. If stone occurs naturally anywhere, I didn't see it. I suppose it must have been brought in by barge from farther south to decorate the most prestigious buildings. The usual building material is a dark red brick. Houses, churches, office buildings are all made of it, some plastered, some plain. Out of this tradition have grown many monumental constructions, but the grandest and most evocative of them all are the *Speicher*, or warehouses. I was already very familiar with the famous examples in Hamburg. These are five- and six-story mansions of commerce, some almost two hundred years old, constructed with all the care and affection lavished on homes, but windowless and inward-looking, being concerned entirely with their contents. Ranged in large communities along the quaysides and canals of Hamburg, they speak eloquently of the enormous respect those merchants had for the goods they housed in such style and at such expense.

In Waren, however, were two *Speicher* of a different sort. The first, which we saw on our way out of the city to the lake, was more recent and more functional. A single gabled roof several stories high covered a simply enormous building. Row upon row of tiny windows, set among the tiles in oval frames like unsleeping eyes, watched suspiciously over the neighborhood. At ground-floor level, piercing the dark brick, were other dusty windows, and through them, just visible in the shadows, I could make out a series of immense timber supports planted on the floor, like the feet of some gigantic fairy-tale monster receding by giant steps into the gloomy interior.

The second warehouse fronted right on the lake and was obviously intended to receive and discharge waterborne goods. It was both older and bigger than the first, and of a more sophisticated form. With its central nave and two wings, it was made in the shape of a very grand human habitation rather than an industrial building. This was clearly not a home for spices and Oriental carpets but for bulk goods, like grain and lumber. Sprawling along the edge of the lake between the city and the water, it had the presence of a venerable and crumbling palace.

It must be the scale of these buildings that excites the imagination. How easy it would be to spin tales of ogres brooding over hoarded wealth, of young adventurers braving unknown terrors and skipping between those monstrous feet to seize a fortune. And with the sky so low and so architectural, why shouldn't a beanstalk carry a small boy up to a castle in the clouds?

Deliberately, I allowed this magical, mythical dimension to color my thoughts. It put me in touch with the Germany that preceded the terrible distortions of recent times, a Germany I had subconsciously absorbed long before political realities intruded on my life. I don't think my mother ever made a systematic attempt to introduce me to German culture. We never spoke German at home, but there were occasional cautionary references to fairy-tale figures, like StruwelPeter (who was too lazy to cut his fingernails or comb his hair) and Hummel, the legendary water carrier of Hamburg. However, she did get me a compendium, in English, titled *Great German Short Stories*, and I read them all. It was there that I became familiar with a gothic Germany of dark forests, ogres and goblins, of Munchhausen and Hansel and Gretel, of Lorelei and the Niebelungen.

The following morning I grabbed a coffee at a mobile snack counter outside the station before we went on our way. The perky little man who served me joked about his roast chickens.

"They come," he said, "from Schlarafenland," which is a fairy-tale land where fowl fly through the air, ready-roasted, with knives and forks planted in their backs—probably the earliest, and by far the best, example of convenience food.

"In that case," I said, "where are the knives and forks?"

"Ah," he replied. "You know the place?"

"Oh yes," I said, without thinking. "I live there."

It was a simple exchange, but it cheered me up immensely to be able to make the connection.

We walked through forests that day, mile upon mile of sandy tracks, with unmarked roads and paths leading off mysteriously in all directions. After several hours we came to a tiny village, just a single row of maybe ten houses, but built curiously like town houses, with common walls, semi-basements, and stairs rising up to the front doors. They looked odd in the middle of the forest.

Nearby was a small prefabricated lock-up shop with chairs and a table outside. A bell push said "Ring me." I rang, but there was no sound or response, and we were about to leave when a man approached silently from one of the houses where the bell must have rung. He sold us some refreshments and sat down with us outside. He was a tall, well-built man with graying blond hair, unusually fit and agile, I thought, and in the prime of life. From an intelligent face he regarded me intently with cool gray eyes in a way I found subtly menacing. His carefully neutral manner was as restful as a coiled spring.

Without Manfred around, I was gradually getting my German back in use. He answered my questions about the road and the region in a fluent but highly accented German that was difficult to understand. As long as I knew approximately what he was likely to be saying, I could follow him well. I asked him whether things had changed much since *die Wende.* He said nothing had changed in the ten years he had been there. These had been the private hunting grounds of the former rulers of East Germany—Erich Honecker, who was then exiled and dying, and his right-hand man, Willi Stoph, who was in the Moabit jail.

"What were you doing here during that time?" I asked.

"I was a gamekeeper," he said.

He gazed at me steadily as he talked, and I had the strange sense, under his glacial regard, that I was being challenged to go too far. Then he began to speak about what lay ahead of us. There was a *Gaststätte* at Ankershagen, he said, where we could eat. Then my comprehension was stretched to its limits and became unhinged. I picked up something about a certain Herr Schliemann, who had apparently brought about the deaths of numerous children ("*viele Kinder umgebracht*" is what I thought I heard). I could think of no way to deal with this information. We thanked him and continued on our way. Under the combined influences of medieval myth and Cold War intrigue, I had the odd sensation that we were being watched. For many miles, as we walked through the forest, lanes and vistas opened and closed to our view and, in them, cars and people popped up and vanished again in a disconcertingly surreptitious way, while I fantasized Deightonesque plots with unregenerate "Kommis" planning their counterrevolution in these woods.

Even so, the walk continued to be beautiful. Farther along, the forest became more deliberately a nature reserve. Signs with an owl depicted on them appeared at regular intervals, pointing to Ankershagen. The dislocation of my senses was sustained by curious discrepancies in the distances they showed, which told us that we were walking backward. 5.5 KM said one. 7 KM said the next. Then 3 KM. Then 5 KM.

"What do you believe?" asked Ginny.

"My feet," I replied, since they were beginning to tire after ten miles, but soon we came to the edge of the village, where we passed through some old-established vegetable gardens, carefully hedged and fenced, with fruit trees everywhere. Ginny, unable to resist the temptation of fresh fruit, dawdled and picked cherries. Afraid of being caught filching from someone else's tree, I wandered on to find the restaurant we had been promised. I was halfway through lunch, expecting to see her arrive under guard, when she turned up, not only at liberty, but very excited about a museum and a medieval fresco she had heard about.

The riddle of the serial child-murderer was quickly resolved. Ankershagen was the birthplace of Heinrich Schliemann, the archaeologist who excavated the site of ancient Troy, and a museum had been created in his memory. Schliemann, I am happy to say, murdered no children. On the contrary, he inspired them, and many had made paintings of scenes from his life and his work. They were being exhibited on the walls—fine, sunny visions that shed bright light over the remnants of old dusty digs. The weather was getting bad again, following its usual pattern of sunny mornings and rain in the afternoon, so we sheltered comfortably in the little museum, which was no more than a large converted cottage. The curator offered us tea and coffee. She gave us a large iron key and sent us to the small and ancient church on a nearby grassy mound so that we could see, painted on the wall inside, where St. George had been fighting the dragon for well over six hundred years.

Another woman arrived soon after us, a very talkative and kindly woman, a true fusspot, who introduced herself immediately as Renate and offered to drive us to Pilenz, where she said she had an old school friend with a room to rent. By now it was raining steadily and we could not refuse. As we rattled along in her modest red car, she told us that Pilenz had been her hometown, where her father, a pastor, had raised her. Then, in 1960, just before the Wall went up, she had gone West to study, and for some years she did not dare return. Things went badly for her father. Eventually she was allowed to visit him, and she came many times, drawn by her childhood ties, but each time she came things got worse. The roads broke up, houses were in disrepair, gasoline became harder to get. She shrugged. Now, at least, there was gasoline.

Unfortunately, her friend in Pilenz was nowhere to be found. We were directed across the road to a fifties-style villa with a tiled porch, where Renate, negotiating on our behalf, told us the price for a night was twenty-five marks. Later it turned out to be twenty-five marks each, but for that we had a basement flat to ourselves, with kitchen and laundry facilities, so we washed all our clothes and draped them over every radiator, pipe, and rail we could find, eventually drying my jeans by suspending them precariously over an electric hot plate.

Our landlady, Helga, was an attractive woman of fifty-something, with a plump figure tightly contained in spandex and a made-up face topped by marcelled bleach-blond hair. She seemed to be pursuing an image that, I guessed, floated halfway between Frankfurt and Miami. The flat we were renting was modern, fully equipped, and very well finished. It had been intended for her children. She and her husband had built it themselves in what was originally just a semi-basement storage area, and they had worked hard and deprived themselves so that their children would be able to stay with them. Then the Berlin Wall came down, their children had chosen to go West, and now they found themselves deserted and alone.

She could not blame the children but she rarely saw them, because they were too far away. All the effort they had made to protect and unify their family now had no purpose other than to make money. Her husband was in the building trade, she said, which enabled them to use their time profitably by expanding their little empire, and she was well set in the brisk, mindless pursuit of material advancement that unification had made possible. But, as she eventually confided to us, their life felt barren.

She had been raised under Communism, and she had to admit that her childhood had been a happy one. They had always had security, there had always been work, and there was always enough to eat—even though there were no "luxury imports." As she talked about it, her face softened and her voice was tinged with regret. People used to be nice to one another, she said. Children were protected. All this had changed. She herself had once been a kindergarten teacher, who had spent her life thinking about children—her own and others'—but there were few children to teach now.

"People are not having children because of the insecurity," she lamented.

The newfound freedom she enjoyed was undoubtedly appreciated. Back in the eighties, she said, she would never have believed such a liberation possible, even in her lifetime. She says she felt the loss of freedom before, but I suspect this is an idea she might not have formulated for herself. Many of her earlier friendships had not survived the change, and she was envied by the less fortunate. People, she said, were driven apart in this new competitive atmosphere. Unemployment was high. In the area around Pilenz there had been 360 working farmers. Now only sixty were employed. The others received, as welfare, 63 percent of their former salary, an amount much smaller than it seemed owing to inflation and because the benefits had counted for so much.

She recalled the general euphoria when the Wall came down, but since then she had spent many nights crying herself to sleep and waking with tears in her eyes, wondering what would become of them in this strange dog-eat-dog world now that all their security was gone.

This confession made a strong impression on me, for she was no weak, ineffectual person. It made me wonder just how I would feel if I was suddenly granted the kind of security she felt she had lost. Would I experience an equal but opposite emotion? Would I go to sleep chuckling and wake with an irrepressible grin on my face? And how would that degree of security affect my behavior? Would it be death to ambition? Would I become as dull as ditchwater?

But a person cannot go on crying and regretting the old days forever. So now this plump, blond mother, who used to think only about children, has buckled on her spandex shorts and is hardening into the kind of domestic entrepreneur we, in the United States, know so well.

As soon as my jeans were dry in the morning, we left to walk through Werde, Püklow, Alt Rhese, and along the side of yet another lake. There we stopped for a moment, brought out some food, and lay back against a stout tree trunk. Then Ginny wandered off briefly and came back to say that she had met a man and wanted me to talk with him. He didn't speak English but seemed interesting, and she wanted to know what he had to say.

I followed her out onto a landing stage, where a large, pale middle-aged man, dressed only in shorts, was lolling in the sun on an air mattress. He had thin, graying hair cut short over a square Saxon face, longer curly hair on his chest, and the kind of bone structure that can carry a lot of pounds. His manner was composed and self-assured, and he had a pleasant smile in which one gold tooth stood like a fence post among the white pickets.

I introduced myself, and as usual, the combination of my appearance and my very natural German accent paired with an obviously inadequate vocabulary piqued his curiosity. When I told him that I was aiming ultimately for Romania because my father had come from there, it all clicked into place for him immediately—and it flashed through my mind as though it were a new idea that for the first time in my journeyman's life, I was planning to travel among people who would always be whiter than me, until I got to my destination.

He turned out to have formerly been a colonel in command of a tactical nuclear rocket regiment. Now he worked for German Telecom, somewhere between Leipzig and Dresden. A good-paying job, he said, and his wife worked, too, so he had nothing to complain about. He had been in the Party, of course. He was still a Communist and did nothing to conceal it, nor had it hindered him in any way. He seemed pleased to have an opportunity to talk, and at my prompting he wandered from one topic to another, delivering what I suppose was the Party line on current events.

As a Communist he regretted what had happened. He felt the press had grossly exaggerated the shortcomings of the previous regime, and retained a stubborn pride in what he claimed was good. The MiG, he insisted, was still the best airplane flying, and the West German air force, he said, was flying them here in the East. For that matter, from his point of view one of the worst things about this new situation was the loss of the balance of power that had existed under the Cold War.

It was true that efficiency in the old Democratic Republic was a joke ("*lächerlich*") because of guaranteed employment, but the underlying structure was entirely viable. As proof he cited those original farming collectives, or L.P.G.s*, in Saxony that had today become very competitive since they were able to reduce their workforce.

As for the hysteria about the Stasi—the old East German secret police, who were supposed to have infected everything and everyone—well, as a colonel he had had to deal with them at various levels, and the idea that everybody was informing on everybody else was, he said, simply nonsense

---

*L.P.G. stands for Landwirtschafts Produktion Genossenschaft.

("*kwatch*"). He spoke with the ease and assurance of an elder statesman handing out chunks of good, plain common sense, and it was tempting to believe him. One meets and hears such people everywhere, but it is impossible to know whether they are describing the world or themselves. Once I met an Old Etonian who was very proud that his school, famous as a bastion of the upper classes, had become so much more democratic. In evidence he observed that everywhere he went in the world, he usually found other Old Etonians. One would need to know, of course, what kind of club "Everywhere" was.

By the same token, how would a nuclear artillery colonel know what the Stasi was up to among the general population? Not through his official connections, certainly. Yet he was apparently sure of his knowledge, and believed that general paranoia had been costly to the country. The most competent people in the East, he insisted, had naturally been in the Party. Throwing them out of government and management had sacrificed the best chance of rebuilding fast. For the same reason, the police were now quite ineffective and unable to keep order. The streets of what had been East Germany, he said, were a total mess.

"Germany without order?" I exclaimed in mock astonishment.

He roared with laughter, and shouted for his wife to bring coffee. When he stood up to help her, his rather lazy, almost plump-looking body uncoiled into a commanding figure well over six feet tall.

We walked fifteen miles that day, the most we had managed so far, and came upon Neubrandenburg at about five o'clock, by way of a landscaped park. We trudged past swings, fountains, a duck pond, and tennis courts, where children and the unemployed were amusing themselves, and came to a ring road, which told us that we were on the edge of a rather bigger urban center than we were used to. What we could see of it had that unmistakable, vacuous look of a city that has been recently destroyed and rebuilt rather than restored. Our eastward route, of course, ran counter to the main thrust of the advancing Red Army, which in 1945 was not upset by the need to reduce to rubble every German city in its path.

Though we did not know it, from the moment of our arrival we were destined (I won't say doomed) to stay at the Wohn Hotel, though we had never heard of it. We crossed the ring road expecting to find a residential neighborhood where we might rent a room, but the new city plan baffled us. Instead we found ourselves in a fancy shopping district. I asked a Turkish taxi driver about rooms, but he seemed perplexed by the idea, as though it were new to him. What about hotels? He named one that I knew would be expensive. No cheap hotels? He scratched his head, and said we should go to the Wohn Hotel.

It took me a moment to get the name right. Wohn, in German, is an active verb meaning "inhabit." As the name of a hotel it has a rather chilling, functional sound. I asked if it was small. Oh no, he said brightly, it's gigantic. It sounded like the place to avoid, and we spent the next hour avoiding it. We walked right across town looking for something else. We found a youth hostel that would have cost us more than we could dream of paying. We phoned hotels in the Yellow Pages—yes, there were even Yellow Pages—but they were either full or too costly. At all of them we were told to go to the Wohn Hotel.

Despondently, we set off in its direction. Even as we walked I made a few feeble efforts to escape. Like a fish flapping in the net, I knocked indiscriminately on front doors to find someone with a room who would save us from the dreaded Wohn, but it was useless. The Neubrandenburgers knew where we had to go, and made sure we went there.

Indeed, the Wohn Hotel was enormous, and consisted of three concrete tower blocks, built and run in the Soviet style, which is to say for the benefit and convenience of the staff. There was no reception desk in the lobby. Visitors entered a room rather like one of those government offices where permits are issued to favored applicants. Yet I must say that there was some evidence of a softening. Behind their manual typewriters, the Wohn bureaucrats, in their well-filled blouses and skirts, were correct but not severe. One of them took only a few minutes to first tidy up her paperwork before attending to me. She gave us permission to stay with something resembling a smile.

In a Soviet elevator, which filled Ginny with misgivings, we made the dangerous ascent to the sixth floor and found our twin-bedded cubicle. It was furnished with nothing to speak of and looked out on little of interest, and we spent an unremarkable night.

If there *was* anything remarkable about the Wohn, it was probably the manager. I met him by chance the following morning as I sat on my pack by the roadside waiting for Ginny to come down. Across the road from the hotel stood a building symbolic of a different but equally disappointing school of architecture, which I associate with the Festival of Britain—England's first attempt at civic merriment after the war. The idea was that if you decorated concrete buildings with panels of brightly colored plastic or ceramic, it would make people feel jolly. We were all starved for color during the war, which I remember as a mainly black-and-white affair (with some unavoidable red). So at the time, in 1950, I was quite charmed by the concept of colored buildings. As long as the concrete stayed white, it worked in a tedious sort of way, but soon the cement was soiled by sooty rain, the colors merely drew attention to the general grubbiness, disenchanted kids with nothing to do threw stones and paint at it, and that was the end of that.

The office building of the *Nord-Deutsche Kurier,* covered with magenta oblongs and fake buttresses that failed to fly, was a late example of this misguided movement, and I was studying it when an even more blatant swatch of color struck me in the corner of my eye. It was a large blue suit, the kind of blue (you could not possibly call it a shade) that was once used to sell politicians and Mediterranean vacations: royal, true, acrimonious blue. The man in it must have bought the material cheap and told his tailor to use it all up, because it was voluminous. It drowned his shoes and overran his wrists. The jacket went almost to his knees, and the pants were like wind socks. There were cuffs and pocket flaps everywhere, and he sported the broadest lapels east of the Oder-Neisse line.

However, he was a big man, big enough even to overcome the suit. He had the rough, red, weather-beaten face and hands of a street trader, and when I discovered that he was the manager of this huge hotel, I had to make some rapid adjustments in my mind. He looked down at me and my pack with a quizzical air.

"Where are you off to with that thing?" he asked, and when I told him the names of the German towns we would pass through, he said he knew them all well, having been a traveling salesman.

"But why are you going to Poland? You must be mad. It is terrible there. You can't get anything. Everyone is poor. Take my advice. Forget it. Stay at my hotel. Spend your holiday here, in this beautiful town. Here you can get good food and drink. People will be nice to you. In Poland you will only be miserable."

His words had a curious effect on me. To my mind this man, in his travesty of a suit, surrounded by ugliness, had no idea what he was talking about. At the same time I knew that forty years earlier I might have been seen wearing equally impossible clothes and making the same large claims about the beauties of contemporary London. Were things really that much better now? Other offensive styles in clothing and architecture have come and gone since then. In the interim, I had become used to a multitude of goods and services never heard of at the Wohn Hotel and it was a shock to be deprived of them at first, but I had to admit to myself that life in the former East Germany had become easy enough. The only real discomforts were ones we imposed upon ourselves. The night before we had had a very nice dinner at a Greek restaurant (though there was not a Greek in sight). In the morning I found good coffee, delicious rolls, butter, fruit, and cheese. The contrast between East and West had been so sharp when we crossed the line, but after only a few days the edge had worn off. The shops, which had once appeared bare, now seemed well stocked, and for us things were not expensive. I no longer cared about the outward appearances of the houses or the lack of things inside, and saw them simply as comfortable homes.

Of course the West offered more choices, more amenities, more luxuries, but we seemed to be managing very well without them. How could the transition to Poland be so much worse? I asked myself. And behind that question lay the bigger one: How much can be stripped away from our lives before they become truly intolerable?

From Neubrandenburg east, the countryside opened up. There were fewer forests, more cultivated fields. We passed immense acreages of wheat, though some of it looked stunted and unhealthy. Many fields were crowded with crimson poppies. Small villages of dark, drab buildings appeared here and there, clustered around impoverished churches. The church steeples, either of open ironwork or metal cupolas, looked as though they might have been bought from a discount catalog. The dominant structures were silos and hog sheds. Strings of rusty red grain wagons stood abandoned on spurs of rail, and the massive agricultural machinery of the collectives corroded silently among heaps of scrap alongside deserted sheds with broken windows and flapping doors.

Between these remnants, our walks were made beautiful by the wildflowers, which had seized their opportunity to retake lost ground. Not just poppies, but blue cornflowers and chicory, golden chamomile, white daisies, wild magenta roses, and scores of others I had no names for. The weather pattern had changed to suit us well, with soft winds and sunshine through the day and showers at night to keep the country fresh and green and delightful.

Bismarck was the last German village on our route to the Polish border, and we arrived there early in the afternoon. In two hours or less we could have made it to the frontier and Ginny would have liked to go on, but I resisted. I am nervous about crossing borders late in the day. It's a habit I acquired in other, more unpredictable parts of the world, where borders could be strangely unstable places and where guards often reacted in rather whimsical ways to travelers in a hurry. I didn't really expect this border to be any kind of a problem, but I thought we might be glad to have plenty of time to find our way in a country where neither one of us understood a single word of the language.

It must have seemed silly to Ginny, but she humored me, and we spent one more night in Germany. Bismarck was a modest community on the main road to Poland, with a few shops, some farms, and a church. The church was nicer than most we'd seen, perched on top of a high hillock surrounded by its own intimate family of tombstones among lush grass and apple trees. One of the shops, across the road from the church, was a long, low building containing nothing but used clothing hung on racks. Behind it was a grassy yard bounded on three sides by high barnyard walls and a house. I asked at the house for permission to camp, and we pitched our tent in a corner and went swimming.

Our map showed places to swim, and about a mile away, deep in a birch forest, we found a lake with a wooden pier. There was nobody about. The only sounds came from birds, frogs, and the wind in the reeds, so we stripped and cavorted about in the deliciously cool water, drying ourselves afterward as best we could with the skimpy towels we carried.

The lake, like so many others we had seen, had great charm. I took a picture of it before leaving, and pointing the zoom lens across the lake, I saw that what I had thought was a floating log was actually an angler seated motionless in a skiff. It struck me as hilarious.

I told Ginny about our audience on the lake, expecting some sort of reaction from her, but she just said, "So what." I should have known better than to mention it. Ginny is full of laughter and good humor, but like most Americans I know, she doesn't think there is anything even slightly funny about the idea of someone catching her accidentally in the nude. I can't say it bothers me, but because I have emerged from a culture that used to find such things acutely embarrassing, the idea of it amused me, like a vignette from an old movie. And strangely enough, I felt a pang of nostalgia and regret at the loss of that outdated modesty. Strange, because I associate it with innocence, whereas most people would have it the other way around.

We ate a picnic supper in the churchyard, and I slept well but fitfully, woken first by a shower of rain and then by the reverberations beneath me of heavy hooves stamping the ground on the other side of the wall.

# Chapter 9

*A*s we started off toward Poland in the morning, I became very excited at the prospect of coming to a country I had never visited before, with a language that was utterly strange to me. Not since I rode my bike into Libya twenty years earlier had I been in that situation—and although Polish, unlike Arabic, employed a familiar alphabet, there were clumps of consonants so impenetrable to my tongue that I wondered how I would ever get around them. What could you make of a word like *trzy?* Or a town named Przemyśl?

The road was busy with traffic, mostly Mercedes cars, coming and going, and almost all with German license plates. If Germans found Poland such a miserable place, why were they going there in such numbers? They made our walk less pleasant, and I tried to divert myself by assembling everything I had heard about the Poles, beginning with Chopin and ending with Wałęsa. I knew they were passionately nationalistic, incorrigibly romantic, and deeply traditional—not a very practical combination. When Hitler's armored panzer divisions poured across this same frontier in 1939, they found themselves opposed by heroic Polish aristocrats on horseback flashing their sabres. We had one of the survivors of that campaign in our house in London at the end of the war. He had been an officer in General Anders's army and was very unwelcome in Poland's postwar Communist society. He was a sweet, melancholy man with no marketable skills whatever, who liked making things from wood. I can't remember his name—we called him Bob—but I still have a rather primitive bookcase he made.

The interesting thing I do recall is that he was deeply in love with a very modern and attractive Jewish girl, who also lived with us then—interesting because of the extremely difficult time Poles had in accepting the four million or so Jews who lived there when "Bob" was forced to flee.

I had another Polish friend, called Freddy, who was definitely not an aristocrat. He had bad teeth, dirty fingernails, was usually unshaven, and drank a bottle of scotch a day when he could afford it. But he was also an inventive entrepreneur and an irrepressible wag who held court at the Troubadour Café and told jokes in broken English. One evening he startled everyone by arriving with a bentwood hat stand upside down on his head.

"Look, ever'body," he said. "I'm a Vicking."

His theatrical instinct was so good that everybody got the joke, and the café fell apart with laughter. One of his pioneering schemes, way ahead of its time, involved delivering homemade sandwiches to offices in his bubble car. He was the forerunner of the quilted wagon. He wanted to make me his partner, but I couldn't get past the fingernails.

So Poles, I thought, were indomitable, spirited, sentimental, arrogant, unhygienic, pale, and button-nosed. They liked sausage and alcohol, which was just as well because, as Germans never ceased to inform us, that was all they had. And of course they spoke a language that was both illegible and unpronounceable. Poland was a big country, almost as big as Germany, but with only half the population. Also, the Poles were unfortunately placed right in the middle of the playing field, so that they were always getting in the way of bigger, more powerful teams—like Russia, Serbia, the Ottoman empire, the Austro-Hungarians, and, of course, Germany. Nobody ever really wanted Poland, because the Poles were such a nuisance, but they were forced to take her just to foil the opposition.

The Poles themselves, for all their pluck, were only gadflies to these European warhorses. Their borders, which were constantly being redrawn, fluctuated like the membrane of a corpuscle. Nevertheless, they must have been made of some irreducible substance because, after centuries of abuse, they were still there, and more Polish than ever.

The border was a disappointment, just a few dreary sheds and some standard street furniture. I shouldn't have expected any different. I can remember only one border post grand enough to evoke the pomp and authority of its function, and that was a wonderful ochre gateway between Turkey and Iran, or rather between the Ottoman empire and Persia, because it must have dated back to those times. By now it has probably been torn down, because it was hopelessly inefficient at dealing with the mile-long queues of commercial traffic. Here in Poland there were no romantic fezzes and twirled mustaches. Some dull guards in compost-colored uniforms processed us like ticket collectors. There were no penetrating glances, no meaningful jokes, no veiled threats, no hints at lubrication. They gave our passports a perfunctory stamp each and waved us on. I should have been glad it was all so routine, but I missed the thrill.

On the other side, some enterprising capitalist had put up a cheap two-story building and divided each floor into dozens of stalls, like a bazaar. I wandered around it in despair. It was crammed with things you would never want—mostly clothing in fabrics you could not wear and colors you could not abide—yet it was this that apparently was drawing all the Mercedeses over the border.

We invested ten dollars in Polish money and got a few hundred thousand zlotys for them. Then we sat in plastic chairs at a tin table while I drank a Sprite, and we tried to memorize currency values. The chairs, table, and soda were the same as we would have found anywhere in the world. The soda, we calculated, cost the same as it would have cost in London or San Francisco. It was depressing. It was not what we had come for, and we decided to get away fast. The first big city was only eight miles away, and we took a bus to Szczecin. Szczecin was more easily read than said, and neither of us had much of an idea how to pronounce it. Two soldiers at the bus stop tried to help us. "Sh-che-cheen" they said, more or less, and we practiced it as the bus took us through a nondescript area of rural and suburban blight. We could have said Stettin, the German name, but we had our pride.

At a big bus terminal on the edge of town we changed to a tram. Ginny had been reading up on the place and took us to a travel agency called Pomerania. That's where we were, actually, in Pomerania, or Pommernland, as my aunts would have said when it was part of Germany. We used to sing a song about it, a simple ditty that went to a tune rather like "Three Blind Mice."

*"Maikäfer flieg, Dein Vater ist im Krieg, Dein' Mutter ist in Pommernland, Pommernland ist abgebrannt, Maikäfer flieg."*

This cheerful little rhyme reads, "Fly, ladybug, fly, Your father is at war, Your mother is in Pomerania, Pomerania has been burned down, Fly, ladybug, fly"—which gives a sense of what life has held in store for the citizens of the region through the ages. In fact Pomerania stretches all the way from Rostock to Gdańsk. The Swedes once sold this particular part of it, including the valuable port of Szczecin, to the Prussians, who celebrated the acquisition by building a triumphal arch now called the Brama Portowa. It was standing there still, big, Baroque, and black with soot, in the center of town, and that's where we got off the tram.

The city itself is very German in appearance—hardly surprising, since it was Prussian for 220 years—and much of the center seemed to have survived the heavy shelling during World War II. We found ourselves among five- and six-story buildings with carved and molded facades from the early nineteenth century, when the city was rebuilt in the Parisian style. The Pomerania Agency sent us to the Hotel Pomorski, two doors down along the colonnaded pavement. Obviously they were in cahoots, and they both occupied the same block, but there was nothing wrong with that. We went through a narrow door into a tiny, gloomy lobby with a wooden desk at the foot of a winding staircase. A tired woman looked up from her nails to examine us with indifference. Well, what could be interesting about thrifty travelers you only see for one night and never again?

She interrogated us briefly. Then we surrendered our passports and lugged our packs up to a room on the third floor, passing on our way a mishmash of assorted enterprises, including a nightclub called the Black Jack, a massage parlor, a beauty shop, a dentist's office, and a tourist agency, where I caught sight of a woman with phosphorescent-green eye shadow painted over pancake makeup. Our room had the usual high windows and ceilings with molded plasterwork, a hand basin, a couple of cheap beds, two chairs, and a table. What more could one want? It had the advantage of being fairly close to the staircase and only a short walk from the bathroom. There were apparently thirty-eight of these rooms, and crooked corridors could lead one off in all directions through this large, rambling block of masonry, possibly never to return. We slept a bit, and I tried to learn some Polish. Then I went out on the town, where I met Alphonse.

He was a student who came to my rescue in the post office. As soon as I went into the post office, I knew we had moved back through another block of time. I recognized it straightaway. It might have been the same post office, on boulevard Saint-Germain, that I used in Paris in 1950, where arrogant, bored, pitifully underpaid employees in faded blue aprons made us all pay for their misery. In Poland now as in Paris then, all foreign calls had to be made through the operator and taken in a numbered *kabina*. The number was shouted out. I had mastered the Polish for numbers "one" and "two," but was still stuck on *trzy*, and the rest were gibberish. If you didn't know your numbers, you were done for. Rarely would an operator take the trouble to point, and if she did, it was with a withering show of contempt.

I desperately needed someone to translate the number when it was called out, and Alphonse obliged. He was an African student who spoke a kind of French, so when we were done and I had left my message on Manfred's machine, I asked him to have coffee with me and talk about Poland. It had started to rain, so we couldn't look far, and ended up, rather wet, sitting under an inadequate awning in the same chairs at the same metal table I had escaped from at the border. I asked him how he came to be in Poland, and in a very matter-of-fact way, he explained his circumstances. He said he was one of four students who had come to Poland three years earlier from Guinea-Bissau, a small country on the west coast of Africa. They had arrived just at the time when the Polish Communist regime was beginning to collapse.

Alphonse was in his first year of law school, with three more years to go. Already he had had to overcome a number of unusual obstacles. First, of course, was the Polish language. Then there was the weather. For almost a year he had shivered constantly, before his metabolism adapted to the change of temperature. And now he had to face the prospect that most of what he was learning would prove to be irrelevant, not only in Poland but also in Guinea-Bissau. His country had been under a military Marxist regime, but only six months before we met, that government too had been toppled and Guinea-Bissau, now supposedly a democracy, would be adopting Western legal principles.

Meanwhile life was not a bed of roses. He had been given a small bedroom, an alcove in which to do his own cooking, and the equivalent of two dollars a day for all his expenses. Money was so tight that for the whole six years of his studies there could be no question of his ever being able to see his family, not even once. He was a very impressive young man with a nice disposition, quite unaffected, lean and good-looking in a stylish pair of jeans he must have starved for. I thought of the easy way we take our privileges for granted and how tough his life was. You could not envy him, and yet there was something fine about taking on such an imposing obstacle course. By the time he had finished talking to me, I was wishing I could order him a three-course meal, and I pressed him to take advantage of me. But he seemed unable even to conceive of such largesse, and wanted nothing from me. All I could get him to take was a cup of instant coffee. There was no cream or sugar.

He told me more about Guinea-Bissau than about Poland. The country, he said, was in economic chaos but rich in minerals, like bauxite. They were planning to dam the river there, presumably for hydroelectric power to produce aluminum—yet another African country being ripped apart and devastated for short-term gains.

He taught me to pronounce the Polish word for "thank you," *dziękuję*, which has curious nasal sounds in it—like djyeng-*koo*-yeng. Then he shook my hand and left.

So now I could say "one," "two," and "thank you." That wasn't going to get me very far. Amazed by my carelessness in having come without even a Polish phrase book, I went in search of one. A big bookshop near our hotel shed a lurid light on the state of commerce in Szczecin. It was run like a literary jail. The shop front, all on the ground floor, was very long, maybe sixty feet, with windows all the way, but the shop itself was only about ten feet deep. You entered a door at one end and had to leave at the other. The shelves were arranged like a series of open cells facing the street, and at the mouth of each cell, with her back to the window, stood a very serious looking attendant, clearly there to make certain that none of the imprisoned books should slip away without being accounted for. Strange as it was to browse under such scrutiny, I got used to it, but of course all the Anglo-Polish phrase books and dictionaries were Polo-Anglish, designed for Poles and not for me.

Hearing a rumor that there was another bookshop somewhere, I wandered off down a busy commercial street and got lost in my reflections on the passing scene. I was immediately struck by how little display material there was to distract from the shop fronts and facades. Many of the shops had the names of their owners above them, still, instead of some catchy, cliché concoction. Through the windows, in their sober interiors, one could even see the owners and the wares they were selling. The original architecture of the buildings was still dominant, unsullied by the cacography of images that blasts out at consumers in America and Western Europe.

True, things had a stuffy, old-fashioned look. No doubt they needed more color in their lives. They were still, I thought, in the pre-Carnaby phase of commerce. I remember the joy I felt at the explosion of color and audacity that struck London in the sixties, when a newly emerging generation discovered that it had tastes and opinions of its own, the energy to express them, and the buying power to support them. It seems on reflection to have been a too willing surrender to superficiality, but it was also a liberation from the muddied mess of dogma, mildewed precepts, and empty assertions of authority supporting a repressive class system.

We were over the moon at being released from the ancient and dreary hegemony of our "elders and betters," who had proved themselves merely older and the worse for wear; who had dragged us up through decades of fear and penury in gratitude to them for having won—barely—a war they had brought about in the first place. Carnaby Street became a symbol, worldwide, for that effervescence. I thought then that from the exhilaration of this shiny new present, we would revisit our traditions on our own terms, like a liberation army recovering our country.

But what Carnaby Street became was as false and sterile as the stultifying traditions that preceded the Swinging Sixties. Before, we had had a culture of hats, umbrellas, wool scarves, twinsets, and tweeds, and poor shop girls mumbling, "Did madam have anything particular in mind?"

Now we have objects of no intrinsic value—like baseball hats, coffee mugs, and posters—as surfaces for commercial icons and cheap humor. Once we paid sandwich-board men to carry advertisements down the street. Now we pay to wear them on our T-shirts. We have, as McLuhan foretold, become the message, but I refuse to believe that it is my message.

When I walk down old streets, like those of Szczecin, I remember my feelings when I walked the streets of London and Paris fifty years earlier—the hunger, the longing, the barely credible expectations I held then for a world of significance that would flower in magical ways, a world I could not even imagine. Now I am left hugging the last remaining shreds of those hopes about me like the threadbare coat of a tramp at the onset of winter.

I turned right, along a quieter street with trees. To my right was a street named Bohaterów Getta Warszawskiego, which I was able to figure out as meaning "Heroes of the Warsaw Ghetto." There has been much written and said lately about Polish and Soviet indifference to the Jewish tragedy, and I was curious about the naming of the street.

I saw facing me four blocks of apartments, side by side, and oddly enough there was something a little ghettolike about them in the medieval adaptations of their facades. The houses themselves, of five and six stories, were not particularly old, but they had sets of ornamental iron balconies, three stories high, stacked above the ground floor and joined together by vertical iron columns. They projected by three or four feet, reminiscent of the way houses in the Middle Ages overhung the street, and in many cases the structure had been filled in with windows and walls to make ornate extensions of the interior. Where they had not been turned into extra rooms, they were crowded with potted flowers, tomatoes, laundry, or people taking the air.

There was a lot of life in this street, out on the pavements, and exuding from the windows. Close to me, a man was spread out in a reclining position on the windowsill of his ground-floor apartment, beckoning amiably and insistently, calling out the German word for "pound." *"Pfund! Pfund!"* he cried. Why did he think I had English pounds rather than German marks or dollars? I was tempted to find out, but I felt a sudden fear of being swallowed up by the life of this street. It seemed as though all eyes had turned on me, and feeling as though I were in the presence of a consuming appetite, I hurried away.

I passed some massive apartment blocks built in the Parisian style, then more buildings originally made to house solid, bourgeois businesses on the ground floor, living accommodation above, and a basement, usually accessible from the street. But, already, new needs had reshaped them. Shops, big and small, were squeezed into basements, hallways, and the upper rooms, where windows displayed cards advertising repairs, wholesale outlets, hairdressers. From the basements to the rooftops people were digging into the structures, struggling for a bit of business. Evidence of the coming change was everywhere.

Only the very biggest buildings resisted this infiltration. There were several huge ones made of brick—always dark, forbidding, and mysterious: cathedrals, warehouses, government offices, the repositories of the past, hibernating through these difficult times.

Frequently dark-skinned women, each with a single miserable child, keened and begged from doorways or on the pavement. Romanians, I was told, but I think what was meant was Gypsies. They had become the migrant beggars of Europe. In the end I gave up looking for the other bookshop, returned to the first one, and bought two rather unwieldy dictionaries. They were heavy and difficult to use, but better than nothing.

That evening we went to see what we could of the monumental aspects of Szczecin, around the castle alongside the river. Walking back we passed another Polish entrepreneur, who had set up shop at his window. He had raised his bed so that the mattress was level with the windowsill, and he lay on it in his pajamas, eating a bowl of stewed tripe. His wares—postcards, guides, stamps—were set out on a counter on the windowsill in front of him. He could get by in English, and we stopped and talked with him for a while—I more for the unusual experience of conversing with someone lying horizontally at eye level.

At the next corner I was enticed by a menu at the doorway to a restaurant. While looking at it we stood alongside a Danish family, got into conversation with them, and decided to eat together. Henryk was a short, stocky man, and he had his rather placid wife, Birtse, and their two adolescent children with him. The conversation, which started with the usual exchange of potted biographies, developed rather strangely. He was a trumpet player who had been with a Danish concert orchestra, but his lip had gone and he could no longer play regularly. He had taken up teaching. His passion was the small family group he had created to perform traditional Danish folk music and dance. A thickening current of bitterness flowed with his words as he described the difficulties he had faced getting support for their art.

"There is no money for Danish tradition," he complained. "Anyone who brings in foreign culture can have grants and subsidies, but not us."

The radio and the newspapers, he said, were always prejudiced in favor of foreign artists, and he was quite certain that the Jews were behind it, because they controlled the media.

He wanted us to believe that this was the objective truth, that he was not racially biased, but he was angry that in Denmark he could not speak openly about these matters. He was a victim of "political correctness." Meanwhile, the Danish identity was being corrupted and swallowed up by these cosmopolitan Jewish sophisticates who were cheapening Danish customs and traditions.

It was a strange experience. He sat facing me, speaking with all sincerity, looking straight at me. I had no idea whether it had occurred to him that I might be Jewish. Was he challenging me, or did he assume that since I was listening politely to his views, I could not possibly be implicated? I argued the matter as though I had no allegiance to any point of view—which was true enough—and said that I thought it was all too easy, when you worked in the media, to attach more importance to events occurring on the world stage than to those occurring in your own parish.

"Why should it have anything to do with race or religion?" I asked, but I could see that I was making little progress.

During the two weeks we had been traveling, I had accumulated a large bundle of bills, obsolete maps, receipts, and other papers that were getting too heavy, and I decided to mail them back to Hamburg. Altogether they made a package about the size of a birthday cake, and it was at this point that I discovered something I would never have observed otherwise. There was no spare cardboard. Normally, I live my life alongside a stream of cardboard. Quite frequently I go to some recycling dump, where my personal cardboard river flows into an ocean of cardboard. There is always a box handy, and if there isn't, the nearest market is only too glad to get rid of one.

The hotel receptionist could not help. It annoyed her that she was practically the only person I could talk to, the inevitable target of all my demands, which I'm sure she thought typical of spoiled Westerners. She had no cardboard, no ideas, and no enthusiasm for the project. Nor did anyone else. Resourceful as ever, I wandered the streets until I discovered a garbage bin on the pavement around the back of a building. In it was one precious carton, not too badly stained and more than big enough. I cleaned it, slit the edges with my knife, and made a box.

But how should I fasten it? If there was no cardboard, there would certainly be no tape. Right! No tape, neither Scotch nor any other nationality. But the girl at the desk was getting interested in spite of herself. She found two short lengths of plastic ribbon.

It had been a long time since I last tied a parcel, but I managed it and took it proudly to the post office. There, a girl in a smock looked at it with open contempt and pushed it back across the counter. What she said was eloquently incomprehensible, but there is always someone ready to translate bad news, and the bad news was that all parcels had first to be wrapped in paper and then tied with string.

Now I remembered. That was what the post office used to do to us back in the old days. In Southeast Asia, as I recalled, it was even worse. There, parcels had to be sewn up in canvas, and men who sat on the post office steps made their living by performing that service.

I went back to my girl behind the hotel desk. Paper? Of course not. And even if I did find paper, these two little pieces of plastic ribbon would certainly not go around again. I went out looking for the sort of shop that might sell paper. No luck. What to do? Out on the streets once more to search for the answer. It lay below me, around the corner. A basement flower shop. The Poles love flowers—flowers and poodles. Poodles can be sold without paper, but flowers? I went down the steps. All I needed was a florist who used paper, spoke one of the more common European languages, had some kind of string, and was feeling well disposed toward the world. Not much to ask.

She was small, fiftyish, friendly, and French-speaking. She was dressed and made up like a Fabergé ornament. She had paper, and she had white ribbon. She also had long, elegant fingernails, and she insisted on doing the whole thing herself. Her fingers tugged and twisted the ribbon into a complex lattice of oblong shapes around my precious parcel. At each intersection, the twine was carefully knotted to ensure the geodesic integrity of the web. I shuddered inwardly, waiting for one of her nails to snap off.

Finally, triumphantly, the work was finished, without injury. It was a fine example of an ancient and dying craft, a projection in paper and string of her own immaculate persona, and a cause for much mutual congratulation. Lacquered, it could have passed for cloisonné. She wanted nothing but profuse thanks, which I gave her, and I carried my trophy proudly back to the post office.

When she saw what I held in my hand, the girl in the smock beamed at me and welcomed me to the ranks of those worthy of consideration, no mean tribute. She weighed the parcel. I said, "Minimum," hoping it meant something. She charged me 73,000 zlotys, which came to a fairly minimal four dollars. A good day's work lay behind me.

# Chapter 10

*I*t rained heavily that evening, and the city shut down. We dodged from one dark doorway to another in search of food until we found a restaurant that was open. I knew we had made a mistake as soon as we passed through the heavy plate-glass doors. It was the kind of restaurant where the waiters glide, the fish float patiently in tanks, and the patrons murmur discreetly into their soup. Our dripping waterproofs were taken hostage at a rather ostentatious cloakroom, and we were sequestered at a small table at the back and left with the menu for a long, long time— long enough for us to agree that this was not our place. We didn't even have enough zlotys on us to buy one decent meal. We collected our coats from the cloakroom and walked out. Nobody seemed surprised.

Several inches of rainfall later, we found the Balaton, named after a Hungarian lake, and famous, or so the menu declared, for its forty dishes. The premises were split into two halves. On the left, people with nothing to say could sit in gloom and cigarette smoke and be deafened by a very loud band. On the right, people could sit in fluorescent brightness at a counter, with rather less smoke and noise. We chose the light. The owner, wearing a heavy mustache and a paprika-colored shirt to prove his Magyar credentials, came to make hearty and pointless conversation while Ginny searched through the menu for something edible.

Traveling with an abstemious vegetarian exposes many illusions. On my own I could adorn the most ordinary-sounding meat dish with promise and soften the subsequent disenchantment with a good bottle. I regard it as a duty to have fun in restaurants, and it takes a really dismal joint to turn me off. Ginny is inclined to approach them from the opposite position. Rarely do they offer anything to excite her. Most of what's on the menu, she points out, has probably been grown in one kind of poison or doctored with another, and alcoholic drinks are just a poor alternative to good water. Subjected to this radical analysis, Mr. Balaton's forty dishes quickly failed the test, and Ginny settled for the only possible choice, a rather skimpy salad. I on the other hand managed to regale and pollute myself with a quantity of spicy pork. It was to her credit that, as always, I was allowed to enjoy it as if she were tucking in alongside me. With the food consumed, there was nothing to do but leave. The light was too bright and the darkness too toxic. Outside, the streets were even blacker, wetter, and more deserted. We went to bed.

The next morning I came down to the Black Jack bistro, where breakfast was served, to find Ginny already in conversation with Marek Kowalski, a Pole from Gdańsk. He was sitting with two impassive men in running suits, whom she called "the Russians." I took advantage of Mr. Kowalski by asking him how to pronounce *trzy*, meaning "three." He obliged, and his lips flowered around his teeth in the effort to project some inner voice or thought that would qualify the "zhee" sound, but I didn't get it. To me it sounded just like "zhee." Polish is difficult, and some Poles told me later, in all seriousness, that many Poles can't pronounce all of it, either.

We packed our two bags, recovered our passports, and bought a map of the region from the girl downstairs. It was surprisingly easy. I had only to ask her a few times before she admitted that there was such a thing. Then we took the tram to the edge of town at Basen Górniczy. It went careering through all the rusty debris of an obsolete port, crumbling workshops, yards stacked with metal stuff rusting in the salt air, most of it halfway to being reclaimed by shrubs and grasses. It was warm and humid, and the scene was South American—like Manaus, minus twenty degrees.

Eventually, on the other side of the bay, we started walking north on the highway. The land was wooded and the trees blocked our view. Drivers in baby Fiats and Volkswagens came whistling up behind us, overtaking wildly and missing us by only a foot or two. At one point along the way a bright red, room-size plastic cube with windows had apparently dropped from the sky, complete with American sodas, sausages, and a sophisticated blond woman in her forties, who was eager to serve us. We waited out a shower with her, and she also tried to help us say *trzy*. Then we walked as far as Kliniska, but by then we were pretty fed up with the traffic and decided to take a train.

Our object was to get to the Baltic coast that day. The map indicated beaches and campsites at Pobierowo. It was Polish vacation time, and with childhood memories of seaside holidays in England in my mind, I wanted to see how the Poles did it. The stationmaster at Kliniska was a short and jolly little man who, in lieu of language, invited us into his command post and let us read the train times from his board. We found a train to Swinemünde that stopped at Wysoka Kamieńska, where we could take another to Kamień Pomorski. From there, we thought, we should be able to walk to Pobierowo. I noticed how difficult it was to keep all these names in memory when they meant nothing and the words were difficult even to sound out in the mind.

We took a big, international train for the first leg and—scrambling out only just in time to save us from a visit to Swinemünde—changed to a funny little toy train that rocked and rolled wildly all the way to Kamień Pomorski. There the weather was worse. We had to spend a long time under a bus shelter while the rain hammered down, so we changed course for a nearby campground at Żółcino. We walked for a mile along a quiet road, meeting only one van, whose occupants screamed something unpleasant at us as they passed.

Polish campgrounds are often furnished with neat little A-frame huts, rented out with bedding at very reasonable rates, but we didn't know that and were pleasantly surprised. We found ourselves on the edge of a big lagoon, in an area lightly wooded with birch, oak, and willow, enjoying a very peaceful evening as the sun set over the lake.

While trying to understand the shower arrangements we met a gentle and pleasant woman called Ewa, who spoke English. She had come from Toruń for the summer months to help her sister, the owner of the campground, and we heard for the first time in Poland a story that would be repeated again and again—of the misery of people on fixed incomes. Ewa had a chronic health problem, a pension, and an apartment on which she had paid a deposit. The deposit was supposed to ensure a low rent, but while her pension remained fixed and had dwindled almost to nothing through inflation, the deposit had lost its value, and her rent was now impossibly high.

Listening to her as she patiently explained her predicament, it became clear that she represented millions of people throughout the Eastern countries, who would face real suffering in the coming years. The glamorous aspects of the collapse of the Soviet empire would soon pale alongside this misery. The collapse of pensions and social security would leave scarcely any family unaffected, and such widespread discontent might have quite unpredictable consequences. Meanwhile, she said, the historic role of President Wałęsa and Solidarity were all but forgotten, and he had lost his following. Everybody was simply waiting to see what the West would do for them.

In the morning, at the camp cafeteria called the Relaks, I took my coffee in the Polish manner, meaning with the coffee grounds in the cup. As I stirred, a fly popped to the surface, but I flicked it nonchalantly aside and drank up, congratulating myself on my acclimatization.

We had a hard but good walk that day along country roads, picking up snacks and apples as we went. It rained only occasionally, and we were able to get to Pobierowo in the afternoon. Walking up a rutted and muddy road to the resort town, we passed several large institutional buildings where workers from factories and mines in the south might spend their vacations, and I was reminded of their presence again as we entered the town because, instead of tar, the potholes and subsidences had been filled in with coal dust. Perhaps the practical benefits of this system were irresistible, but it seemed like a really bad idea for a seaside resort, and rather discouraging to anyone who might think of walking barefoot or in sandals. It certainly added to the general sense of crisis.

Pobierowo was crowded and wet. We found two campsites, but here there were no idyllic little huts under trees. In two fenced areas of nondescript, uneven ground, hundreds of small tents and tiny cars were jammed, peg to peg and wheel to wheel, with scarcely room to walk. We were charged twelve dollars for a night—an outrageous amount in Poland—given a metal registration plate to hang over the tent pole, and left to find a patch of empty ground if we could. There were several permanent buildings for cooking, laundry, and showers, and a cloud of thick coal smoke, burbling from the boiler room chimney, swept down over the site. Fortunately, our minuscule tent allowed us to hide away at the edge among the shrubs, where the smoke was less of a problem. Then we made our way to the seaside.

The beach scene really was a window on my childhood. For one thing, the vacationers displayed a forgotten indifference to physical beauty and fashion. Like in the old days at Brighton and Blackpool, men put knotted handkerchiefs and newspaper hats over their heads to shield their baldness from the rays of a rather weak sun. Some rolled their pants up to their knees and waded. Women tucked their skirts into their knickers. Potbellied men with scrawny legs and alabaster skin scampered merrily into the freezing waters. Three-generation families played tag together, with every sign of hilarity and enjoyment. We sat back among the dunes watching, and I shivered at the thought of removing even one piece of clothing, but there was a cool beauty in the pale sands and milky light as the sun dropped to the horizon.

As night fell so did the thermometer, and we became seriously committed to finding a hot drink. Our efforts were symptomatic of what everyone in Pobierowo was doing. Food, clothing, and entertainment were all triumphs of improvisation. The kids took their old jeans, shirts, and socks, and ripped, burned, shrank, painted, and sewed them into punk, grunge, and all kinds of hybrid hip. Then they swarmed and clustered on the streets and beaches with whatever they could get to make them happy. The only indoor place we could find was a villa that had been converted into a café, and it looked full of promise. In fact all it delivered was MTV, but the kids sat in the half-darkened room watching the screen and chattered happily over sodas. We managed to contrive our own happiness with a can of black-currant juice and a glass of hot water to mix it with, and then went to bed.

It rained again, heavily, in the night, spreading the coal dust more evenly over the streets, and went on raining fitfully through the morning. The vacationers sat in their tents drinking beer and playing cards. We carried our stuff to the kitchen between showers, and packed it there. Then we took off, with one pleasant surprise. When I returned our registration plate, I got half my money back, too. It was only a tiny stroke of good fortune, but it had a surprisingly uplifting effect, and helped overcome the misery of trudging unnecessary miles through the rain, following half-understood directions to a bus terminal.

Meanwhile, I was not feeling at ease. I had been trying to resist a growing impatience to cover the distance to Russia more quickly, but now it had to be faced and understood. We had spent only four nights in Poland. Continuing this way as far as Gdańsk, we could have traveled profitably for a week or more and learned a lot about Poland, and Polish, on the way. The journey with Ginny was in itself fun and informative. She kept me alive to things I might have missed, like the scent of flowers, the songs of birds, touches of color in the scenery and, equally important, aspects of ugliness in our surroundings that I am inclined all too easily to gloss over in the interests of comfort. She was truly a good sport, grumbled less than I did, and left me free to pursue my solitary thoughts. In short, she was a perfect traveling companion. Had there been any sausage factories for me to investigate, I would have felt no inhibitions.

So what was my problem? I was sharply aware that this was still just a preamble to the main event. The crux of the journey for me lay in the six hundred miles between Russia and Romania. Troubling me a great deal was the hardening conviction that I would have to make that journey alone. It upset me to have to recognize that. For one thing it finally exposed, as badly mistaken, all those nice, warm thoughts I had started out with about the pleasures and rewards of company. Worse still was the pain I knew it would cause Ginny.

How would I be able to explain my reasons to her when I could hardly explain them to myself? It was certainly not a reflection on our relationship. If anything, it was precisely because we got on so well together that I was having qualms. There was much in what Manfred had said: The relationship got in the way.

As a traveler, I was not always more effective on my own. Ginny often reminded me of useful information I had forgotten. It was frequently helpful to have another hand, and always interesting to have another point of view. Yet my purpose was not to travel in the most efficient way or even to be the best informed tourist on the block. My purpose was to experience things, good and bad, and write about them—to dip myself into cultures, like a strip of litmus paper, and read the results. It turned out that I couldn't read them so clearly in company. During my previous journeys—and particularly, of course, during the four years I was making my way around the world—I had developed a way of looking at things as a solitary being. The fault was undoubtedly with my vision, but it could not be helped.

I was not discounting what we had achieved so far. Learning how to walk was something done best in company. We had seen things and met people of great interest, but soon the journey was going to become much more personal to me. I needed to start on it soon, and alone. I would have to tell her, and I didn't know how.

From Pobierowo we took a bus sixteen miles to Trzebiatów, where there was a railway station. It was a medium-size town, where we saw outward signs of a renaissance. Some old buildings were being restored and there were indications of new money coming in, but I knew that here, as everywhere, the pain and misery would be hidden. I saw one striking figure on a bench outside a churchyard wall that seemed emblematic of Poland's predicament. A woman—I presumed an old woman, though I could not see her face—was seated, bent over, with her head in her hands. She was very small, and so still that she might have been carved out of the same material as the bench beneath her. A scarf wrapped and hid her head. She wore a thick gray coat. Under it about eighteen inches of chocolate-brown skirt material, in the tight floral print that we used to call a granny pattern, came down to cover the tops of her knee-high rubber boots. Silent, subdued, apparently bowed in complete resignation, a woodcut from a story of the days of serfdom: What could there be for her in this new Poland?

That afternoon the train took us another thirty-five miles to Koszalin, a garrison town near the coast. To our surprise we found ourselves staying at a hotel next to a barracks, and the hotel was apparently owned by the army. There was a great deal of confusion at the desk. Nominally in charge was another of those plucked, polished, and painstakingly resurfaced women who seemed to represent Poland's current ideal of femininity. It was not at all displeasing—Western women had made much the same effort after the austerities of war fifty years earlier—but it somehow became difficult to take them seriously. This particular woman did her best to support my prejudice. She misunderstood, inexorably, everything we said for twenty minutes, but we ultimately got what we had asked for in the first place—a pleasant room for two.

The next morning I told Ginny what was on my mind—that I would have to go on alone after Gdańsk. It was deeply distressing to her, as I knew it would be, but we got through it somehow. I had always believed she would be able to understand. As a serious painter, she would know that some things have to be accomplished alone. The difficulty lay mainly in persuading her, and myself, that I was actually engaged in some sort of artistic endeavor.

We spent an extra day there making up for the pain. The city was a beautiful place to walk in. A river ran through the middle of it, and parks with glowing flower beds had been landscaped along the banks. The sense of having been transported to an earlier age persisted. We passed a woman scrubbing the steps of a school. She was doing it on her knees, with a bucket and a brush. What was more, she actually seemed happy doing it. A little further along a woman in her late forties, dressed in black, with bright red hair, held her hand out to an older man, whose own thinning strands were oiled back over his head in outmoded aristocratic fashion. He took the hand and raised it to his lips in a gesture at once perfunctory and stylish. His action left no doubt that kissing hands was de rigueur in Koszalin.

We were finding our way with a map from the back of a brochure, which emphasized the city's religious life, the cathedral, the many modern churches, and the pope's visit. However, there seemed to be a large student population, too. We noticed a small shop specializing in English books, where I at last found a simple Polish phrase book published by Penguin. The bookshop was run by a young student who spoke some English, and we talked about various things, including the Bosnian Serbs—"animals let out of their cages," he thought—and my journey. When I said my mother had been German and my father Romanian, he was amazed. How was it possible then for me to be British? he asked. I said there were British people from all over the world, wonderful people of all races, including people from India, Pakistan, the West Indies, and Africa. He laughed, innocently enough, assuming that I was being facetious.

"No," I protested. "Why not? Why should they not be wonderful people?"

Hard-eyed, he looked at me and said: "You must have very different ideas."

It was instantly clear to me that he was not stating a personal position but rather what he understood to be the normal attitude. It was what you might call an "uh-oh moment," which immediately brought my conversation with the bigoted Dane to mind.

That night there was no piped water in Koszalin. Apparently it was all pumped from some central station, and the *centralny* had broken down. It must have been a common occurrence; we were the only ones who appeared to have a problem with it.

We took the train to Gdańsk the next day, a three-hour journey that brought us in at fifteen minutes or so before seven. We had read that Gdańsk was a popular and expensive city, and Ginny had found in our guidebook a reference to an office "opposite the train station" where private rooms could be arranged, but it was said to close at seven. At great cost to her composure Ginny raced across the street, but although she got there with plenty of time, it was closed, and looked as though it had never been open.

She need not have worried. Lily was there to take care of us. Lily Wisniewska was one of a flock of ladies hovering at the edge of the little park near the station. Although she was the smallest of them, her vivid orange hair marked her out. As soon as she saw us, she came chugging over like a little tug in pursuit of salvage and launched into me in rusty German, entreating, promising, singing the praises of her room. It sounded expensive, but she was implacable, and driven, as we discovered later, by the fear that if she didn't make a few dollars that summer, she would not survive the winter. We could not hold out for long, and soon she was steaming away proudly with her two big prizes in tow.

The room was indeed a marvel, a museum of granny objects. Behind sliding glass cabinet doors was a welter of cut glass and china. Windows and surfaces were festooned in lace and alive with plants. Mustard-yellow furniture anchored a swirling multicolored acrylic rug to the floor. The furniture had been arranged to make a separate alcove where we slept, and we had the use of her miniature kitchen, a six-by-six-foot box. It was only the next day I discovered that Lily, who was barely five feet tall, slept on a tiny mattress partially under the kitchen table. I saw the necessity for what she was doing and put my scruples aside. We could help her best, I thought, by simply accepting the arrangement.

She told me her story in fragments during the short time we were there. Her husband, she said, had been a fisherman in Gdańsk before the war and, being half-German, had been allowed to continue his work until the German army became so depleted that he was dragged into service on the eastern front. He was taken prisoner by the Russians. After that, she said, he did not live long, and she had had to bring up her children and struggle as best she could to hold on to her little flat.

Actually, it proved to be a bargain. She lived in flat number 5 at 1a Minogi Street (she asked me to mention the address) in a quiet area very near the most interesting parts of town. Impatient as I was to get on, I had to get my visa for Russia first, and we had several fine days in Gdańsk on that account. Nothing I had ever heard prepared me for this city. All the tremendous events of 1989 and later were concentrated on the shipyards, the grim-faced workers of Solidarity, and the bitter industrial strife that led to the collapse of Soviet rule. There had been nothing about the other face of Gdańsk, which is a city of exceptional beauty.

Most surprising was the tremendous effort that had been made by the discredited Communist regime to restore it from its shattered wartime condition. Cobbled streets and squares, elegant stone houses, graceful bridges, and ancient city walls and gates had been lovingly remade, and the once independent city-state buzzes with vitality again. We were in and out of galleries, bookshops, and cafés, took a ferry to see the harbor and the shipyards, climbed to the cathedral roof for a wonderful view of it all, and listened to live music in the streets at night. Ginny had been quick to recover her spirits and, true to her word, made other plans that excited her. She made contact with a friend in Germany, who agreed to come and meet her at Kraków, in southern Poland, and travel with her into the Tatra Mountains. On her way she would visit Toruń, a city of celebrated beauty, where Copernicus was born. Then there was another friend in the Peace Corps in Lódz. We agreed we would each leave word with my cousin in Hamburg so that we could arrange to talk in a month or so, and eventually meet again in southern Romania.

So dense with glorious experience was that short time in Gdańsk that I can scarcely believe we spent only three nights there, but on Sunday morning at dawn I kissed Ginny good-bye. With a lighter backpack, having decided to sacrifice my sleeping bag, I walked through the cool streets to the station. In spite of all we had done already, this, I felt, was really the beginning.

# Chapter 11

*J*ourneys are made in the imagination: The rest is drudgery.

On the station platform at Gdańsk, which my grandmother knew as Danzig, the journey I am about to make shimmers before my mind like a protozoan life form on a slide, wriggling in and out of focus, inflating and contracting, widening and elongating. I can't explain why I see abstractions as shapes, but I always have. Many decades ago, when lysergic acid was still only a laboratory curiosity, I remember seeing all the workings of society vividly represented before me as an intricate three-dimensional construction of cubes. I was quite conscious walking from the air force canteen to my billet, and it made perfect sense to me at the time. I suppose the baffled and insecure mind will resort to any stratagem to reassure itself.

So I am trying to imagine this unimaginable thing I intend to do while I wait for the train to Russia, but at the same time my eyes are fixed on a pair of lustrous black high-heeled shoes decorated with cherry-red polka dots. They appear, brilliant as lacquer, at the end of tight, tapering black slacks worn below a red bolero jacket. This cheerful and immaculate ensemble of carousel-colored clothing adorns a young mother, who has red lips to match and is handing her daughter up onto the Warsaw train. She has the figure and the vitality of an acrobat, and even though her actions are all quite mundane, she performs them as if under a spotlight, and every gesture brims with enhanced significance. Her vibrancy is all the more stunning because it is quite unreasonably early, somewhere between dawn and sunrise, and the world is still yawning.

As she follows her child into the compartment, I can't help but imagine that she is setting out on a momentous adventure. I am envious of her presence, the excitement she evokes, the delicious expectancy she projects. I'm the one who should be glowing with such a heroic aura, for it is I who am embarking on a momentous adventure, while she is almost certainly going home from a banal visit to an aunt. If she were to glance in my direction at all, would she get even the slightest hint that I am contemplating anything more romantic than breakfast? And if she did know what I have in mind, would she not dismiss it as a foolish digression? I suddenly remember those stern posters that admonished me from every station platform as I traveled around wartime London in my childhood. IS YOUR JOURNEY REALLY NECESSARY? they demanded.

Memories of war, the collapse of Germany, all that gray chaos and misery, come to mind more and more frequently as I move east. It becomes quite natural to summon up the ghost of my long-gone Prussian grandmother, who almost certainly traveled west through this very station a hundred years ago, who probably changed trains here and feasted her eyes on this same Victorian marvel of a station building that faces me across the tracks. If she were looking down on me now, perhaps from that copper-clad cupola, I know she would be appalled at what I have in mind.

"*Du kommst unter die Räder,*" she would say. It was her direct warning, her illustration of the terrible dangers that lurked everywhere beyond what was familiar. "You'll come under the wheels." For most of her life, the threat of being trapped and crushed under the ironclad wheels of a horse-drawn cart was very real. It must have been one of the more common accidents to befall ordinary people in her time, and a very public and gruesome fate. I once watched helplessly in India as a small girl fell under a grain cart in one of the narrow streets of Agra. The great size and closeness of the revolving wheel forced my eye to follow every shuddering instant of the event as the iron tire ground, so slowly, over the child's rag-doll body. Comparing such perils with today's automobile accidents is like comparing hand-to-hand combat with sniper fire.

And I realize, with an inward start, that this is not idle rumination. I have stumbled up against something fundamental about then and now, about the life I have lived and the journey I am making, about modern alienation from the mortal condition and the familiarity of death, disease, and disfigurement in those earlier times. I want to go on and think about what we may have lost that was good by shielding ourselves so carefully from what is awful, but an insistent image recurs of two men painstakingly driving a wooden stake lengthwise through the living body of a prisoner in Bosnia. As usual, I am myself transfixed by the thought.

Although the image was drawn from an account of much earlier events, it represents so exactly the quite unbearable horrors of the Bosnian conflict. My incomprehension in the face of so much frenzied cruelty was in part what brought me to Eastern Europe. Like many others, I'm sure, I feel a heavy weight of responsibility without having any idea of how to discharge it. Already I perceive that traveling alone will make me much more vulnerable to these reflections, and going to Russia is also highly significant. In terms of distance, I will be moving farther away from Bosnia, but this is for me the definitive break between West and East, and the effect is to bring me closer. It demonstrates rather well the power of culture over geography. Since I am drawn inward and preoccupied by these thoughts, the arrival of the Kaliningrad train takes me by surprise. Then I'm kept busy counting carriages, looking for my reserved seat, as Granny's ghost slips off the station roof and into the caboose.

This is an excellent train, much like the trains I took through Europe after the war, when cars and planes were too rich for me. There is a smoke-filled corridor along one side, where people lurch, drunk or sober, to reach the toilets and where the border police advance along the train like beaters through the brush driving wild game out of cover. Behind sliding glass doors each compartment is a castle, to be guarded from invaders by ruses suggesting that all the seats are taken or that those already inside are dangerous imbeciles. But this train is half empty, and those already on it have packed themselves convivially into a few compartments, where they are stuffing themselves with sausage and curing themselves in tobacco smoke. Eastern Europe is where smokers come to take revenge. Quitters like me are a despised minority. In an empty nonsmoking compartment I spread myself over the cloth seats, chew on my Polish sausage and bread, and watch more of my grandmother's Prussian landscape unfold.

This is a big, flat country of grain and potatoes, marshes and rivers and storks, fringed with broad sands and a cold sea. It is a natural continuation of the country I have been traveling through ever since leaving Hamburg weeks ago, a land of lakes and soft light, of dunes and rushes, but the sky is getting paler and the air feels thinner. At first the train follows the track to Warsaw, south across the Vistula River. Soon afterward a massive redbrick fortress looms up beside a different river, and the train stops at Malbork. To my grandmother this was Marienburg, one of the great strongholds of the Teutonic Knights, the self-appointed soldiers of Christ, who roamed the Continent from the Mediterranean to the Baltic seas eight hundred years ago, those same monstrous horse-borne tanks that Alexander Nevsky lured onto thin ice and sank to the throbbing music of Prokofiev.

I wonder whether my grandmother was impressed by all the steely heroism that was so much in fashion in her youth. She lived through three wars that ravaged the Continent. By the time she emerged from the ruins of the second one, in 1918, she had already had a bellyful of bellicosity, although in truth her belly and the bellies of all her six children were achingly empty. But that first war, the Franco-Prussian War of 1870, was the victorious one, fought far away from her home when she was a child. No doubt there was much "Fi-Di-Rum-Bum-Bum," with flags waving and bands playing and spiked helmets gleaming over cavalry whiskers. It must have been a popular war with those who weren't bereaved by it. Perhaps, since it set the seal on Bismarck's greater Germany, it was one reason her family was drawn west to Hamburg and a chance for a better livelihood.

So I imagine that from the luggage van of the train, where she was seated on a laundry basket to save money, she looked out on Marienburg castle with some wonder and pride in her Teutonic heritage, whereas I see blood and bigotry and pain. On the other hand, my sentimental affections go out to the land, which is lovely and mild and full of flowers and beehives and hand-pitched haystacks. It cannot be very different from what she knew, and as a peasant girl I suppose she would scoff at me and remind me of the unremitting labor and bone weariness it represented to her.

The Polish border formalities are carried out at Braniewo, where the train is surrounded by indolent soldiers in speckled camouflage and curious brown boots that have leather puttees sewn onto them. Everyone seems to be smoking. I declare my sausage (for want of anything more interesting) to a young customs officer with a pleasant smile. He speaks a few words of

English, but not enough to help. Soon we will cross the Russian border at Mamonowo, only a short distance from Kaliningrad, and I do have a number of questions I would quite like answered.

The way I often find myself approaching strange cities would not appeal to most people—too untidy and tramplike, if you can imagine a tramp with two thousand dollars in banknotes dotted about his person like garlic on a pork roast—and here I am again, alone on the brink of a country I've never seen, completely unprepared, with no friends or contacts to call, no maps or guidebooks, no phrase books or dictionaries, and no language unless I'm lucky enough to find someone who speaks mine, no local currency or any idea of what a ruble is worth, not even the name of a hotel, not even the certainty that there *is* a hotel.

Of course, I didn't put myself in this situation deliberately, not quite. Nobody would actually plan to be so disorganized, and I have plenty of excuses. I really didn't have time to read about it. I thought for sure I'd pick stuff up along the way. And in Gdańsk everything happened so unexpectedly fast. But my excuses don't convince even me, because the truth is, I'm enjoying it. I'm a little apprehensive, maybe even a bit scared, but definitely thrilled.

What kind of irresponsible, nutty behavior is this? you may ask. To take so much trouble, spend so much money, go so many thousands of miles, only to drift in like an amoeba on the tide without even knowing whether there is a museum worth visiting or a historic quarter to marvel at, or some unique tradition of artisanry to plunder. How extravagant. How risky. How absurd!

True, all true. I hardly know how to defend myself, and yet I keep doing it. What lures me on, what allows me to conspire with myself in letting this unruly state of affairs occur, is the anticipation of an incomparable moment—it may only be a moment, but sometimes it can be drawn out exquisitely in time—when my fate is revealed. I see myself plummeting suddenly into this exotic environment, as though by parachute, stripped of all the normal social equipment (What about the money, you say? I'll get to that) and forced back on my most fundamental human resources. Somehow I have to make a judgment, spin a wheel, hear a voice, call it what you like, and insert myself into the life of this strange metropolis. Out of this crowd I have to choose someone. Who will it be? Tinker, tailor, soldier, sailor, rich man, poor man, beggar man, thief? And then, what will follow? Until the choice is made, anything is possible. One of the rules of my game is that I must not use money to ease my predicament. I must make a connection, and then I must follow where it leads. So there is this moment of extreme vulnerability, like a moment of rebirth, when I have to learn my way in the world afresh. Metaphors abound. An insect bursting from its shell, a girl discovering she's a woman, an idea that explodes in your mind and transforms everything you once knew. Then the die is cast and, if I play the game right, it leads invariably to some kind of revelation.

I think many travelers must know this moment. I'm not going to argue with the Buddhists, and others, who say that *every* moment of life is a new beginning, but I am too shamelessly attached to the things of this earth to float so freely above it. I carry baggage, and I love to rummage about in it, digging up theater tickets and love letters and expressions on the faces of old friends I had forgotten. I drag my past around with me, but it slows me down, and to be able to put the burden aside every now and then and rediscover myself in the present seems to be a ritual necessity. It is not without risk or pain. Often I wonder whether a time will come when I can no longer face it, when my spirit is too feeble and scurries for cover. I think of men (yes, mostly men) I admired who killed themselves, and I wonder whether that was perhaps the reason.

For now, at any rate, the spirit seems resilient and willing. Everything is shaping up nicely. I'm on a train from Poland to Russia that three days ago, in Koszalin, I was told did not exist. I have learned maybe twenty words of Polish and not a word of Russian. So far I have encountered nobody on the train who speaks anything else. All I know about Kaliningrad is that my grandmother took a train out of there a hundred years ago, when it was a Prussian city named Königsberg. I don't expect this information to be immediately useful.

I'm loaded with cash, in dollars and deutsche marks, which is supposed to keep me going for months. I don't know whether I'm allowed to bring this money in, whether I have to declare it, whether that will limit my ability to exchange it, or whether some genial customs official will simply call it his own. I don't know what rules there are about anything or whether the rules apply. I have no way to ask or answer any of these questions. When it comes right down to it, since Russia may be in a different time zone, I don't even know the time of day.

After one of those long, inexplicable pauses characteristic of rail travel, the train moves out of Braniewo and plunges into a forest, and here's Russia now, behind one of those terrifying borders, familiar only from war movies, defined by two towering wire fences with a broad no-man's-land of carefully mowed grass between them, where one can almost see the perforated bodies of escapees dangling on the wires or lying spread-eagle on the ground. I have crossed many borders on many continents, and even though this installation has a museum quality now, I can't remember passing through anything so intimidating before. Soon afterward the train stops in the middle of the woods. On either side, the trees have been cut back and posts erected along a quarter-mile of track to support floodlights. It is broad daylight, but the presence of the lights suggests a trap. There are no buildings anywhere that I can see, and yet there are Russian soldiers all around us in camouflage fatigues and very broad peaked caps with green tops. They peer under the train, between the carriages, and into every nook and cranny. It's the set piece of spy stories, of desperate Cold War border crossings and double-crossings. How strange to feel the shiver without the substance.

The soldiers are surprisingly thorough and alert, and I'm struck by the quality of their high, black, supple leather boots. Both are contradictions of the story of moral and material decay that I have been hearing along the way. They are evidently going through the train very carefully and take a long time to get to me, but eventually a party of soldiers, including a grim-looking woman, appears out of nowhere to board my carriage. Two of the men come into my compartment, but they speak only Russian and all I learn from them is that the hotel will stamp my visa. After a moment, another young soldier comes in with an embarrassed grin and asks for a cigarette. Then yet another man, this one in a light civilian suit and with a fine show of gold teeth, hands me a form to fill out. It appears to be printed in Romanian. Perhaps they saw the Romanian visa, or perhaps they looked at me and saw a Romanian. I don't speak Romanian—well, not yet—but it is a Latin-based language, and I can guess that this is a customs form and has to do with currency. It takes me much time and anxiety to decide what to write on it, but I need not have bothered. Nobody will ever ask for it, and months later it will be just another of the many pieces of paper I carry away with me.

The train moves on, and there is not much to see but trees and twenty or so telephone lines strung on poles. Then the telephone lines sag abruptly and vanish in the undergrowth. A little farther along they struggle bravely up again, only to collapse once more. After a few more sad attempts they give up entirely. (I hear urgent voices from the past . . . *"The lines are down. We're cut off."*) Soon we pass a graveyard for railcar wheels. Nothing but massive iron wheels joined by axles—hundreds, maybe thousands of tons of them, jumbled together and spread over acres of land. Then the bedraggled outskirts of Kaliningrad intrude on the countryside. Two derelict brick warehouses and a water tower, abandoned in an industrial wasteland, are all I can see that remains from earlier days. The train passes through a marshaling yard with dozens of overgrown tracks carrying stranded rolling stock. Strings of decrepit sleeping cars, their pale green paint powdering, stand on spur lines like decaying caterpillars. Through makeshift curtains I see jars and bottles and cramped interiors bulging with torn mattresses. Everywhere there are men, women, and children picking their way over the rails and through the rubbish, and my guess is that they live in the cars.

In stark contrast to the Prussian pomp of Danzig, Kaliningrad station looks like a defunct recycling facility. The platforms are filthy. Steps marked EXIT lead down instead to a locked gate, garbage, and excrement. Unlike the railroad stations of the West, with their winsome little bars, cafés, kiosks, and boutiques, here there is nothing to charm the traveler and make him linger. The station foyer is a maelstrom of people struggling to get through with enormous bundles of goods brought back from the relative prosperity of Poland. I look in vain for any sign of an information booth or tourist office, for wall maps or posters or guides of any description. With Granny's spirit flitting overhead, I let the surging crowd flush me out of the station doors into what is now, officially, Russia.

# Chapter 12

*I*found myself facing a wide-open space, vaguely ornamented here and there with shrubs and benches, crisscrossed with pathways along which intersecting streams of pedestrians flowed. At the edge of this space were roads and traffic, and beyond the roads stood nondescript concrete buildings. I saw nothing that resembled a hotel or restaurant or café, or any other place where transients might congregate. There was no indication whether I was in the center of town or at the edge. There was no map visible anywhere, and I could deduce nothing from the movements of the people, which seemed random and inscrutable.

Out of the crowds that flowed past I chose Volodya. He was young, maybe eighteen, tall, slim, fair, and poetic-looking, and he seemed a little less determined to get somewhere than the others.

"Do you speak English?" I asked, in English. He went into mild shock, and stared at me for a moment through pale eyes between even paler lashes. I noticed that his nicotine-stained fingers were trembling.

"I yam stoodgie English grammar," he replied, as though in a trance. He was carrying a blue nylon duffel bag in one hand and had a cigarette going in the other. He wore a yellow shirt and brown trousers, and his brown lace-up shoes were scuffed and dusty. I asked, as simply as I knew how, for a hotel. I thought *hotel* was a pretty international word, but it didn't mean anything to him. I tried different pronunciations, and he watched with tense incomprehension. We were like animal and trainer, though which was which would depend on the point of view. Eventually we found some words in common, and agreed on a definition of a hotel as a "sleeping house for tourists."

He had sensual lips and a faint, adolescent mustache. There was a nervousness about him that I resented until I realized that it wasn't directed at me and that his jitters were probably chronic. He managed to convey to me that I could help him study English grammar.

"Certainly," I replied. "Why not. At the sleeping house?"

I introduced myself, and he told me his name, Volodya. Suddenly decisive, he set off at a great pace and barked, "Come on." He repeated it several times, with the emphasis on the second word, like an impatient order to a reluctant subordinate. We charged through the hurrying phalanxes of people going hither and thither until we arrived at last at a road and joined a queue. A yellow tram tottered up, leaning over toward the pavement, so tightly packed with passengers that not even light showed between them.

"Come on," he ordered, and made straight for the impenetrable wall of people guarding the tram doors. Remarkably, the bodies gave way and, like the mouth parts of some marine creature, seemed to draw us and my bulky pack in. It was like being absorbed and digested by a huge crustacean, and I traveled blindly in it for fifteen minutes or so, pressed up against its various internal organs—chests, hips, buttocks, elbows, and armpits—all surprisingly odorless and malleable. There was never any question of a fare being offered or collected. I was coughed up eventually onto an even vaster concourse than the one we had left, and Volodya said to me, with a little smile: "You are good man." I was glad I had done something to earn his approval.

Looking around, I saw that we appeared to have crossed a river, which ran behind us under a bridge. To the right, looming over an expanse of wasteland, was a monstrous cube-shaped concrete block many stories tall, weather-stained, sullen, and obviously untenanted. Modules stuck out of it at various levels, so that it might have been an obsolete space station fallen to earth in disgrace. I resolved to investigate it later, and turned to the only other large building in sight, a hundred yards ahead of us. Big Russian letters along the roofline spelled out: K-A-L-I-N-I-N-G-R-A-D.

"Come on," commanded Volodya, and through the big, blank doors we entered the hotel. Most people by now have read descriptions of that oxymoronic institution the Soviet hotel—the curious role reversal that makes the guest feel like a supplicant and the sense that it has all been organized to serve some quite ulterior purpose. Even without the Cold War, the feeling persists, but the purpose today is no more sinister than a scheme to keep redundancy at bay and capture as many dollars as possible.

Across a sweeping, if unswept, dark marble floor was an extremely long and massive counter, intended more as barrier than furniture. Two homely ladies behind it attempted, and failed, to match its grandiose and portentous presence. They spoke some German, and I learned that a room cost twenty-two thousand rubles. That was a lot of money in Russia, and I would have liked to find cheaper accommodation, but first I had to change some dollars. Not here, said the ladies, pointing to an empty cashier's cage, and they began explaining something to Volodya in Russian. Even without understanding a word I could tell there was something weird going on, but it didn't seem threatening, and when Volodya rapped out his "Come on" order, I followed him meekly into the street.

Apparently we were looking for money changers. I could not remember ever being so bewildered by urban geography before. Nothing was recognizable. With only a few exceptions the shops were invisible to my eyes, hidden and unadvertised, and Volodya found money changers in the oddest places. None of them seemed at all interested in doing any business. It was like fishing for abalone. You had to have an instinct for the kind of rock to look under.

Even stranger, when he did flush them out, he rejected their offers, one after the other. "Not good," he said. "Come on."

How could they all be "not good"? If we knew they were "not good," how could they be good for anyone else? But I could not frame a question he could understand. In thrall to my ignorance, all I could do was follow as we walked quickly for half a mile along the principal boulevard, named Leninskij Prospekt, and across a broad intersection. A little farther on he found a changer who was "good." Unfortunately, this time it was the changer who rejected us. He took my twenty-dollar bills and fed them into a little black box, which buzzed and flashed and spat them out.

Was it possible, I thought, that my rural branch of the Wells Fargo Bank was handing out forged twenties? No, Volodya explained. That was not the problem. But the changer didn't like such small bills. He wanted hundreds. I pleaded. Volodya argued. And finally the changer relented and took forty dollars from me, enough for one night and a bit of change.

Now that we had the money, Volodya quickly turned to something else. Vodka. We had to have vodka. On the way we had passed small clusters of people, usually women, selling items of packaged food and clothing. They sat on low walls, kicking their heels and talking. Most of the vodka he was offered was also "not good," but finally he found what he wanted—Stolichnaya Russian Vodka, with the label printed in English: the very same label I saw on the shelves of my local Safeway. I wondered how far it had traveled to find its way to this wall in Kaliningrad, but now another problem emerged. Volodya's money also was "not good." I was the only one with good money. Dread suspicion tainted the atmosphere. Just a cheap setup, I thought, and was immediately put to shame as the whole story came out.

I had arrived, unwittingly, on the very day that all previously issued Russian banknotes would become obsolete. Yeltsin had decided, on deliberately short notice, to issue an entirely new series of ruble notes, all with 1993 printed on them. At midnight all others would become worthless. All over Kaliningrad people were queuing up at banks to convert their money, and Volodya, who, I already knew, lived some way away from the city, had come there that day specifically on a mission to change his mother's savings into new currency. I caught my breath at the thought of the disaster I had so narrowly escaped. I could have changed a small fortune and lost it all.

The price of a bottle of vodka, thirteen hundred rubles, seemed like a meager offering in the circumstances, but as soon as Volodya had the bottle in his hands, he became desperate to get back to the hotel room. This undisguised urgency in so young a person made me a little uncomfortable. He rushed me through the formalities at the hotel desk, and we rose up in the elevator to the sixth floor, passed through a plush waiting area where some businessmen were pecking at canapés, and on to room 617. There was an expectant flush on Volodya's face as he opened the vodka and poured it liberally into two tumblers. Then he drew himself up with the utmost gravity, and staring into my eyes with stern resolve, as though he had just spun the chamber and put the pistol to his head, he threw the vodka down his throat.

Of course I'd seen this done countless times on film, usually by effete czarist officers, and never really understood it before. Where is the pleasure in it? I asked myself. Volodya's single-minded devotion to the ritual was a turning point for me. I have drunk toasts, and been toasted often enough, sometimes with much ceremony, but this was different. This was life and death . . .

Our conversation was limited by various shortcomings. For instance, he did not know, could not grasp, the meanings of the words *why* and *because.* Without them I was getting nowhere. Doggedly, I constructed examples of their use.

"*Why* did the chicken cross the road? *Because* the fries were cheaper at McDonald's."

He could not get the concept. Time and vodka flew by, and I had to persuade him that he needed to get going, before his mother's money turned to dross. So he went, leaving his bag on the floor and promising to be back soon. We would go out to eat, he said. What did I like to eat? Fish? Good. He knew a restaurant . . .

With some relief I closed the door after him. I liked him, and he had helped me. I knew how significant my sudden appearance in his life might seem, what an opening it might represent, and I did not plan to shirk my obligations, but I needed a brief respite. The room was small, fairly narrow, with a telephone (useless to me) and a TV that screened only talking heads. The bed was monastic, the bathroom white-tiled, with a single swiveling waterspout that served both shower and sink. There was hot water in abundance, and I rejuvenated myself beneath it, but only just in time.

Volodya was back sooner than I expected. "Come on," he commanded, and we charged off again to get food. Once more he demonstrated his talent for finding the right door in a maze. How could he know? Faced with unidentified facades and blank doors, he chose, unerringly, the right one, but we were out of luck anyway. Both of his first choices had nothing to offer. The third was a bar that tempted us with small bowls of cabbage salad, rissoles on half rolls, and hard-boiled eggs. We bought two of each and a liter of beer in a brown bottle. None of it was delicious. The beer was thin, though it claimed 11 percent alcohol.

We sat and continued trying to decipher a little more of each other's thoughts. I found out that he worked as some kind of baker, but not for many hours or very often. He lived with his family in Kornevo, some distance from the city, and had come in by bus. His father, I gathered first, was an army officer. There was a tank regiment. His father was the commander.

Something terrible had happened quite recently. A man had died. It could have been suicide. A general had come to inquire into the death. His father had been severely reprimanded. Volodya used a crudely expressive gesture, slamming an open hand down on his clenched fist, to show what the general had done to his father. Now his father was working overtime to correct the problem, though what the problem was I could not divine.

Volodya hated his father, who was repressive and violent. He flushed with resentment as he spoke. Volodya's complexion was so pale that it registered every emotion with a flood of pink, and you could measure it by the area and intensity of the blush. We finished the beer, and Volodya insisted on buying two more bottles. There was not much time. His bus was due to leave at six, and his bag was still in my room. Already I had a premonition that Volodya would not be too distraught to miss the bus, but I was determined to get him on it.

Volodya's appetite for attention would leave me little room for thought, and I needed time alone in this strange city. He handed me one of the bottles, grabbed the other, and, as we walked out onto the sunlit street, immediately hoisted it to his lips in an extravagant movement of abandon. I realized how conditioned I had become by America's taboo on public drinking, and looked around reflexively for the forces of law and order, but if there were any they were certainly not concerned with us. I joined him more to challenge my inhibitions than for any pleasure it gave me, and we boozed all the way to the hotel.

In my room Volodya made his pitch.

"Tonight sleep here, on floor," he said, with more firmness than he could have felt.

"No," I replied, just as firmly. "You must take the bus," and I bullied him out of the room. Downstairs in the lobby, I looked around desperately for a way to let him know why I had to be alone tonight. I thought the New Age concept of "needing space" might be hard to translate, too hard for the venerable ladies at the reception counter, but they said, "Inter*pret,*" and pointed to a small wooden kiosk in the corner behind the door. It had been deserted before, but it now contained a young woman who, as it turned out, spoke moderately good German. So I was able to explain to Volodya that as a writer, it was essential for me to have eons of time to myself, and the room was too small to share except in an emergency.

The bus stop was not far, across the square. We sat on a low wall, like everyone else in Kaliningrad, and exchanged addresses. I promised to write. He started talking about a young sister who lived in Kazan with his grandmother, and the beauties of the Tartar language, which I presumed was spoken there. Then a bus arrived, less crowded than the tram we had taken earlier. He made his last-ditch attempt to stay, saying it was too full, but I bundled him onto it mercilessly. I shook his hand as he stood squeezed into the doorway and said, with a grin, "You are good man." He gave me a pained smile. As the bus carried him away, he lapsed into an attempt at stoicism that failed to conceal the disappointment in his eyes. I thought I would not see him again.

The interpreter's name was Irina Svintitskaya, and the obvious thing to do was to go back and talk to her as much as possible. She was studying German, and happy enough to practice speaking it, though a little nervous about what her boss might think. She explained that Germans came to visit Kaliningrad in large numbers now, mainly elderly people who had been driven from their homes fifty years before, when the Red Army broke through at the end of Hitler's war. Stalin had repopulated this entire piece of old Prussia with immigrants from other parts of the Soviet Union. Now the Germans, relatively prosperous, could afford to make sentimental journeys into their old lives, while Russians struggled to put food in their mouths. Though it was a strange reversal of fortune, she was not bitter. Like everyone else I met, she could not help talking about how much things cost and how little she earned. Volodya had already told me that his father, a full colonel, earned a hundred thousand rubles a month, currently worth a hundred dollars. I think it was a constant source of wonder to them all that things could have become so bad so quickly.

Irina explained that there was virtually nothing left of the Königsberg I had hoped to explore. As for hotels, there were some cruise boats tied up in the river and converted to hotels for German tourists, but they were more expensive than this one. We talked more about shops and prices, and I had to answer a torrent of questions about myself and America. California was pure magic. Foreign currency enchanted her. As for the workings of credit cards, if I had brought out Aladdin's lamp and conjured up a genie, it would not have astonished her more.

The curiosity was mutual. Irina was twenty years old, strongly built, with dark, curly hair and soft brown eyes. She had an obvious physical confidence and an attractive personality, and I thought I would enjoy her company, but she treated me with a degree of reverence that seemed to raise a barrier between us. Of course, I was more than old enough to be her father, and I had come as a friendly alien from another planet, bearing mysterious tokens of an unknown civilization. Perhaps she felt overwhelmed, but there was a strong sense of old-fashioned rectitude about her that reminded me of the way well brought up girls used to behave, and in particular of the young women my mother employed in her London kindergarten after the war.

I told her as far as I was able what was happening in the world, and learned from her what I could, but the language difficulty and her own inexperience were very limiting. By the time she left, I was hungry for some kind of interaction with a real, live adult and wandered around despairingly until, hidden beyond the elevators, I noticed a door I hadn't seen before, and through it heard the unmistakable hum of a bar in action.

The counter, which took up half the room, was crowded with well-dressed men and women from a dozen European countries speaking mainly English. I hung around the edge of the crowd looking for a way to join the company when I heard a very British voice behind me declare:

"Well, of course I couldn't agree more, but then they'd never admit it, would they?"

I turned to see a rather short, very upright young man in a blazer addressing a taller, thinner man who, I guessed by his accent when he replied, was probably German. My rather obvious first assumption, when I introduced myself, was that they were visiting businessmen, but I was wrong. They were military attachés from Moscow, some with their wives, who had come to attend the celebrations of Russia's Navy Day at the Kaliningrad naval base.

The Briton was Lieutenant Commander Gary Newton, R.N., and during a spirited conversation I managed to tell him a good deal about myself and what I was doing while he managed, at some length, to tell me virtually nothing, replying to most of my questions about naval matters with "Well, I really couldn't say" and an enigmatic smile meant to imply that he could but jolly well wouldn't. Nevertheless, he handed me around the company generously, and I heard lurid stories of mob crime in Moscow, of cars hijacked and drivers kidnapped or found dead at the wheel.

Some of the women spoke of these dangers with a strange relish, at the same time as they listed, for my admiration, the truly colossal quantities of booty that they were buying up with their hard currency and shipping home. Fabrics, antiques, jewelry, works of art—they were packing them away by the boxcar load. They seemed to look on their purchases as a kind of tribute due to victors, and by romanticizing the violence that surrounded them, they could somehow validate these shopping coups. They might have been the consorts of conquering generals rather than the wives of low-ranking diplomats from supposedly friendly countries.

It all had a rather hysterical and unsavory air about it, and I noticed that it made the German a bit uncomfortable too. He was an air attaché, and I told him of my meeting with the colonel in the former East Germany who had insisted that the MiG fighters were more effective than NATO's Lockheeds and Mirages. He disagreed vehemently.

"I was a fighter pilot myself," he said. "It's true that the MiG's might be a little bit faster, but they are so thirsty that they can't stay up long enough. In any case, their electronics are not very reliable."

Then we turned to more interesting matters. I asked about the concrete monstrosity standing alone near the hotel.

"It is a terrible thing," he said. "I really can't forgive them. You know, it is built where the old Königsberg castle was situated. It was a very historic, very ancient castle. It was where the old kings of Germany were crowned. Of course it was in ruins, but it could have been restored. Many ruins in Germany that were even worse than that have been restored."

He was speaking with some passion now, diplomatically distraught, I thought.

"But instead the Russians wanted to wipe out the German presence, and they flattened everything and put up this horrible building. It was supposed to be the new town hall of the new Kaliningrad, but they failed to investigate the foundations. Now it is tipping over and sinking into the ground. It is completely unusable."

I couldn't help laughing at the image his story suggested. It seemed as funny as it was poignant that those ancient monarchs from the Dark Ages should reach up and make a mockery of Stalin's pretensions. I was interested, too, by this man's forthrightness. It was quite unusual, even brave, for a sophisticated German to talk about forgiving, or not forgiving, the Russians. Of course he had not even been born during Hitler's war, and I would no more fasten responsibility for it on him than I would on my younger German cousins, but political correctness still required every decent German, however young, to wear a hair shirt. I wondered if he was one of many who were finally taking theirs off. I thought it would be a fine thing if they did. Hair shirts are no defense against the dangers that threaten us now. And besides, when worn too long they can provoke unpredictable and violent behavior.

Eventually, I dragged myself away from the bar and went to my room, knocking back a shot of vodka and scribbling some notes before I lay down. I wasn't ready for bed, but in this spartan cell of a room there was nothing else to do, and eventually I slept.

The hotel restaurant, in the morning, was noisy with older German tourists eating a set breakfast of bread, cheese, sausage, and jam. Most of them had brought their own supplies of instant coffee. I persuaded a hotel functionary, much too bossy to be called a waitress, to let me have breakfast as well, and then wandered out into the lobby. There was no problem changing money this morning, and I was buying another fifty dollars' worth of rubles in the hall when the functionary chased me down and demanded two thousand of them for the breakfast, which I had fondly imagined she was giving me. Then I booked the room for another night, got a cheap map of the city, and went out to visit what remained of the city from my grandmother's time. Irina had told me that one small section still stood, not too far from the hotel.

For a thousand years Königsberg has had great significance in this part of the world, and the evidence is still clear to see. It must have been one of the most heavily fortified strongholds in Christendom. The map showed twelve moated forts ringing the city, as well as fortresses, towers, bastions, redoubts, gates, and of course the castle itself. All of them are in ruins, and were last put to use by Hitler's General Lasch. He was the unlucky recipient of one of Hitler's enthusiastic orders to hold Königsberg at any price and fight to the last man, dog, and rat, something he tried, but failed, to do.

Like Stettin, Königsberg stood at the mouth of a river, the River Pregel, where it empties into a huge lagoon. This long stretch of sheltered water, extending two thirds of the way to Danzig, could obviously harbor a fleet of any size. As a naval base Kaliningrad gave the Soviet Union its most westerly access to the North Sea and the Atlantic, so from a naval point of view it had, and for Russia probably still has, enormous strategic importance. Although now cut off on land from the main body of Russia by Lithuania and Belarus, it is of course directly connected to Leningrad/Saint Petersburg by a thousand miles or so of sea.

The old parts of town I meant to visit were called Hufen and Vorderhufen, and the names themselves indicate their antiquity. A *hufe* translates as a "hide," which in ancient English, as in German, was a measure of land, supposedly sufficient to support a family. There is also a connection with the hide of a cow, because supposedly at one time this was as much land as could be girdled by a thong cut from a cowhide, an interesting test of ingenuity, aptitude, and perseverance—not to mention magical powers, since another definition of a hide of land was approximately a hundred acres.

Vorderhufen was at the other end of Leninskij, only a ten-minute walk away, but I took my time, hoping along the way to solve a more mundane mystery that was puzzling me. Where did people get their food? In my rapid excursions with Volodya the day before, I had not seen a single food shop, although other shops were plainly visible. I came no closer to the truth this time. At the first corner was a hairdressing and beauty salon, with big plate-glass windows, where I stood for a while and stared rudely at numbers of ladies under dryers having their hands manicured. I saw sparsely stocked bookstores, kiosks, street vendors, and so on, but never a thing to eat.

The big boulevards had been rebuilt on that sterile, monumental scale that was so wearying to the eye and the feet, and when I came at last to Vorderhufen, it was a relief to find myself in an area of older buildings and narrower streets, with gardens and shade trees. The gardens were shabby, the houses sometimes semi-derelict, but it felt almost like home. I wondered what would distinguish the people living in these older houses from those in the great, ugly blocks of workers' apartments I had seen from the train. Did they feel themselves privileged or victimized to be living in them? Why weren't the gardens being used to grow food? And how did these Russians feel today, cut off so completely from their motherland? In their terrible economic plight, exposed to the relative prosperity of neighboring Poland (an ironic reversal) and to the even more prosperous Germans on their nostalgic trips down memory lane (doubly ironic), would they not begin to feel more like an independent entity than a part of Russia? In the short time I would have in this town, what hope did I have of answering so many questions when, so far, I had not even discovered how to buy a loaf of bread?

At that very moment I was lucky enough to spot a woman actually carrying a loaf of bread. She was coming away from the side of an apartment building, and I tracked her path back to the only door that she could have come from, a solid wooden door with no windows. It looked like a service door to the apartment block, but there was lettering above it. I pulled it open and, eureka! Inside, barely lit, was a bakery attended by a phlegmatic woman in a headscarf. There was little to choose from—maybe three or four different kinds of bread. Pointing and smiling, I bought myself a small brown loaf for thirty-four rubles, a pitifully small amount of money. With the dollars I had in my pocket, it would be hard to starve in Russia.

As I left, I cleverly noted down the Russian word above the door to add to my vocabulary. I needn't have bothered. It turned out to be the baker's name, Tatiana. But I had been granted a clue at last. Maybe food was always sold in unlit caves behind solid, unmarked doors.

Most of the houses were detached villas, but coming back to the new part of town, I passed between two rows of taller redbrick buildings that appeared to house apartments and offices. The ones on my right were built over semi-basements, each with its own set of steps leading down from the pavement, and I glanced down at them as I walked past. Only two of them had their doors open to the street, two successive ones as it happened, and through them I glimpsed scenes that were as startling as they were different.

The buildings were unwashed, unpainted, forlorn, and dowdy in the extreme, so that what I saw through the first door had the impossible brilliance of a futuristic vision, an incongruous spectacle as insubstantial as a hologram. The room was so brightly lit that it shone. It was immaculately painted, and in it, openly displayed or stacked up in cartons, was a profusion of modern electronic equipment and office supplies such as I had forgotten existed. A youthful man with a hundred-dollar haircut, who could have stepped directly out of a *Forbes* magazine advertisement in his striped and monogrammed business shirt and cool gray worsted pants, stood at the center of this entrepreneurial dream, holding a stylish new phone to his ear. A sign identified him as the Kaliningrad agent for Hewlett Packard. He might as well have been their angel as their agent.

At the bottom of the next set of steps was a room of hideous appearance, a scene from the lower depths. Before I had even understood its significance, I was oppressed by a sense of fear and misery. It was in every sense the antithesis of the radiant tableau next door, a throwback to all that was most demeaning in the old, menacing, authoritarian worlds of the past. Between grimy, encrusted walls of a sickly mustard color, on a filthy floor, stood shabby, downcast people, mostly women, waiting in grim resignation with packages in tattered paper or frayed and faded bags. A heavy door swung open, revealing bars and an aperture. I heard a male voice muttering a brief command, and one of the women shuffled forward to unwrap her parcel and push the contents through the grille. A stale odor wafted up the steps. She turned wearily away and another woman stepped forward.

I walked down to interview the angel and confirm my deduction. Yes, he told me in pretty good English, next door was a KGB prison. They were in the building across the road, too. It didn't bother him, of course. He had celestial immunity. The two scenes were like a medieval diptych, the antechambers of heaven and hell, separated only by a brick wall. But if you took the wall away, undoubtedly the whole building would collapse.

Then I was back on Leninskij, among the crowds of pedestrians and the women kicking their heels on the low walls. One of the tasks I had set myself was to find a functioning post office. The main office, a big building like a department store, had been temporarily closed, for what reason I never knew, and there were women inside washing down the floors. I was sent to another but couldn't find it. Men in leather jackets met and talked on street corners, but whether they were just chatting or doing deals I couldn't tell. There was a disjointed atmosphere about the place, of people trying to keep busy with nothing to do.

I went off to find a statue of Immanuel Kant, Königsberg's most famous native son, recently restored to public acclaim after years on the Soviet hit list. Not that I much enjoy looking at statues of dead males, but it was on the way to the bunker. Two very cheeky young boys of eight or nine surrounded me at the statue and whisked me off to the bunker with a spirited chorus of yells, whistles, and solicitations. There wasn't an ounce of respect in them, and I enjoyed their irreverence immensely, but the guardian of the bunker was outraged and shooed them away.

The underground labyrinth that General Lasch had used as his command post was a graphic record of the horrors inflicted on this city. The Royal Air Force flattened a large part of it. The Red Army destroyed most of the rest. Lasch had slogans painted everywhere saying he would never surrender. Then, when enough people had been killed, he did.

I came out hoping the kids would still be there to bring me back to life, but I'd lost them for good, so I made my way back down Leninskij toward the hotel. On the way I found three solid, unmarked doors and behind each one I discovered a food cave. In the first I found a great hoard of pickled cucumbers in jars but nobody to buy them. The next was offering some skinny roasting chickens, and a few people were inspecting them mournfully and muttering to themselves.

Behind the third door was a room packed with people. Light filtered through two lace curtained windows, making it a little less gloomy. Beyond the crowd, working across a counter, I saw two unhappy-looking women, one large and one small. They wore white coats, with lacy white coronets on their heads, which contrasted frivolously with their sour expressions, and they were hacking up some pallid sausages of great girth and some even more massive mounds of cheese. The people were arranged in two queues starting at the door and following the walls around to the counter, so I attached myself to the end of a line and watched.

About twenty people were ahead of me. Many of them appeared to know one another, and they kept up a constant hum of conversation, interspersed with laughter. Some delivered long and plaintive monologues. A stocky woman with thin orange hair moved up a few places to direct animated, and I thought hostile, remarks at a shrimp of a girl with a pointed nose. Some older women, also with dyed hair, sat on the window ledge to rest their feet. Among the younger women, miniskirts and short pants were popular. Some had friends or relations who came in occasionally to hold their places in the queue, and one man went outside for a smoke, making me suddenly aware that here, if nowhere else, smoking was frowned upon.

There was a lot of movement back and forth within the queue, like waves in water, but the queue itself shuffled along at a painfully slow pace. I spent some time trying to grasp why progress was so slow. The women behind the counter were quite vigorous, hacking off two- and three-pound slabs of quivering sausage and chunks of cheese, weighing them on the old white enamel scales with the big swinging needles, and wrapping them in thick gray fuzzy paper. They sold milk as well, and there was some business with bottles that required them to disappear into a back room at times. Dealing with the money seemed to take a long time, too. As I edged around the room, I studied every nuance and attitude of the people in front of me, rehearsing the few words I would use. Perhaps it wouldn't have seemed so long with friends and relatives to entertain me, but I arrived at the counter thirty-five minutes later bored and tired.

I bought enough cheese and sausage to feed myself for a couple of days. There were still about forty people waiting when I left. Among us all, I calculated, we had spent a working week in there. Well, what of it? Work isn't everything. But I was getting a little fed up with having to invent Kaliningrad for lack of anyone to talk to. Irina was at her post in the hotel lobby, and I asked if she would have dinner with me and tell me more about the life of the city, past and present. I had made up my mind to leave the next day unless something turned up, like a cheaper room or a good reason to stay. Maybe Irina would have an idea. We made a date for six o'clock, and I went up to my room to sample the sausage.

I had been there only a moment when there was a knock on the door. Even as I was opening the door I guessed. It was Volodya. He had come back on the bus and had brought a friend along with him, a shorter man with wavy dark hair, wearing a leather jacket. The friend's name was Andreas, and he was maybe a couple of years older than Volodya and seemed steadier and more mature. His brown eyes looked me over carefully, but he had an infectious grin with just the faintest trace of a harelip. Best of all, he spoke some German.

Volodya announced the purpose of the visit straightaway. They wanted to take me to a museum and show me a famous collection of amber ornaments, and they wanted me to come to Kornevo, where I could stay at Volodya's house. I took out my map. Kornevo was southwest of Kaliningrad and about twenty-five miles away. I pointed out the route I had to follow to go to Warsaw. It crossed the frontier at Bagrationovsk. Kornevo would be about twenty miles out of my way, but Andreas confirmed that Volodya's father really was the commander of a Russian tank regiment, and the idea of visiting him intrigued me. Andreas said someone would be able to drive me to Bagrationovsk the next day. He was holding something wrapped in plastic, and he passed it to me.

"Volodya said you like fish. Is this good?"

There were three kippered herrings in a plastic bag.

"Feerst," said Volodya, "we drink." He brought two bottles of beer out of his blue bag and then produced a statue of Lenin, which he presented to me with much reverence. It was a foot tall and weighed a ton. I didn't know whether to laugh or cry, and of course I didn't do either.

He took the tops off both bottles, thrust one in my hand, and said: "Lenin!"

If it had been old Joe I might have drawn the line, but I didn't mind drinking to Vladimir Ilyich. What I wouldn't do, though, was carry him. I set him down on the table, and poured beer into the tumbler from the bathroom. Andreas refused. He said he was in training. They insisted that I taste the fish, so I cut a little off one of them. It had a good strong smoky taste. All this business had taken too long.

"We must go to the museum now," I said, "or it will be too late."

"Come on," said Volodya. We walked fast from the hotel through pleasant parks beside a long lake, but the museum, housed in a fortress, was already shut when we got there. By the time we got back to the hotel, I was already late for my meeting with Irina, and she had left no message. I was annoyed, but at the same time resigned. I realized that things had worked out pretty much as I expected, which is to say they hadn't worked out at all.

The boys came up to fetch their things, and I explained to Volodya, with Andreas's help, that Lenin was a little too much for me to hump across Europe. He took it like a man, and I accompanied them to the bus stop, promising to arrive at Kornevo in two days' time.

There was a chance I might still find Irina. She had told me that her boss was often at a cruise ship moored on the Pregel and used as a floating hotel and restaurant for German tourists. I walked down to look, and though she wasn't there, I stayed for dinner. At the next table was a family group from Germany, including an old man. I listened in shamelessly to their conversation. They had just come back from a visit to the village where the old man had been employed before the war, and he was telling his children incidents from the life he had lived.

He had been indentured to a minor nobleman, a *Graf*, and he chuckled as he recalled the hard times he had endured.

"They never gave us enough to eat. We had to steal it. The *Gräfin* was always trying to catch us. One time I had to hide in a cupboard when she came into the kitchen unexpectedly. They were the meanest people you could imagine."

Irina came into the restaurant just then and, walking over toward me, greeted the Germans as well, so I was able to confess that I had been eavesdropping on their conversation and explained why. The old man, proud of his eighty-two years, was happy to go on talking. Perhaps there was no direct link between his reminiscences and whatever childhood my grandmother might have known fifty years before, but as he went on describing in detail the numbers of cows, the disposition of the buildings, the hours he worked, the hard winter weather, and the irritating affectations of his superiors, I thought her life couldn't have been very different. I realized then that she hadn't been on my mind much since I'd arrived. Granny's ghost must have taken one look at Kaliningrad and fled on the first train back. Perhaps, as the old joke went, she had decided she couldn't face a Russian winter.

# Chapter 13

*A*t seven-fifteen the next morning, on a fine, sunny day, I stood outside the barracklike doors of the Hotel Kaliningrad and hoisted the thirty-five-pound pack onto my shoulders, cinched the waiststrap tight above my hips, loosened the shoulder straps, and felt it sit down nicely into the small of my back. Without the sleeping bag it seemed light. The boots felt comfortable and strong, like a second skin. The vest of many pockets carried my many little necessities easily. Maps, wallet, passport, notebook, tickets, receipts, glasses, address book, pens, Band-Aids, and small change were all distributed separately and weightlessly about my person.

For the first time since I had begun walking in Möln a month earlier, I felt fit and ready and competent to do this thing. My spirits were all the more buoyant since I had convinced myself that this crossing I was about to make between the two poles of my patrimony would have a genuine significance. This was the crux of the whole matter. Everything before had been a preparation, physical and philosophical. I did not see how it could fail, either as an adventure or as a rich source of clues to my own hybrid nature.

Even though I once used to admire it, through my mother's eyes and as a wartime ally, to me Russia was always a monster. When I was still a schoolboy just after the war, I had the idea of going there. The Russian consulate (I never really got used to calling it the Soviet Union) was near my home, and I went to see whether I could get a visa. A heavy-set man in a black suit sat behind a ridiculously dainty table set on an Oriental carpet in the ornate lobby of the building. I stuttered my request, and he raised his enormous bulk up on his feet, looming over me and pinning me down with a baleful glare. His voice was deep, resonant, and incredibly loud.

"Who ARRRRRE you?" he bellowed.

I don't know what I said before I left the building. Perhaps I gave him my name, but a truthful answer at that moment would have been "I have no idea." A monster, to my mind, is any creature with the power to strip you of your identity, and for a while, under that man's oppressive interrogation, I lost mine.

So though Russia and I have had a long relationship, it has never been an easy one. It was a bit like discovering that your godfather was, well, a God-father. And even now, when the old monster had apparently lost his teeth, I could not help some nervousness about wandering alone into the Russian countryside. Just two days in the city of Kaliningrad were enough to convince me that the Russian Bear was too exhausted and anxiety-ridden to be bothered with me. It worried me at first that old habits might be hard to break and that some resentful bureaucrat or ignorant official would detain me for "unauthorized pedestrianism" or some such nonsense, but I soon put those thoughts aside.

It felt very good and brave to be stepping out like this, dependent on nothing but my feet to take me across an unknown land. Not brave as heroes are brave, but more in the sense of bravura—as though I were accompanied by an invisible brass band, with my spirit strutting and twirling its baton in the sunlight, full of confidence and excitement.

Over the sacred and desecrated ground of the old castle I went, gamboling like a mountain goat among crumbling cement terraces riven by weeds and subsidence, fancying I heard the curses and groans of ancient kings in their subterranean tombs as they strained to cant the hated concrete monolith above them one more degree toward the river. Scrambling down a slope, I met the road and crossed the New Pregel River on Oktyabrskaya. On my right I passed the ruins of a big cathedral, its red bricks darkened to the color of dried blood. On my left was a derelict circus. It seemed sadly significant to see both fun and devotion in such a state of neglect.

Streaming toward me from their beds, bathrooms, and breakfast nooks were numerous Russian naval officers in pale yellow tunics and big peaked hats, carrying briefcases and wearing the worried frowns of bureaucrats late for the office. Some were chasing uncomfortably after buses, some were cadging lifts from the few cars going their way, most were hurriedly walking. They did not look enthusiastic, and it was not difficult to empathize with them. How could they feel anything but defeated? They were forced to share in the humiliation and poverty of their countrymen, and yet they had not fired a single shot or sailed on a single active mission. What an ordeal Navy Day must have been for them. And to be gloated over by chubby naval attachés from the other side, with the buying power of moguls. . . . In their place I would have been sorely tempted to kick young commander Gary Newton, R.N., over the side.

The road crossed a second bridge over another branch of the Pregel and turned into Dzerzhinskogo, a broad and filthy highway with tram lines running down its center. After a while a park opened up on the right, behind an old brick wall, and my map told me that this was the site of one of Königsberg's many fortified city gates, the Friedländer Tor. The direct road to Kornevo led off here and I followed it, past some kind of electronic communications complex, through a belt of nauseating odors from a fertilizer factory, to the railway bridge. No naval officers here—just drably dressed workers. A woman of about forty, with a red windswept complexion, in rough work clothes and a headscarf, pushing a cart and wielding a broom, was sweeping the gutters belligerently toward me. I remembered the absurdly sophisticated machinery I had seen polishing the cobbles of the market square in Mainz. Street Sweepers of the World, Unite: the Panzers are coming to run you out of your jobs.

Kaliningrad is surrounded by a ring road, and after an hour and three quarters of walking, I came to it. According to my map, I was moving at the rate of four kilometers an hour—not rapid progress, but quite adequate. In ten hours of walking I could be in Kornevo. If I kept it up, I could be there in one day. Since Hamburg I had dreamed of covering twenty-five miles a day. Only my feet had prevented it, and so far they felt fine, in the sense that they were not complaining. Perhaps it was that which made me register how peaceful it felt on the road. There was traffic, of course, and there were people, but they were sparsely distributed and their energy was not intrusive. The vehicles were mainly commercial. To my surprise, even in this bankrupt nation there was a lot of heavy construction going on. Concrete mixers, sand and gravel trucks, loads of prefabricated slabs were all heading out to a satellite community of apartment blocks on the horizon, where I could hear the thumping sound of pile drivers.

Beyond the ring road things got quieter again. A motorcycle rumbled up behind me and passed, with a sidecar attached. The driver was a man of middle age with a serious, set expression. He was well wrapped in everyday clothes, but with leather gaiters below the knee. On his head he wore a brown leather helmet shaped like half an acorn, with leather flaps that tied under his chin. In the helmet, with that purposeful look on his face, he reminded me of Snoopy as the Red Baron. In the sidecar was a large female passenger. They soon disappeared ahead of me, but after five minutes or so the driver returned with his sidecar empty. Not much later I turned to see him once more coming up the road behind me, with a different large woman in the sidecar. Difficult times foster strange enterprises, I thought. By this time I was far enough along to see where he turned off the road, on a dirt lane between gardens and fields. There was no house in sight, nor could I see a heavy concentration of large women. I was tempted to investigate, but I did the sensible thing and went on walking. It did strike me, though, that my curiosity was not reciprocated—a marked change from other rural areas, where my passing always drew attention. Perhaps it's all been too much for these people, I thought. They don't care anymore.

A small tanker truck came toward me slowly, stopping frequently at the edge of the road. Where Americans mount their rural mailboxes, I saw small wooden platforms and, standing on them, a pleasing assortment of cans, pails, and churns containing, I realized as I got nearer, the yield from the family cow. The driver stopped beside them, climbed up on his tank, and emptied them through the hatch. His final action was to ream out the cream from the rims of the containers with his forefinger and flick it into the tanker.

The walk continued—uneventful but crowded with events. It grew warmer, cloudier, with some breeze. I walked alongside hedges and deciduous trees. Storks circled overhead. As the sun rose higher, the clouds commenced to mass, promising rain. A fleet of dump trucks carrying sand made up almost all the traffic now, and the same drivers passed me several times. I could not imagine what they thought of me. After four hours of brisk walking in beautiful weather, I felt happy and well. Although my feet were already hot and aching, any nervousness I might have had was gone, and by the time I arrived at the first village I was sure there was nothing to fear. Of course it could never have crossed my mind that, before nightfall, I might have to save myself from a far more ferocious animal than a supine bear.

It was just after midday when I came to the first cottages of Medovoje, fourteen miles south of Kaliningrad. Medovoje was such a small village that I could already see through to the other end of it. I walked on a narrow, raised footpath between the road and the cottage gardens. The large gardens were defined by knee-high picket fences that offered more decoration than defense, and the cottages looked like models of rustic charm in wattle and daub, set well back from the road amid outbuildings and vegetation.

Looking more carefully, I saw that the cottages were very small and primitive, and I had to remind myself how easy it is to project blissful fantasies on life in a rural setting. I told myself how hard it would be to work one of these half-acre life support systems. For a moment I forced myself to dwell on the frustration of packing a family into a space hardly larger than a Western living room, but the summer noon in Medovoje seduced me away from these tiresome thoughts with birdsong, soft breezes, and a feeling of tranquillity and ease. There was nobody about, but the people made their presence felt by the flowers in the gardens and the washing on the lines. I walked on looking for a likely house to call upon. I needed water. I had refused to fill my bottle with chlorinated water from the hotel sink in Kaliningrad, hoping to find a more appetizing source along the road. Now I was really thirsty.

A little way into the village, the far sidewalk veered off to the left and encircled a pond that was shaped like an eye and fringed with a thick band of tall green rushes. I crossed over to where the houses seemed closer to the road and more approachable. A rectangular steel kiosk made from an upended shipping container, painted bright blue and displaying a sign, MAGA-SIN, stood at the gate to one of the houses. It was small and neat but very incongruous, a bold hint of big changes to come. Although it was battened down and padlocked, I guessed it marked the focus of Medovoje's enterprise zone. There was no door at the front, so I walked around the house and saw my suspicion confirmed by a shiny blue tractor, obviously new.

Through the back door drifted the plangent tones of the Beatles singing "Lovely Rita." A teenage girl in a tightly fitting blue tracksuit answered my knock. She was athletic and good-looking and reminded me of all those old Soviet-bloc Olympic teams. My appearance seemed not to surprise her at all. Fed with so many lurid tales about crime waves in Russia, I still somehow expected the locals to scatter in alarm at my arrival. And if they weren't going to be nervous, then surely they should be curious. I would have bet money that no other foreigners had hiked through this village for a long time, yet I was treated, then and later, with matter-of-fact courtesy and only token interest. I was forced to conclude that these people, however depressed they might be, were after all in the habit of feeling secure. This was not a country, I thought, where a stranger could be shot for calling at the wrong house.

The girl filled my bottle happily enough, but when I strung a few words together to suggest that I might buy food at her shop, she shook her head regretfully. There were no goods to put in it; the cupboard was bare. The harbinger of a consumer culture had arrived before its time. I lingered a moment, hoping for a way to continue the conversation, but she showed no interest, and reluctantly I moved on through the village.

On my way out I passed an older, more conventional co-operative shop, which was also closed, and then began to climb a hill, but as I looked upward it became clear to me that the clouds were getting darker by the minute and would soon burst. My short glimpse of the village attracted me strongly, and the green pastures spreading out around me like a billowing emerald sea beckoned me to anchor my bed there for the night. I thought I would put up the tent, wait out the showers, and then return to the village in the afternoon and explore it more thoroughly.

I chose a spot in a shallow dip that concealed me from the road, and as the first short shower came rattling down, I sat it out wrapped in the fly sheet of the tent, watching the changing skies and the wandering beams of sunlight flashing between cumulus castles. In the short lull that followed I had the tent up, and before the first crashing chord of thunder announced the main performance, I had my boots off and was munching on bread, sausage, and cheese while I examined my aching feet.

My feet were a great disappointment to me. After all the walking I had already done in Germany and Poland to get this far, they were still not ready to take me the daily distances I wanted to cover. Old blisters were causing trouble on my right heel and the ball of my left foot. Would they never toughen into the hardy instruments I needed to take me the hundreds of miles I wanted to go? Like all living organisms, I presumed, they would eventually adapt to what was demanded of them, but would they come through in time? Impatience with my feet was all that disturbed me. The weather was no problem. I was dry, I had food and water, and I was still happily ignorant of how the day would end. At five the clouds blew away in a fine display of rainbows, and with five hours of daylight left I clamped my boots back over my sore feet and set off down the hill to the village.

To my surprise, I found that the village was already printed in me. Quite where in the anatomy of my soul that oval pond with its green lashes resided was a mystery. Queen Mary said Calais would be found engraved on her heart. Others receive instruction from their brains and take counsel from their guts, but Medovoje didn't seem to inhabit any of those locations. It hung rather like a hologram in my inner space, an interference phenomenon between present observation and imagined memories. Fragments of literature, both Russian and German, refracted the light from the past. A silly song learned from my aunts about the egg-laying habits of carp and chickens put an extra kink in the image. The rushes were a defining feature. So were the cottages, in their appearance and also in their distances from one another. Not huddled together for protection or so far apart as to contradict a sense of community, they reflected a nice judgment on neighborly relations. Villages I have loved around the world flashed by, and Medovoje slipped into the stack with ease, before I had even considered it. I walked back down the hill to discover why I liked it so much.

The streets were still quiet. I supposed people were out working, though I had seen none in the fields around. In the middle of the village, a dirt road went off to the east and I followed it past a few more cottages, drawn by a huge yellow sun painted on the wall of a bigger building further on. Two toddlers playing on the steps saw me approach and disappeared, giggling, behind the heavy wooden doors. I was able to read the word KULTUR among the signs outside and guessed that this was a community center.

Medovoje is no bigger than Elk, the small village on the California coast where I lived at the time, and Medovoje's community center was about the same size as Elk's, with the addition of a small library. I found the children waiting for me in the shadows behind the door, clinging together and bubbling with words and laughter. I heard something about a babushka, so I followed them into the library, where she sat, bent over her files, working. She raised a secure, stress-free face—those were the characteristics I recalled most clearly—and smiled. We had a pleasant exchange about nothing at all, which left us both feeling happy.

From the community center the village school was visible, only a hundred yards or so away, and I walked over to it. It was a two-story building, impressive for such a small community. It was locked up for the summer, but through the windows I could see how clean, tidy, and nicely decorated the classrooms were and, annoyed with myself, muttered silently, "Well, what did you expect?"

A steady rumbling of machinery caught my ear, and from the back of the school I followed the noise, which seemed to emanate from buildings closer to the main road. Under a high asbestos roof an invisible motor was buzzing noisily, constantly. Two rectangular shafts made from long wooden planks rose up from a large, elevated bin and disappeared among the shadows under the roof. Climbing up and peering over the top of the bin, I saw it was half filled with grain. From the other side of the bin a man with disheveled flaxen hair and a heavily veined complexion regarded me with clouded eyes and little interest. He was deep in argument, responding angrily to another voice, equally vexed, whose owner was out of sight. I advanced to see that a ramp led up to the bin. A dump truck was backed up the ramp, with its bed raised, having just emptied its load. The driver was leaning out of the cab, shouting abuse, but I didn't know why.

Beyond him at ground level was another roofed area, open on all sides, with a concrete floor, and on the floor stood a mountain of wheat, attended by three women with brooms. The women all wore headscarves, jackets, and long pants under skirts. As I stood and watched, the truck came down the ramp and stopped alongside the grain heap. A blue vacuum machine with a swan's neck sucked the grain up and expelled it into the truck bed, while the women swept the grain toward the machine, moving in a slow ritual manner, like acolytes at a ceremony. The truck circled around again and backed up the ramp, and the dissolute-looking man I had seen first came out and nervously poked a stick in front of the rear tire of the truck. The driver released his foot brake, the truck settled forward on the stick, the bed of the truck tipped up, and some of the grain fell to the ground between the truck and the bin. They began shouting at each other again. Clearly the man with the stick was afraid of losing his hand under the truck, and the drama between them was quite tense, yet the women seemed completely indifferent to them.

Strangely they paid no attention to me, either, and simply went on sweeping in that calm, dedicated manner. Then a fourth woman, with a young girl by her side, wandered over to the grain pile and lay back in it. She seemed to be luxuriating in it, rolling in it like a cat among olives. She sank deep into it and spread her arms and scooped up the grains, letting them trickle through her fingers. She lifted some to her mouth and then looked over to me, smiling broadly, and beckoned me to come and do the same.

I lay back beside her, nibbling on the grain and savoring the remarkable vitality of the flavor. Very patiently, with scarcely any words in common, we communicated our mutual regard and our pleasure in the ripe harvest that cushioned and enveloped us. All the women exuded a warm contentment over the wealth of the yield, while the men were cut off in an alien world of their own, barking and grumbling over their machinery.

Eventually, my companion and I ran out of simple truths to convey and she showed signs of boredom with the charade. It was only the effulgent fruitfulness that had momentarily made me part of her world. Intrinsically I was of no interest to any of them. It was early evening as I worked my way back to the main road. The air was still, the machinery noise soon became inaudible, and I was drawn instead by the murmur of voices coming from the direction of the pond. Seeing a willow alongside the water, with one bough low enough to serve as a bench, I decided to spend the rest of my time there peacefully absorbing the sights and sounds of the village. I could see the fishing rod extended out of the reeds over the water. How deep was it? I wondered. What could be down there? Didn't every pond in these parts conceal a carp? Perhaps the carp had been there a long time. Perhaps it was enormous, and had been there since the war—a German carp that no one could catch, the Monster of Medovoje. For half an hour I sat, listening to the voices, watching the stork on the roof, and pondering the beauty of it all until, as the clouds gathered, I rose to keep my appointment with the bull.

# Chapter 14

Strung up to breaking point by my ordeal with the bull, I now had to wait out the cows. They could not get over their fascination for my tent. They went on licking it and slobbering over it and shoving their noses up underneath it, and as long as they were pursuing their infatuation, I never for a moment felt that the danger was over. When a huge wet black nose pushed in too far for safety, I pricked it gently with my knife, and its owner went bounding away in fright, but another would soon take its place. Where the bull was now, I had no idea, but I had to assume it was still nearby. Then at last, as the sun finally went down and the light began to fade, they left me alone and seemed to have wandered away, drawn, I suppose, by the need to assemble for the night. They left me in a strange state of mind, convinced that I had escaped death by the narrowest of margins, but with no one to tell and no way to mark the occasion. I was wrung out, still not quite daring to believe it was over.

I remembered the last time I had felt that my own violent death could be imminent. That was in Brazil, when the *Federales,* under a notably brutal military dictatorship, had convinced themselves that I was a revolutionary or a spy or maybe both and had locked me up. The ordeal then lasted much longer, all of two weeks, and it was impossible to maintain the same level of fear, but it certainly had its moments, when the signs looked particularly bad. Eventually, thanks to outside intervention, they let me go, and their unctuous chief talked to me as though it had been nothing more than a mild inconvenience. If it had not been for the many people who later confirmed how easy it was to disappear forever down that totalitarian sewer, I might have thought I had imagined it all. In any case, it was a humiliating experience, a kind of defilement, and I was sickened by it for some time. That was when I had come closest to feeling like a disposable human being—close enough to give me just an inkling of how degrading and humiliating it is to be helplessly in fear of what others might do to you.

Give me the blind fury of a bull anytime. With huge relief I stopped crouching like a sprinter on the blocks and lay back on the ground. It was getting chilly. I pulled on all my clothes. Then the cowherd's voice hailed me. I looked out, and he stood there grinning down at me. I don't remember the words he used, but I understood them quite plainly.

"They won't bother you anymore," he said. "They will be sleeping over there." He pointed. I affected to be totally nonchalant.

"*Dobra*," I said, and smiled back.

He said good night, and walked away. A little later, as the dusk folded in around me, I stole out of the tent and crept up the rise until I could peer over the neighboring fields. Under the branches of a copse, I saw the animals gathered together in a somnolent pack. I went back to the tent promising myself that long before even the thought of breakfast crossed their tiny minds, I would be far away.

It was easy for me to wake up in time. It was too cold to sleep deeply. At half past three in the morning there was already a smudge of light in the sky, and I rolled up my dew-drenched tent and crept away to the road. Dawn broke just as I started marching toward Kornevo. As my body loosened up and got warmer and my pace quickened, I realized that I might easily get to Kornevo by seven. Twenty-five miles in twenty-four hours. Not quite what I had meant by twenty-five miles a day, but close.

Although my feet still ached, I felt wonderfully alive and well. In the gathering light, the countryside came to life around me, growing more lovely by the minute. I walked past beautiful fields of hay, pasture, and glistening corn stubble. Bursts of birdsong echoed the song in my heart. I passed through woods of mixed deciduous trees, including the biggest birches I had ever seen, and saw in a clearing what looked like a gypsy encampment, but with nobody stirring. After an hour or so, sand trucks began to pass me on the road, empty and going north. What on earth would those drivers make of me? I wondered. They must have passed me a dozen times yesterday. Then they went home to their borscht and cabbage, their wives and their warm beds, slept, got up, tossed back a vodka or two, came out on the road, and there he still was, the eccentric figure in the peculiar vest, plodding along.

Every now and again I would stop for a while to rest my feet, but whenever I took the weight off them, some kind of healing process would begin, and to start walking again was even more painful for a while. What a joy it will be, I thought, when I don't have to be reminded of my feet. I will have no difficulty then walking as far as I want in a day.

Only once along the way did I catch sight of a large horned beast in a field, and an electric shock of fear shot through me. God, I thought, it's only a cow—but I was branded. I wondered how long it would be before the memory of my terror faded.

I had been walking for two and a half hours when the asphalt road turned to cobblestones. Soon after, I saw a rusty enameled plaque that read TANKODROM. Then I heard male voices singing, like a massed choir. Another sign told me that I was entering Kornevo. Through bushes on my left I saw a parade ground and barracks and then the upper stories of some apartment blocks above the trees. The road led on past them, but looking ahead I could see no other buildings anywhere.

Volodya had scrawled an address into my notebook, and I dug it out and looked at it. It was in Russian, but easy enough to read. First came the district, Kaliningradskaya Oblast, and a postal code number. Then he had written "Bagrationovski P-H." Bagration—a name hard to read without a smile—was the nearest biggish town. It was where I would have to cross the border. After that came "p/o Kornevo—1" and then some numbers. "D 11 KV 64," and finally a name, Fursov Vova.

There was no street address. The numbers, I guessed, referred to buildings and apartments. It seemed to me quite possible that the buildings I was looking at were the full extent of Kornevo, and I turned in off the road to ask.

I had never examined my expectations, but it was clear to me as I looked around that I had not been expecting this. Perhaps my own distant experience of the military had surfaced from my subconscious to tell me to look for guard posts, signs with meaningless acronyms painted on them, pole barriers, swept paths, uniforms of course, and maybe even some of the bullshit stuff that I used to resent so much, like whitewashed curbstones and polished fire hydrants. At the very least I thought there would be some sense of order and superficial cleanliness, things marked out, painted, and dusted off. After all, the border guards had been smart enough, and so had the harried naval officers of Kaliningrad.

There was none of that—not any of it. I looked around me in dismay at a scene of desolation. There were two rows of apartment blocks—four or five stories, I think—facing each other. Once, no doubt, they had been white. On the architect's drawing, if there had ever been such a thing, they might have looked neat. Not pretty or distinguished or intriguing in any way, but at least neat. Now they were in a state of collapse, with filthy, peeling walls and crumbling steps. Only the glass in the windows and, in some cases, the curtains behind the glass indicated that they were inhabited. The ground between the buildings was a wasteland, all the worse because there had obviously at one time been flower beds, grass, paths, and playground facilities of some kind. If I had been visiting some run-down council estate in a depressed part of England or a housing project in Chicago, I would have thought it bad enough. That it should be a military establishment seemed inconceivable.

I wondered if I was in the wrong place entirely. If these really were military quarters, they must be for the lower ranks. But where did the officers have their quarters? There were no uniformed personnel in sight, but an elderly woman in a headscarf and coat came along the side of the buildings. I said, "*Dobre dan.*" She answered with a smile. I showed her the address in my notebook and she became very animated.

"*Da, da,*" she said, "*moment, moment,*" pointing back to where she had come from, and from the other sounds she made I gathered that someone was about to arrive. Around the corner came another woman, younger but also well wrapped, hurrying along with a shopping bag. She began smiling too as she approached, and since she seemed to know who I was, I guessed that she must be Volodya's mother. It had worried me a bit that I had turned up so early in the morning. I thought it would be hard to explain that I had been chased there by a bull, but she seemed delighted to see me. She reached out immediately to relieve me of my pack, which was on the ground, and I had to grab it to stop her from carrying it off. She made happy, inviting noises and led me up some dilapidated steps to a horribly scarred and battered wooden door, which she heaved open.

I had hardly absorbed the thought that she must, after all, live here when the smell of the staircase hit me. The dominant aroma, I suppose, was of cat's pee, aged and reduced to its essence, but there were other, darker ingredients, too, which I associated with our own species, and it required a triumph of the will on my part not to hold my nose. As we tramped up the filthy cement steps to the third floor, my astonishment was complete. I couldn't grasp the experience.

In this stinking slum tenement building lived the commanding officer of a tank regiment in the army of a superpower. His wife, obviously a very nice woman, with good manners, was somehow completely oblivious to the smell. The colonel himself, I presumed, walked up and down these stairs several times a day. Even if he couldn't get whitewash for the curbstones or brooms to sweep the paths or paint to touch up the door, surely he could get a couple of men and a few buckets of water to wash down the stairs?

Madame Fursov opened her apartment door and ushered me in, and I experienced a huge sense of relief when I found that the smell had stayed outside. She very soon showed me where the bathroom was, and with a slight blush of apology said something about "*voda.*" The bathtub was filled with water, and she showed me the bucket I should use to scoop it out. I had been wrong in my judgment. Whether the colonel could get a couple of men or not was beside the point. There was no water to spare for washing down the stairs. I finally began to appreciate the extent of the emergency.

The colonel's apartment had an unexpected familiarity. It was similar to the one my mother and I lived in through the war years in London. A solid front door opened onto a small, unlit hall, about ten feet by three, with coats, scarves, and hats hanging on the right-hand wall between the bedroom and kitchen doors. The bathroom door was at the end of the hall facing the front door. Glazed double doors led into the living room to the left, and they were the only hint of luxury I saw.

All the rooms were small. The living room, where I slept that night, was the biggest. A polished wooden bookcase with cupboards concealed most of the left-hand wall. I remember a table, some chairs, a large TV on a chest, and a couch. The couch was a simple affair of two upholstered panels hinged together so that the back could be folded down to make a bed. When I arrived, Volodya was still asleep on it.

The kitchen was smaller, maybe only eight feet square. A table that would seat only four comfortably stood in the middle of the floor, and around it on the walls were a painted wooden cupboard, a dresser, counters, a sink, and the kitchen stove, leaving just enough room to move about. Most of those fixtures would have been ripped out and replaced decades earlier in the majority of Western homes.

The bathroom, a windowless cubbyhole at the end of the hall, was no wider than the tub, which half filled it, leaving barely enough room for the sink and a very small toilet. It was crammed with stuff, including drying clothes. The painted surfaces were old, worn, and dingy, and the sense of clutter was overwhelming. The plumbing of this entire block, inhabited only by officers as I later learned, had broken down, and all the occupants had to commission their bathtubs as reservoirs. There was no immediate prospect of repair, either.

I did not get to see the bedroom, but it would have to have been quite small. Probably the building had been put up in the fifties or sixties, before Colonel Fursov had even joined the army, and I can only guess that it was representative of the general standard. It seems most likely that as he climbed the ranks, things were gradually getting worse. I saw no objects in that house to suggest that the Fursovs had ever known a fraction of the prosperity that a successful career officer in the British or American army would have enjoyed.

I have not spent much time with military people, but I remember two occasions when I visited officers of roughly equivalent rank. In 1975 I was the houseguest of a U.S. submarine captain and his wife, a remarkably modest and contented couple, who were certainly not propelled by greed or a need to keep up appearances, although he was second-in-command of the military establishment in Panama. It would be only a slight exaggeration to say that the entire Fursov apartment could have been fitted on the captain's living room carpet.

Twenty years earlier still I had been invited to take tea with the group captain who commanded the R.A.F. station where I rather unwillingly served. He was a decent and unpretentious sort of chap, a former Battle of Britain pilot, who was once famously in trouble for flying his Spitfire *under*

London Bridge. Life was still quite spartan in Britain when he had me over to his bungalow, but with its immaculate grounds, its cut glass, porcelain, and polished oak antiques, it would have seemed like a bishop's palace alongside the Fursov home.

I knew very well that Russia was economically wretched, that the bureaucracy was paralyzed, that most things were either in short supply or unobtainable. I had heard that the army couldn't pay its soldiers more than a pittance, and I had expected to find the Fursovs struggling. What shocked me was the evidence that their conditions must have been deteriorating for many years, since long before the collapse of the Soviet Union. I was simply not prepared to find a high-ranking officer in a great peacetime army living in a slum.

These dismal observations were made during the first few minutes after my arrival. Writing them down I feel a touch of guilt, as though I were abusing the Fursovs' hospitality by splashing abroad such sorry details of their life, but far from wanting to shame the Fursovs, my purpose is to praise them. Sharp and disconcerting as my reaction was, it was dissipated almost immediately by Mrs. Fursov's wholehearted enthusiasm. She was in raptures over the arrival of this exotic personage, myself, and all the practical difficulties of life evaporated under the warmth of her regard.

I have no idea whether Vova Fursov felt herself to be deprived. Even if she did, she would not have revealed it to me in the short time I knew her, but I can read bitterness and self-pity in a face, and there was none of it there. It was a very pleasant, comforting face, not beautiful or refined—though she had surely been a pretty young woman—but a strong country woman's face brimming with honesty and goodwill, despite the signs of overwork. Her clothes were utterly plain and practical. The thought of putting her alongside such regimental "first ladies" as I had seen in the West was laughable, though I would have been laughing at them rather than at her.

In fact she projected the almost impossible simplicity and selfless innocence of a Dickensian heroine, focusing entirely on pleasing and providing for those around her. Perhaps she shared some of the inadequacies of those rather one-dimensional creatures, too, but for the moment I could only benefit by her virtues. I was the object of all her attention, and she turned her cramped kitchen into a source of great comfort and strength. There was little we could say to each other. She knew the German for *breakfast,* so I knew some kind of meal was on the way. She made tea. Volodya came in, looking very solemn, and shook my hand formally. She said something to him, clearly a request, and he said to me, "Come on." I followed him out of the flat and down the horrifically malodorous stairs. Then we walked diagonally across the wasteland outside to the end of the facing row of buildings and around them to a gate.

"Family garden," said Volodya, and took me inside.

It was a big fenced plot, maybe a hundred feet long and half as wide. A path ran along one side where there was a shed and a chicken coop. Vegetables grew in transverse rows across the rest of the ground. The size of it was the first and only indication that Fursov's rank entitled him to any privileges. Few other families, if any, could hope to have such a large kitchen garden so close to their home. Volodya had been sent to get some herbs and carrots, and he was able to communicate, in our broken fashion, that his father worked the garden himself. Indeed, without it, said Volodya, they would have starved.

I have done a lot of digging, too, and few things give me more pleasure than being in a productive garden, which this certainly was. Everything you would expect to find in a temperate climate grew there—potatoes and onions in plenty, and all the other root crops; peas, beans, lettuce, chard, cabbage, cucumbers, and so on. I noticed that trees to the north hid the garden somewhat from the buildings, while to the east and south there were glimpses of the rolling, wooded countryside. It was a sanctuary from the man-made mess, and I strolled about in it as Volodya harvested his carrots.

Suddenly a loud and angry roar burst upon the tranquil scene, and I jerked around looking for the bull, but this was a mechanical sound coming from the east. At the brow of a low hill, in a clearing among the trees, I saw a tank. It was too far off for me to register any detail. I could make out only the general shape of it—rather flat, with a low turret and that long gun barrel—but it was moving in the most astonishing way, not like tanks as I knew them, but with enormous agility. It was climbing and whirling around and bucketing back and forth like a wild animal. Also like an animal, it gave the impression of effortless muscularity, and the surging roar of its engines sounded ferocious. I only saw it for a few moments before it disappeared behind the trees—I am sure I was not supposed to see it at all—but I was left with the impression that for all its violent movement, the gun barrel remained pointing always in the same direction, like the needle of a compass. It was a chillingly impressive glimpse, and I reflected that if the soldiers weren't getting enough to eat, the tanks were certainly well nourished.

We climbed back up to the kitchen—oh God, that smell, but it bothered me less, I noticed—and as soon as I sat down at the table a lake of hot, earthy borscht appeared in front of me. I beamed my gratitude at Mrs. Fursov and lapped it up. It was immediately replaced by a hill of steaming noodles. Feeling challenged, I summoned up what remained of my appetite and went to work on it, but she called my bluff and a mountain of pork rose up alongside the noodles. I fluttered my hands in defeat. She made insistent sounds and put a piece on my plate.

"Okay. *Basta,*" I said. "No more. *Genug. Spassibo.*" Everything I could think of except "nyet," which I thought would be too rude. She relented.

"*Chai?*" she questioned. So we had more tea.

Although it was Volodya's breakfast too, she deliberately made it seem as though the whole meal had been created just for me, as a celebration, and they would reluctantly dispose of what I left uneaten. It had been a long time since I had met anyone with such a talent for hospitality. I managed to ask Volodya, at one point, when his father would come home.

"Very busy," he said, with a tragic droop of the eye. I was impatient to set eyes on this colonel. A picture of him was forming, unbidden, in my mind, constructed from the various clues I had been picking up. Volodya's anger at him, the hints of violence, his wife's submissive personality, the general sense of things military having come to some crisis, the vague story of a suicide in the ranks. I thought I would not be surprised to meet a loud tyrant with a drinking problem and a short fuse, overweight, overbearing, and over the hill. Whatever this problem was he was dealing with, it was keeping him on the job around the clock. I could only contain my curiosity and hope that sometime he would appear.

They were very solicitous. They thought I should rest. Sleep. Volodya had to go out. He would come back. With Andreas and friend. The friend speaks German good. Now, sleep!

Sleep did not seem like a bad idea. I was coming down from the exhilaration of my lucky escape, and a short, cold night in the tent had left me feeling drained. I tried to tell them the story of the bull but failed miserably. So Mrs. Fursov put me to bed on the couch, and although I was a good deal older than she was, I still had the uncanny feeling that I was being tucked in by Mum. Before I fell asleep I reflected that she had driven from my mind all thought of the deprivation that had hit me so hard on arrival. Wonderful, I thought, how a generous spirit can transform circumstances.

A few hours later Andreas did turn up with his girlfriend, a student named Elena, who really could speak some German. Volodya, I discovered, had to work at the bakery and would not be back until evening. I was to be taken for a walk, to look at the ruins of Tinzen.

"Tinzen?" I asked. "Where's that?"

"This is Tinzen," said Elena. "This was Tinzen in the old days. Now there is very little of it."

We began walking from the building. As we went we collected another boy, a lighthearted kid who joked a lot. A quiet girl named Larissa tagged along as well. We came back to the cobbled road, and I began asking questions I had stored away. What was this story about a suicide?

"No, no. Not suicide." They laughed. "An accident. A soldier was killed by accident. It was bad, careless, lack of discipline. Volodya's father had to take responsibility for it. Now he was working night and day to raise the level of discipline. He had not slept for twenty-four hours."

Was the colonel a good man?

"Yes, yes, very good man," they all agreed.

"There," said Elena, pointing to a place among the trees and undergrowth. "That was the post office."

I could barely discern a rectangular outline beneath the weeds. A little later we came to where the railway station had once been, but whatever remained of it was lost among the trees and shrubbery. So it went on. Here was the mayor's house. Here was the church. There were the shops and houses. Here was the public swimming pool. Only two or three brick houses, a water tower, and a part of the church remained standing. As they talked among themselves and passed on to me what little they knew of it, there was no mistaking their fascination for these faint traces of an extinct community and culture.

Elena said she had heard that the stone from these ruins had been shipped to Leningrad—now Saint Petersburg again—for the restoration after the war. They undoubtedly experienced a sense of loss. I was sure that if only all the rubble of Tinzen could magically reassemble itself, like a demolition movie played backward, it would give them great satisfaction. All the horrors of the Nazi period were forgotten as they conjured up their images of a neat, prosperous, and orderly town, a place with some aesthetic

153 — The Gypsy in Me

value as they imagined it, even if only through the materials of which it was built. Elena transmitted to me a collective longing to be part of some such tradition, to leave behind the miserable dwellings they now inhabited and rejoin a culture, any culture, with its roots in a more civilized past, even if that culture was able to produce such an abomination as Hitler.

I didn't think that fascism concerned them very much. They were as far removed from World War II as is our own "Generation X." It was a strange and moving experience to walk with them among the shadowy remnants of old Germany, feeling their desolation as they coped with the catastrophic collapse of their own society.

I asked them what they did in their spare time and where they could go to enjoy one another's company. Elena asked the others, and as they grimaced and shook their heads, I remembered my own adolescence in wartime London, the barrenness of that social landscape and my own intense frustration. Her pretty face registered hopelessness. There was one café, she said, but it was impossible to go there. She herself would never go. The drunkenness made it too disagreeable.

I wanted to do something to show my appreciation to the Fursovs, and I asked if it would be possible to buy something somewhere for us to take back and drink that night. They took some money and promised to try. They said they would come over to the flat later and bring it with them.

At the flat, when I got back, I found Mrs. Fursov alone, preparing a dinner. She made a great effort to talk with me, and I also tried hard to dredge up the little Russian I had learned so many years before. She was very excited about the actor Mickey Rourke. She laid a fluttering hand over her heart, and sighed extravagantly. "Ah, Mickey Rourke, Mickey Rourke." He was her heartthrob, which amazed and embarrassed me, because at the time I had never heard of him or seen his films.

She told me—I don't remember how—that she worked in the unit library every evening, and she dragged me to the bookcase to show me her favorite books translated into Russian. It was an extraordinary selection. She loved Iris Murdoch, Theodore Dreiser, Jacqueline Susann, and Thackeray. She was nuts about *Vanity Fair*. Russian authors, she said, did not interest her.

All this took a long time to convey, with much emotion on both sides, and I was amazed and humbled by the amount of energy and enthusiasm she could bring to our conversation. I might have been Mickey Rourke in person. Then Elena, Larissa, and Andreas came to the door with a bottle of some kind of liqueur or aperitif I could not identify. We were already sitting at the table when Colonel Fursov suddenly arrived.

Without meaning to, I had let my imaginary portrait of him assume some substance, so that when the real man appeared before me I was pleasantly startled. He was much younger than I had expected, of medium height, with sandy hair and a lithe, tough-looking body. He seemed untired in spite of a long period without sleep, and moved with great vigor and decisiveness. He was obviously extremely fit, and his uniform was impeccable. Most interesting of all to me was that there was no hint of vice or brutality in his face. On the contrary, he had a frank, open expression, almost mild, but I was immediately aware of the quick intelligence behind it. In short, he looked like a man at the height of his powers, on top of his job, and the exact opposite of the caricature I had created.

He sat down with us and ate, and we toasted each other in the rather sickly liqueur, with the colonel excusing himself from taking more than one nip. He had a very rudimentary knowledge of German, and used it to explain that he had been stationed in East Germany for a while. Then he asked me if I would like to come down to the garden with him while it was still light. Encouraged by my interest, he showed me around in a very thorough way, so that I was left in no doubt that he really did take care of the garden himself. He picked a handful of peas to nibble on, invited me to do the same, and then we sat in the shed for a while as he smoked a cigarette.

As I watched how he moved and how he handled the problems of conversation with a stranger with virtually no language, I warmed to him more and more. In particular his genuine feeling for the plants and the soil touched me deeply, so I believed him without reservation when he contrived to say how much he wished tanks could be used in agriculture rather than warfare. The conflict was all too apparent. He was fascinated by the machines. He had a wonderful new tank, he said, that he was putting through trials. He wished he could show it to me, but sadly, since I was a foreigner, it was impossible. I didn't mention what I had already seen, for fear of embarrassing him.

He apologized for having so little time to give me, but the death was a tragedy that must never be repeated. I told him what a help his son had been to me, and to draw out his feelings I tried to convey that Volodya was a "good kid." Fursov nodded, rather mechanically I thought, and for the first time his expression looked tired. I think I understood. Fathers always expect so much of their sons. Then he shook himself awake and stood up to leave his refuge. We went back to the others, and soon afterward he shook my hand. He had to go back on duty in two hours and was going to snatch some sleep. He had arranged, he said, for a car to pick me up at seven in the morning to take me to Bagrationovsk and the border.

We had had very little time and even fewer words, but as I lay on the couch again that night I felt I had learned a great deal. Indispensable as words may be, when it comes to judging people, there is often more to be gained in silence. Brilliant conversation might have brought other rewards, but I felt more solidly connected to the Fursovs for the lack of it. I thought I understood them, and through them something of their culture, the better for having had to fall back on the simplest forms of expression.

Much of what I had picked up was nonverbal. I felt I had a good measure of the frustration the young people felt, but it was very different in kind from the discontent of their counterparts in the West. For one thing, they demonstrated a more tangible sense of their own self-worth. They were not surrounded by models of egregious affluence to emphasize their own failure, as is so often the case in Western countries. It was the society itself that had fallen apart, and it was clear that they thought of themselves as part of the solution.

Even Volodya, the dreamer and the most troubled of them all, who still clung to his faith in the old order, was responsible enough to be trusted to take the family savings to Kaliningrad and come back with "good money." As for the colonel, that most impressive figure, I could make no judgment of his competence as a tank officer, but if intelligence, attitude, and physical presence were the criteria, he would make a damn good one. I could only sympathize with a man in his position, who began his career when the Soviet Union, having buried Stalin, could still convince some of its own people at least that it represented the future hope of mankind, only to see it disintegrate.

I doubt very much whether the majority of Russians see the collapse of Communism as it is seen from outside. Their view may be much more comparable to the way Americans saw America when the stock market crash of 1929 led to the Great Depression. There are similarities. Many Americans thought that the rich had been too greedy, that the capitalist system had been abused and needed modifying. The entire capitalist "bloc" went into shock. Organized crime, which had been semi-tolerated during the years of

Prohibition, clamped down on the American jugular with a grip that has yet to be dislodged. Socialists thought that capitalism was in its death throes and had proved itself to be a cruel, unworkable system. They were confident that socialism would replace it.

Today, America's talking heads are saying the same thing about socialism, but I don't think the people of the Eastern bloc are any more convinced of it than Americans were convinced of the opposite. They may see the need for private ownership and the profit incentive, just as Americans saw the need for the New Deal. Russia will come back from this collapse (just as America, Germany, and Japan did), but not, I think, as a fully capitalist society. Clearly, a few days spent in the European tip of Russia are no basis for such a judgment. My belief is formed more by extrapolation from many years of travel through all kinds of countries and cultures, combined with much curiosity and reading. Nevertheless, my experiences there did give me an underlying confidence in that future. You could say I was bullish.

Volodya, solemn as ever, had to leave the house early. He said his good-byes to me with much restrained emotion and coloring of cheeks. My difficulties with the statue of Lenin had been forgiven. He gave me an enameled badge from his days as a soldier. It was a pure Soviet icon, the red star, the hammer and sickle, and all. His mother said it meant a lot to him. She brought forth newly raised mountains of noodles and pork, which I attempted in vain to scale. Then she cut off a large chunk of smoked pork fat and wrapped it for me to take along. The name of this food in German is *Speck,* and I had not thought about for a long time. It is something everybody I know in the weight-conscious Western world would only expect to be seen dead with. It was a direct connection with my grandmother's time, and tremendously evocative of that old German peasant culture that she had been raised in. It was much admired at a time when butter was a luxury and people still spread beef drippings on their bread. I thanked her for it, but she wanted to give me more. She brought a book out of her shelves, a book of reproductions from the Hermitage collection, and offered it, but I declined. If she insisted, I said, she could send it to me at home. She agreed enthusiastically, but of course it is not the same thing at all to wrap up an object later, when the emotion of parting has cooled, and send it off into the uncertain void of the Russian mails, so I am not surprised that it didn't arrive. I imagine the five-thousand-ruble note I slipped under the fly sheet to cover postage is still in there, undiscovered, and I wish I had thought to put it somewhere where it would be seen. It was only five dollars, but it was also 50 percent of the colonel's monthly income.

At seven the car did not come. Nor at eight, or nine. At nine-thirty a messenger came to say the car would not start. They were looking for another one. It struck me that as far as I could remember, during the whole of our walk yesterday there had not been a single car on the road. It was ten-thirty when Vova came to fetch me. She kissed me on the cheek, and I went down the foul-smelling staircase for the last time, knowing it would haunt me.

A thin, gentle-looking man was standing outside in front of a small van. He looked poetic, with his wavy brown hair and brown eyes, set in a narrow, thoughtful face of darker complexion. Maybe Armenian, I thought. He wore a brown wool cardigan and brown boots. In fact everything he wore was brown. He greeted me in French.

"*Bonjour,*" he said. "My name is Anatoli. Fursov asked me to take you. We are good friends. Please get in—I'll put your bag in the back."

It was a very small van and it rattled a lot, but it worked and we drove off at a comfortable pace.

"Fursov told me about you," he said. "It was clever of him to put us in contact. How fortunate that we share the same interests. He was sure you would be interested in our project."

"Yes indeed," I said, a little bewildered. Was I supposed to go along with this? Maybe this was how Fursov had fixed the lift. "Can you tell me more about your plan?" I asked.

"Well," he said, "we want to do it in the American way, you know. Very efficiently. Like a factory. I have six hundred acres, so land is no problem, but we don't have the expertise. You will be able to advise us, and perhaps you will be able to bring in the latest equipment. Everything must be the latest thing, very up-to-date. Of course that would be part of the investment. What do you think?"

"This could be very interesting," I replied, as much in the dark as ever. "How much are you thinking of putting into this yourselves?"

"Ah, we will have to talk about it. When we get to Bagrationovsk I will introduce you to my associates. In the present situation our money is not very useful. But we have the land and the labor. As a farmer yourself, you will understand the value of that."

"*Ah, oui. Absolument,*" I said. So I was a farmer, apparently, but what was this about factories?

"How about markets?" I asked. "Where will you sell . . ." It? Them? What the hell was it, or them?

"There is no problem. People must eat. The question is only how far to go with the product."

"Naturally," I agreed. "It is always difficult to know how far one should go. But what are the choices?"

"We will have to build our own slaughterhouse, of course, but then we must decide whether to make our own products. That is where the real profit would be, to be sure."

It was dawning on me. Slaughterhouse? Products? Bingo! They took me for a hog farmer. And one of the nasty kind too, apparently. A factory farmer. An imprisoner and torturer of poor porkers.

"There is much to think about here," I said, truthfully enough. I sat back for a while and contemplated a future in pork bellies. Then I asked him more about himself. He said he was a farmer, too, though he was shy about the details. Assuming that in the present chaotic circumstances an officer might employ unorthodox methods to feed his men, I speculated that Anatoli might be an unofficial supplier to the regiment. He told me that with two associates he also had a business in Bagrationovsk—a bakery.

As he talked, I watched the countryside go by. We were on a narrow road winding slowly between hedgerows. Every size and variety of weed, flower, shrub, bush, and tree seemed to be growing at the roadside. I thought I recognized hazel and hawthorn and various plum trees among the taller bushes. There were chestnuts, beeches, birches, and oaks. Behind them the fields were largely pasture, with some cattle, but the land had a relaxed, sleepy feel, with the little sign of human presence. Only the road and the vehicle kept us in the present century.

Because I had been cast as a farmer and did in truth have an interest in the subject, I began to think what a wonderful opportunity was opening up in these "liberated" Eastern countries for anyone from the West young enough to want to make a new start on the land. So what if the amenities of our overdeveloped, consumer-driven society were absent? Here in these big, open lands you could build your own life and grow with a reborn society. Whatever restrictions there were could surely be softened by money, and Western money today was so absurdly overvalued in the East that even a modest amount would be a fortune. What a pity, I thought, that only big corporations were raiding this new old frontier, bringing in the same dreadful mechanistic approaches to life that had ruined most of America and much of Europe already. This guy Anatoli shouldn't be thinking of factory farms. I had the beginnings of an idea . . .

Bagrationovsk is named after the Marshal Bagration, who fought in the Napoleonic Wars. English speakers are inclined to laugh at the name, but when pronounced correctly, with a rolling *r,* a "ts" sound for the *t,* and a swoop on the last syllable, it sounds more martial. We rattled into town over wet cobbled streets at around twelve-thirty and stopped outside Anatoli's bakery. It was a two-story building of red brick. The bricks looked new and for the most part were still bare, inside and out, and although the color and texture were attractive, the house looked as though it had been thrown together in haste without enough mortar.

Inside was all bustling activity, with women carrying trays of baked goods in from the ovens at the back. We passed a display, and Anatoli asked me to choose what I wanted before we went up some bare steps to an office, where his two accomplices were sitting at a table with a third man. Perhaps they had been advised of our arrival. All three were very different from Anatoli—big, burly men with lined faces and a tendency to look either blankly hostile or condescending. One of his associates was an older man from Moscow. The third man was introduced to me as a Polish sausage entrepreneur—that is to say, both he and his sausages were Polish. I did not get the names, which failed to survive translation into French, but it scarcely mattered as I was pretty sure we would never meet again.

Anatoli spoke to them in Russian, while a girl came in with coffee and the cakes we had ordered. Then he invited me to comment on their idea.

"Anatoli," I began. "You speak of wanting to employ the latest, most up-to-date methods, and it is not your fault that you are not au courant with recent developments in the hog field. It is true that until lately the factory method was thought the most profitable, but there has been a dramatic reversal, prompted by changing demand, nutritional factors, and so on. It so often happens, does it not? Today's imperishable truth becomes tomorrow's quaint superstition."

I was beginning to feel quite fluent. French seemed to suit my subject well.

"The leaders in this field no longer lock the animals up in those expensive installations. Remarkably, it has been shown that it is actually cheaper and more efficient to let the pigs run around in a state as close as possible to their wild habits."

While I was warming to my idea, Anatoli's face was registering some concern, wondering perhaps whether his French was deficient.

"In the first place, the flavor and consistency of the meat is superior, and there is much less fat. You may not see the advantage of this yet . . ." I was thinking of the *Speck* in my pack, "but you will. Believe me.

"And then, the equipment is so much simpler. All you need are really strong perimeter fences, well buried. You see, you have the land. And the beauty of the system is that the pigs do half your farming for you—they dig and they fertilize. Then you move them on and plant what you like. Feed costs are minimal."

Anatoli was trying hard to keep his face outwardly calm, but there was evidence of a great struggle.

"Of course," I added, "there is also the music. That is essential."

"*La musique?*" he asked, in half-strangled tones.

"Yes. It improves their attitude tremendously. There must be loudspeakers mounted at the corner posts. Baroque seems to work best, but some people favor light opera. Perhaps you would like to translate what I have said so far, before I go into more detail."

As he spoke, I looked at them intently. Their faces became set in rigid frowns. The man from Moscow snorted. The other Russian spoke to Anatoli briefly, and he turned to me. To my surprise, the subject of hogs was dropped entirely. He said they also had some land on the Baltic coast, north of Kaliningrad. What did I think of a hotel, maybe, or a beach resort?

I said I had no idea, though it sounded nice. The Muscovite laughed and spoke in a patronizing way.

"He says there is a house there you can stay in as long as you like. It has no electricity or water."

I guessed that they were not entirely won over to the pig liberation movement and that it was time for me to move on.

"Thank you," I said. "The cakes were delightful. I wish you luck. You have my address."

"We will write to you with our proposals," Anatoli said politely. We all shook hands. The Pole looked me in the eye and grinned. I grinned back and went down the stairs, and Anatoli drove me to the border.

. . .

A line of cars was waiting to pass through a gate set in a fence. A guard stood there to wave them on, one by one, to the customs shed and to Poland. It was still early in the afternoon. I sat on my pack for a few moments to make sense of the past four days before going on.

Clearly, I was leaving two countries simultaneously. The people were certainly Russian, but only in Medovoje did they seem to belong. Even though my only connection with this fragment of territory on the far edge of Europe was through the childhood of my grandmother—and then only one of two grandmothers—she gave it an identity that was more real than the Russian one. Just in that same way, most people with an ancestral home would probably identify it in some way as being still theirs, however many interlopers may have inhabited it since. To my mind it was the German history of this place that was significant.

As I contemplated the matter, I felt myself to be on the edge of a deep and dangerous subject fraught with violent emotion. If I, a wandering soul of mixed origins transplanted to a new world, could feel the pull of that ancient connection, how much more intense would be the feelings of those entire families who traced their origins to this—or any—piece of land, and more recently, too? To be dispossessed and chased off a piece of land, even a small piece, perhaps especially a small piece, would leave an inconsolable hurt—like the pain of an amputee, who lives always with the fully imagined existence of that missing limb.

Someone who has lived on and from land for a long time knows it in the way a tree grows rings. The knowledge is ingrained year by year, season by season. He knows where the soil is loose and best for carrots, where the frost hits hardest, where the springs are, where the drainage is bad, where the grass is most succulent. She would know where the wild herbs grow, which fruit is best for keeping and where to keep it, what kind of wheat to grow, which predators to protect her chickens from. They would know where and how to build the next barn, what they had planned to do with that piece across the road, how much better life would be if they could only get such and such a crop established. Worse even than the loss of what they had would be the aching loss of their dreams for the future.

The more agricultural the area, the more peasant the traditions, the more deeply imprinted in the owners' souls would be the nature of the land. And there was a further consideration, peculiar to certain kinds of country and terrain. The scale would be of great importance. It might matter very little to a corn farmer in Nebraska whether he owned this or that thousand-acre parcel of prairie. They are probably rather the same. In much of Europe, however, there could be more variety in one acre than you would find in a square mile of America or Africa. Sometimes this was through human improvements—by hedges, ditches, roads, trees planted, stone walls erected, and water diverted. Or the natural topography could change so much in such a short space that a single farm seen through the wrong end of a telescope might look like the state of California.

Such miniature worlds require a great deal of study and familiarity to give their best results. Naturally, we grow most attached to those things or people that demand the most from us and offer the most in return. My experiences in this offshoot of Russia that was once Prussia had exposed a surprising depth of feeling in me about the meaning of land, and I understood myself better for it. In all my travels, as I passed through landscapes that touched a particular chord in me—I'm thinking now of parts of Brazil, Chile, the Colombian Andes, Zambia, the Indian hill stations—it was never enough for me just to admire it. I wanted to *have* part of it and to *be* part of it, and most of all I wanted to do something with it. My thoughts would turn always to what could be grown there and what kind of life could be made there.

Although I laughed at Anatoli's presumption that I was a hog farmer, he was not far from the truth. It came as something of revelation to realize that there was more than a little of the peasant in me, and I had no doubt which side of my family it came from. One thing I now felt sure of: Neither Granny nor her family had owned land out here, or they would never have left. She had no stake in East Prussia, and it was easy for her ghost to turn back at the railway station.

In the Second World War the Soviet Union lost 26 million people, more than half of them civilians. Germany lost 3 million, and a large proportion of those were not combatants, either. They were civilians—mainly women and children—and many had lived in places like East Prussia, places that were once German. Stalin, who knew all about peasants and their obstinate attachment to land, would not have wanted a bunch of them running around in the West, mourning for their German land. What was the slogan through the ages when you seized someone's territory? "Kill all the men and rape all the women." For fun? Not really. It was to abolish the threat of reprisal and to breed a new generation with divided loyalties.

Seen from this perspective, horrors of Bosnia became a little more accessible. If you wanted to take land away from Muslim peasants and deter them from wanting it back, what would be the next best thing to killing them all? It would be to do such ghastly things to a few that fear would overcome their attachment. The extraordinary thing, of course, was that such ancient practices should reappear now in Europe, after so long a period of dormancy. I would put a bet on it, I thought, that it was not the peasants who had initiated these horrors. I had no doubt who the criminals were. It was leaders like Milosevic and Karadzic, with soft hands and hard hearts, who got the ball rolling. But once it starts, one horror engenders another.

Transfixed as usual by the bloody scene playing endlessly in the Balkans, I stood up to shake off the nightmare of "ethnic cleansing" and got ready to move back into Poland.

# Chapter 15

As I walk up to the gate, the soldier shakes his head at me. It's pretty obvious what he means, but I walk right up to him anyway, and gesture toward the gate. He's friendly enough, but adamant. I can't go through. He points to my feet and says something with *nyet* in it. He points to the waiting cars and I hear the word *machine.* I don't like to give in too easily.

A vivid memory plays in my mind, of riding up to the Livingstone Bridge across the Zambezi, twenty years ago, wanting to cross from Zambia to Rhodesia. I knew it was forbidden, but there was no barrier, only an armed guard. Just a few hundred yards ahead of me over the bridge was where I wanted to go. It seemed so stupid. I could see it. The only alternative to crossing this bridge was a hundred-mile detour through a third country. The guard waved me back with his rifle. I thought, If I just ride across will he really shoot me? A good question . . . but the answer didn't seem quite significant enough to be worth risking my life for. I rode the extra hundred miles—what's a hundred miles out of sixty thousand?—and was glad afterward that I did.

Why am I thinking about this now? It's not as if I planned to make a suicidal dash for the other side. But borders hold great fascination for me. There is so much arbitrary power concentrated in so few hands. Merely on a whim you can be put through the most grueling ordeal. As a foreigner you have no rights. You can be refused permission to enter, or to leave, with no reason given. You can have your possessions destroyed simply on the pretext of a search. And those who wield this frightening authority, do they look like the mature, intelligent, good-humored people you would trust to decide your destiny? Not often.

Ninety-nine times out of a hundred you run the gauntlet without harm and squeeze through the bottleneck smoothly, but the potential for trouble is always there. These are the fault lines of society, where the nations rub together like tectonic plates, building up tensions that can pop at any time and plunge the innocent voyager into a nightmare. Nor are unpredictable officials the only denizens of this unstable zone to be wary of. Many others are drawn, like vultures to a carcass, to this meeting point of incompatibles, to feed off the fears and appetites of travelers. Some are licensed raptors, like the official currency changers who offer absurdly bad rates. Others, unauthorized, offer absurdly good rates, payable in currency that is forged or obsolete or, sometimes, of a different country altogether. Many are freelance opportunists, cabdrivers, smugglers, prostitutes, pimps, and agents of one kind or another, who, under the guise of helping, can complicate your life at great cost. And all these glittery-eyed birds of prey provide patronage for an array of seductive aviaries where naive passenger pigeons may get their wings clipped or their throats cut.

But I am thinking of the most colorful examples I have known—in Africa, Asia, Latin America. By those standards Bagrationovsk seems tame, almost tedious. Just a line of fairly prosperous-looking cars, mostly with Polish plates, empty of merchandise. Near the front of the queue is a single male driver with his window down. I ask if he speaks English? *Deutsch?*

"*Ja. Bisschen Deutsch,*" he says.

"They won't let me walk through. Can I ride with you?"

He is pleasant, offhand. "Sure, I can take you."

His name is Bogdan, and he has been in Russia on some mysterious business that he can't, or won't, explain except that it has to do with taking advantage of anything that comes along to make a zloty, since business in his usual line as a building contractor has hit the basement. He's going home to Olsztyn, a large town about fifty-five miles south of the border. Like every other town in these parts, it has another name, Olstein. Another reminder that, from Granny's point of view, I am still just traveling through Germany.

We soon start moving forward through the gate, and I feel pretty pleased with myself—until it strikes me suddenly that I have a stack of five-thousand-ruble notes in my wallet, and I seem to remember that Russia is one of those places where you're not allowed to take them out of the country. Cursing myself inwardly for being so complacent, I fumble them surreptitiously out of the wallet and stuff them down under my belt, where I hope they will stay. I could ask Bogdan, of course, but if it's illegal I'd be compromising him, too. The operation is barely completed in time as we drive up under the eye of the next guard at the customs shed.

At minor border crossings, where uniforms and languages are unfamiliar, it is often hard to tell who is interrogating you, what his function might be, and even what nationality he represents. I say "he" because they always seem to be men. The only woman I've seen was the grim lady on the train at Mamonowo—and I'm sure she was there only to strip-search suspect females. Usually, but not always, you are still in the country you're leaving until your passport is stamped, so I assume that this customs facility is Russian.

There is a cement platform with a canopy over it, and counters raised along each side, where luggage can be inspected. I noticed that none of the people ahead of us were asked to get out of their cars. The guard simply looked at their passports and waved them on. I'm feeling smug again, but when we draw up, the official says something to Bogdan, and Bogdan tells me I have to get out and put my pack on the counter. Praying that the money will stay where I put it, and moving awkwardly to keep it there, I take the pack from Bogdan and lay it down. Now I'm really furious with myself. This could have been a simple, harmless event. Instead, I have a sinking feeling directly above my belly button.

The feeling becomes even more pronounced when I see that the man I face across the counter isn't in uniform. He could be anybody, and that seems like bad news. He certainly isn't nobody. In fact, he's a startlingly theatrical figure in a long black cloak and an astrakhan hat. He's a strong fellow in his forties with a very self-assured, even swaggering, stance. His broad face is clean-shaven, and he has those piercing eyes that I hate so much in a snooper. He's obviously several cuts above the uniformed men around him, and looks cultivated, with a professionally amiable expression on his intelligent face. I think he might look just as amiable slamming the cell door after me, but I am not being totally objective in my judgments as I feel the rubles descending toward the crotch of my pants. To me, now, he's the timeless model of the secret policeman. Victor Hugo would have loved him, and so would le Carré.

He smiles at me across my pack, showing even white teeth.

"Well, what is this here?" he asks, and to my further discomfiture, he asks it in pretty good English.

Keeping my face as straight as I can, I say: "Oh, just personal things. Clothes. A tent."

"Ah," he says. "May I look in here?"

He's already got his fingers in one of the outer pockets before I can reply, and pulls out a small flashlight, toilet paper, and the smoked herring.

"Very nice," he murmurs, sniffing his fingers and rubbing them on his cloak. "And what are you doing here, if I can ask?"

I tell him my tale, about traveling and being a writer. He raises his eyebrows and assumes an awed look. I'm in a mood to suppose he's mocking me.

"Perhaps you are a famous writer I should know?" he suggests.

I laugh. Sweat seems to be holding the rubles in place.

"I don't think so," I say, and tell him about *Jupiter's Travels* and riding a motorcycle around the world. He looks slightly surprised.

"Do you have the book here?"

I tell him that unfortunately I have just given my only copy to a girl in Kaliningrad, but in any case that was in German. I've got his interest now, and I relax—too soon. The notes slip another notch.

"Oh dear," he says. "I am reading many English books. Dickens, Jack London."

"Thackeray?" I venture.

"Yes, of course, Thackeray. English is my hobby."

It's a strange encounter, because right up to the last moment I have the definite feeling that he is playing with me and that his eyes are searching for something. Then abruptly he loses interest.

"Have a good journey. Good-bye."

I make it back into the passenger seat just before the first bright-red five-thousand-ruble notes slide past my knee to my ankle.

"There seems to be a hole in my pocket," I say weakly. "Will I be able to sell rubles in Poland?"

"Maybe," Bogdan replies, looking straight ahead, "but it will not be easy. There is not much demand for them, as they are always sliding down."

It's raining, on and off. He offers to drive me to the first town past the border, Bartoszyce (Barto-*shee*-che). How can I refuse? It's only fifteen minutes, but by the time we arrive, the clouds have gone and it's a lovely afternoon. He puts me down outside a neat little hotel, runs inside to check out the price for me, shakes my hand, and takes off.

Actually, it looks more like a converted house with add-ons, but it's just my style. I get a small room with a bed and a window overlooking the garden. There's a restaurant down the road a little way. Walking there I see that the houses look clean and cared for. Nothing fancy. A lot of do-it-yourself, but tidy. And the gardens are neat, too. Someone's been trimming hedges, mowing grass. Compared with Russia, this is prosperity. How did it ever get around, I ask myself, that the Poles are badly off? I can't believe how my perspective has changed since I first crossed over into Szczecin.

At the Stodoła Restaurant, there is not much variety on the menu—pork, potatoes, cabbage salad—but the food is good and so is the beer. All for four dollars. And the hotel costs eight. Back in the lobby, which is just a room, really, with a counter built in, the young female receptionist and a male guest are watching TV. He's leaning on the counter and she's behind it, sitting down. I sit by the wall and watch with them, and she automatically brings me tea and lemon. Just naturally, like that. No charge. A talking head stops talking, and gives way to corny music. Some computer-generated star-wars visuals buzz around the screen looking for a way out. Then a movie begins, in English with Polish subtitles. There's something in the credits about *Playboy*.

It's such a pleasant thing to be doing, sitting, sipping, watching a movie, that it's a while before I realize that it's in black-and-white. It takes even longer for me to admit that the movie is not only bad but absolutely disgusting. Apparently, it's a Turkish-American co-production, starring four hefty Playmates from the Corn Belt and a bunch of exceedingly nasty Turkish men who, with the help of a nasty Turkish woman, lock the girls up in jail and do horrible things to them. When the girls aren't naked, being tortured and raped, they are romping around in fashionable leisure wear exchanging girlish confidences and experimenting with alternative forms of affection.

The other viewers gaze at it idly. Every now and again the woman gets up, goes through a door to fetch more water or visit the bathroom, and comes back to watch. Why doesn't she rip off her blouse? Why doesn't the man leap over the counter and rip it off for her? He doesn't even have his hand in his pocket. What is the point of it?

I go to my room to make notes and plan my journey to Warsaw on the map I bought in Gdańsk. I've given it little thought up to now. I know it's about two hundred miles, with no great physical obstacles on the way. Now I see that I am going to be among lakes again for much of the way. A broad band of them stretches right across the map, labeled POJEZIERZE MAZURSKIE. I try to pronounce it. Poye-*jyair*-jeh Ma-*joor*-ska, but the *j* is soft, as in "measure." Polish is full of splashy, cheesy sounds like that, spelled in at least twelve different ways—I counted them—with a *z*, a *d*, a *c*, or an *s*, either alone or in combination. To make it still more interesting, when you put a dash or a dot on top of some of the letters, it shades the sounds too. I don't have a bad ear for languages. I speak several, and have learned and forgotten a few more, but I can't hear the differences in the sounds at all. Often they get strung together in chains—like Szczecin, for example—and it begins to sound like a waterfall. They must find it hard to hold on to their saliva. Is that where the lakes . . . no, no, bad joke.

These lakes and the lakes in Germany are really all the same country. They make nonsense of the political boundaries. I remember reading long ago that the European wild boar migrate from Bohemia to Spain. They cross borders without a thought. They don't even know whether they are in the Czech Republic, France, Germany, or Switzerland. Maybe they go south of the Alps through Slovenia and Italy. I absolutely delight in the idea of those hairy black tuskers trundling through woods and vineyards, completely unaware of the countless wars and unmentionable slaughter that these frontiers have provoked. And we are the higher beings?

So, back to the lakes. Looks like I'll be walking between them for about fifty miles. There are dozens of them, and a good deal of land around them is forested. Once I get past the lakes, there's more forest, another fifty miles or so, with many marshy areas to avoid. Then, about halfway to Warsaw, somewhere around the unpronounceable town of Przasnysz, the country starts to get crowded.

One major highway runs through Bartoszyce. That's obviously the one I don't want to walk on. East of it is a web of smaller roads joining up towns and villages. A likely route to follow would go through Reszel, Mrągowo, Szczytno, Chorzele, Przasnysz, Ciechanów, and Nasielsk. I hope by the time I get to Przasnysz I'll have learned to say it. The next thing is to find out whether there are places to stay. I go back to the hotel lobby with my map and phrase book. I'm relieved to find that the movie is over and the receptionist is still fully clothed, with no visible bruises.

"*Tak,*" she says. Yes, there is a hotel at Reszel, and at these other places too. We smile and nod at each other a lot and I get another cup of tea. So, tomorrow Reszel. A nice challenge. It's twenty-three miles, and I don't plan to sleep in any fields along the way.

The TV is now showing dead bodies, blasted buildings, and haggard men being herded somewhere in Bosnia. More than fifteen hundred people have been killed in Sarajevo since it was declared a safe zone. The chosen solution is as grisly as the problem: to put a cordon sanitaire around them and run the show like a cockfight, with the UN setting the rules.

"Now, you can kill people here, in such and such a fashion, but if you do it there, in a different way, we'll have to slap your wrist."

Again and again you hear: "Oh, you can't do anything with them. It's fatal to interfere." But aren't we deluding ourselves when we say that they—the Serbs, the Muslims, whosoever—are different from us because of these ghastly things they do? We can't let this go on? But the real question, as always, is: Who do I mean by "we"?

As to how it can be stopped. That requires a degree of insight and inspiration entirely beyond me.

It's a late start. At nine in the morning, after a little breakfast, I'm off. This country is not quite as flat as I thought. The first five miles are uphill on a straight asphalt road, but the going is good all the same. According to road signs, I am averaging three and a half miles an hour. Another lovely day, warm but with some cooling breezes and a few clouds. The road is lined with shade trees. Ripe grain ripples all around me. Traffic is light—small cars and few of them, but many more than in Russia. I'm feeling great, full of energy, no pain, as if I could walk forever, and after two hours I'm already a third of the way there. Time for a snack. I've got bread, cheese, the rest of the fish, water, and of course Vova Fursov's parting gift, the *Speck*.

The *Speck* tastes wonderful with the bread, as if they were made for each other, as they probably were. I reckon those peasants knew what they were doing. If only I had more. I'm sitting in a field—having made sure there were no large animals around—with my boots off. They really are fine boots. Except for a little soreness on my right big toe, my feet feel all right. It's a pity they aren't symmetrical. That right big toe sticks out farther than the left one. I hope it will adapt.

Leaning back on my pack, I look at my feet stretched out in front of me. How little credit feet get these days. They aren't fast enough for us. They've gone the way of other inadequate antiques, like candles and horses, that we use only for emergencies or recreation. What kind of a life would we lead now, I wonder, if we had to walk everywhere? If everything were more or less within reach. Funny thing is, we've arrived at the stage, technologically, where we could do it. Most people could work at home or live close to work. We don't need monster industries anymore. When you think about it, most of them are related to transport anyway. Not just the automobile and truck industries, either. Take domestic appliances, for example. Why ship those hulking refrigerators all over the country? It's more efficient, and a lot quieter, to build an insulated cupboard into the house. Then all you have to ship is the coil and the compressor. Or kitchen ranges. Same thing. Build them in local materials, stone and clay, and just ship the rings and pipes.

Transport only *seems* to be cheap. We pay a huge price for it in other ways, but it's made artificially affordable. It costs the same to send a parcel across Britain—three hundred miles—as across America—three thousand miles. Why? So that one manufacturer in one place can supply the whole nation. That was how the Industrial Revolution worked. That's what got us where we are, but that was a hundred years ago. What we need now is the industrial *devolution*, but we can't get there from here, because we're locked into cars, trucks, and highways.

Tragic, really, to think what traffic and the oil business are doing to people and the planet. It's one of the best reasons for walking. I know the world looks different this way. I hope it will put me in touch with an earlier time, when people walked all over this earth. Everything worth thinking about has already been thought about by men and women traveling in sandals, with sticks. Apprentices walked around Europe. It was part of their training to do so. Peasants drove their cattle, pigs, sheep, and turkeys to market on foot. America was explored on foot. Religious processions, pilgrimages, and crusades were always made on foot.

I remember Manfred saying he thought there was something sacred about walking. Ginny, I know, draws spiritual sustenance from it. I understand that it is the humble way to progress across the earth, and that wisdom and clarity are impossible without humility. In that sense it is almost the antithesis of my last big journey. Circling the globe on a machine was an arrogant act, though I didn't intend it to be. Hubris could have overwhelmed me at any time. I chose the smallest machine I could and made it as dirty, difficult, and dangerous as possible, just to keep myself down-to-earth.

It was a compromise. We are always compromising. Even now there is rubber between me and the road. Manfred, too, wears boots. I'm not a fanatic, or I'd be doing this thing barefoot or on my knees. But every time a car passes me by and I realize that it will arrive where I'm going within minutes, I have to remind myself that getting there is not the point. What matters is what happens along the way.

There is no question that I mean to walk at least the two hundred miles to Warsaw, and then later from Lvov to Romania. It's all I can hope to do in the time. What if someone offers me a lift? Shall I refuse on principle? It depends. I want to meet people, too. If it's just a few miles down the road and the people look interesting, why not? It doesn't look as though I shall be showered with embarrassing offers. So far not a single driver has shown any sign of even slowing down, and that suits me fine.

I guess I'll rest for an hour, then walk two more, and so on. Seems like a nice, practical schedule that should get me there at about five. A good working day, nine to five. The next shift begins well enough. To the south, on my right, the country opens up into very big fields. There are hundreds of acres of wheat, and they've started cutting it. Five red combine harvesters move through it on parallel paths, the first leading the next by fifty feet or so, and so on down the line, big machines working in formation as a team. After all the stories told about drunkenness and ineptitude on the collectives and after the broken and abandoned machines I saw in eastern Germany, it's a pleasant sight to see it all working the way it was supposed to. I half expect at least one of the machines to break down in front of me, but they continue functioning smoothly as they pass out of sight.

This is a very peaceful and rich-looking country. Of course it is similar to the land I recently came through, though drier, more golden, and less green. I do pass some pasture (and feel that jerk when unexpectedly I glimpse a large horned animal—the trauma is still with me), but most of the land is in grain. Big brick barns fit comfortably into the folds of the softly undulating landscape. Trees are plentiful, but as individual providers of shade rather than in copses or woods.

I am the only person walking on these roads as far as I can see. The country changes hardly at all as I move through it, and my thoughts move off in all directions. Are they the same thoughts, I wonder, as I used to have while seated on a motorcycle? Very similar are the time frames and the isolation. My feet are to Poland as the bike was to the world, in the sense that it takes as long now to walk between villages as it took to ride between the townships of, say, South Africa. Which is exactly what I planned and hoped for. Then, as now, the landscape was empty and virtually unchanging. What was going through my mind then? As I recall, I was celebrating my own good fortune, having survived the length of that continent intact. I was a little anxious about the bike. I was anxious to share my experience, wondering what it would take to persuade others to interrupt the routines of their lives and set off on a journey like the one I had just begun. And I was thinking hard about apartheid, having already run into some rampant examples of it.

So there is very little difference, really, in the subject matter. I'm enjoying myself tremendously. I'm a little worried about my feet. I think it would be splendid if more people could do what I'm doing. And I spend a lot of time thinking about Bosnia. As to the quality of my thoughts, I have to say that they feel more, well, pedestrian. Since my feet can't take me so far, the horizon of my possibilities is closer.

It's been getting warmer. I have come almost two thirds of the way now. A few minutes ago I turned right at a crossroads to climb another gentle slope. But my feet are hurting quite badly. I have to set them down carefully at each step of the way.

Just a little while back, I passed a turning off to a small village. Coming toward me was the first pedestrian I have seen today. He was a slight man in his thirties, with refined features and a Mediterranean complexion. He had a ribbon tied around his forehead and wore a blue athletic suit. He was holding the hand of a tiny girl and leading her slowly along the road with an expression of utmost concentration. But the strangest thing about him was that he was wearing a pair of sandals with extraordinarily thick wooden soles, so that he appeared in danger of toppling over at any moment. In fact it was almost as though the little girl was steadying him. This strange combination of the androgynous and the Oriental in his appearance left me puzzled. I could simply not account for it.

I have paused for a moment's relief from pain, and also to look around me at what is really gorgeous scenery. As I do so, a man riding a small Yamaha comes up the road from the village as though to pass me, but he stops and talks. He has his visor up, and I can see enough of his face to know that he must be in his early twenties. I don't know what he wants until he pats the seat behind him. Good Lord, he's offering me a lift. Do I want to trust my life to this man? Sure. It's one of the rules of the game as I play it. You do what comes along, unless it's plainly suicidal.

I climb on, and the weight of my pack all but whips me off the seat as he accelerates. I have to hang on like grim death. He makes no concessions, swooping along at a good speed. If I were driving I'd love it, but I'm a lousy passenger. Every time he twists the throttle, I topple backward, top-heavy, unbalanced and distinctly nervous, but exhilarated too. I wish I could talk to him, introduce myself. What a nice, spontaneous gesture on his part. I don't think I would stop my bike to offer a lift to some old geezer with a backpack. I'd use the lack of a helmet as my pretext. Interesting how often the law can be used as a pretext to stifle generosity.

At the next crossroads he puts me down. I scribble my name and the title of my book on a scrap of paper. It only confuses him. I suppose I'm hoping that by some lucky stroke he might make the connection one day and that it will give him pleasure. He's saved my feet three miles. Only another three to go. There's no denying the pain, but the great thing about this pain is that as soon as you sit down, it stops and a beautiful glow of well-being suffuses you.

I'm basking in it now, in the Zamkowa Restaurant, on the public square of Reszel. I'm in a big, shady room, where white light filters through lace curtains onto red-and-white-checkered tablecloths. I've already been to the hotel. There is only one, a fairly recent cement job along the lines of a cell block, with metal window frames, spartan rooms, and the kind of bathroom facilities you find in a sports stadium. In fact, they are getting ready for a big sports reunion tonight in their cavernous restaurant, with balloons and fifty-foot tables. I hope I'll be tired enough to sleep through it.

The map says there's a historic castle here, so after a dinner of pickled herring, beer, potatoes, and sausages, I wander off to find it. It's amazing what a difference thirty pounds of weight makes to my feet. Without the pack, my only problem is the persistent soreness of that big toe. I wish it would go away.

# Chapter 16

*R*eszel is an attractive town, of low buildings gathered around a central square. It seems to be well kept and restored. The painted wooden shop fronts are tidy, and display goods in their windows that one might actually want to buy. There are benches in the square with their seats intact. There are few holes in the pavement, and where I do see rubble, it is because something is really being built or restored. Where does this superficial prosperity come from? Aren't all these Eastern-bloc countries supposed to be cracking up under the strain of free market economics?

No doubt the worst of the hardship and poverty is hidden, as usual, with the elderly and infirm starving and shivering out of sight on pensions that have lost most of their value. But Reszel keeps a bold face for the tourists. The castle stands on a rise just outside the town, an imposing structure, foursquare with a great arched gate and a cobbled courtyard. This interior space is very pleasing. Some sensitive minds have been at work here. The inner walls have many doors and upper windows opening onto the courtyard, and the stone frames are particularly fine and harmonious, while the wooden joinery set into these apertures is fully up to the same standard.

The rooms can be rented, and although they cost more than the pittance

I am paying (by Western standards, of course), they are a bargain for any conventional tourist. I sit for a while on a stone bench sketching one of the windows in my notebook, so taken with it am I. Then, dissatisfied with my effort, I close the book and go back to town, drink a half liter of beer at a bar, and buy some food and drink at the grocery next door for tomorrow's lunch, since I plan to start early on the twenty-mile hike to Mrągowo (*Mrang*-ovo). Back in my room, I hear the celebrations booming through the hotel. They don't disturb me, but I am beginning to wonder about Polish sheets. They are all too small—so small that they can't be tucked in under the mattress. Unless you sleep as still as a mummy, you'll wake up with the sheet rolled under you in an uncomfortable sausage. It makes me wonder what Poles do, or don't do, in bed and what I might have to do to find out.

At six-thirty I'm off to Mrągowo, or so I think. I am hardly out of town before my built-in alarm system goes off. Where's my notebook? I don't have it. I'd rather lose anything—passport, money, plane ticket—than the notebook. It's the only thing that can't be replaced. I go back to the hotel, but it's not there. In a sweat of anxiety, I race to the castle. I must have left it on that stone seat. There's nobody around—it's too early—and of course the notebook is nowhere in sight. My desperate hope is that it was picked up and put away. Who would want to steal it? A woman comes to open the café, but she says if it was found the fellow who locks up would have it, and he won't be here until later. I have no choice but to sit and wait.

Two Germans, a man and a woman, come down from their room to take breakfast. Some Poles from Warsaw join them. They haven't seen my notebook, but they invite me to eat with them. The breakfast is comprehensive and delicious. How can I refuse? Halfway through our lordly repast, I am struck by the realization that I must have left my notebook at the grocery shop last night. I excuse myself and run there. They are so happy in the shop to see me. They bring it out, smiling and nodding as though they know how precious it is. Immensely relieved, I return to my new friends. By now they have convinced me *not* to go to Mrągowo today but to go just four miles down the road to Swięta (*Svyeng*-ta) Lipka, or Heilige Linde in German, meaning "Holy Linden Tree." There, they say, I will witness one of the glories of Christendom, an absolutely splendid Baroque Catholic church with a famous organ I must not miss. And besides, they add, the *meteo* forecasts heavy rain this afternoon.

Telling myself my toe needs the rest, I take their advice and walk to Swięta Lipka. I was not misled. The church is absolutely the pinnacle of religious kitsch, while the organ is a quite incredible confection, a pageant of animated figures spinning, bowing, and blowing their horns as the organist plays. Despite all these special effects and wedding cake decorations (or maybe because of them), the acoustics are marvelous. This same evening four musicians from Polish orchestras and academies prove it with a concert of Baroque music in the church. They call themselves Pro Musica Antiqua, and they play exclusively in churches and museums. Their music is so seductive that I am drawn afterward to seek them out in the vestry and join in the general congratulations. I have memorized a phrase in Polish— "*Czy ktos tu movie po Angielsku?*" or, "Does anybody here speak English?"— and to my amazement the oboist, Jerzy Szafrański (Sha-*fran*-sky), not only understands me but answers, "Yes, a little."

He plays first oboe for the National Philharmonic Orchestra in Warsaw, and seems very pleased that I took the trouble to compliment them. It's often difficult to make the effort and risk the intrusion—and possibly, in the case of celebrities, it would be misguided to try—but people who have made sincere attempts to do something well are almost always grateful for the acknowledgment. I would rather take a chance on being snubbed than be too inhibited to express my admiration. The musicians are in a hurry to leave for another town, but Szafrański says I can usually find him at the Philharmonic building in Warsaw, and he'll be glad to see me there, so I've racked up one good contact in the capital.

Impressive as the church and the music are in their different ways, what really astonishes me most is the enormous crowd of German tourists in this town. A large square faces the church, and the roads around it are lined with German tour buses. As soon as one leaves, another takes its place, while just as many private cars from Germany clutter the adjacent streets. All the usual souvenir vendors and snack counters are on show. The Teutonic hordes stay awhile and then move on. Not far from here is the great underground complex that Hitler used as his command post for the eastern front—the one he named Wolfsschanze, or "Wolf's Lair"—and it exerts a magnetic attraction.

It's obvious now that the prosperity, so noticeable first in Reszel, is due to the flow of deutsche marks. It amazes me that the Poles are so hospitable to a nation whose leader, not too terribly long ago, declared that the Polish people were expendable and then did his best to expend them. It is, I suppose, a good thing to let bygones be bygones, but you can't help noticing that forgiveness comes a lot easier when you can afford to pay for it.

All this suggests a simple, pragmatic solution to the Bosnian question. First bomb the stuffing out of the Serbs, devastate their entire territory, and give a large chunk of it away to Bosnia; hold war-crimes trials until they feel guilty as hell; then rebuild their economy with help from Coca-Cola, General Motors, and Time Warner, among others, until their affluence is even greater than their guilt. Then they can come back to Bosnia as rich tourists and be forgiven. All is sweetness and light. End of scenario.

I'm joking, of course. What? This is no laughing matter? You're right. Sorry. Forget you ever read this. What shall we do about Bosnia? Gee, I don't know. Let's talk about it . . .

The Poles I meet are not very interested in Bosnia, or other people's problems in general. They think they have too many problems of their own. In fact they have had nothing but problems since their country was abolished two hundred years ago. They got it back only in 1918, after their famous Polish Legions had fought, at different times, on both sides of the First World War. Being lucky enough, for once, to end up on the winning side, they were awarded a country of their own again, but it was about a hundred miles farther east than it is today. Poland was given large slices of Ukraine and Belarus, and an equally big slice of what is Poland today was still in Germany then.

Even so, there were large numbers of Germans living inside Polish borders in the south and millions of Ukrainians who really didn't want to be Polish at all. The Poles were very nasty to all these minorities, and particularly to their four million Jews. In fact, they had the reputation of being more brutal with the Jews than any other nation, and that is saying something. The country had a large peasant population, 95 percent Catholic, and was run by an aristocratic landowning class that thought of itself as a superior species. Soon after they got Poland to themselves again, they put a military dictator in charge, and from 1926 on, Poland was totalitarian and opposition was repressed by jail, torture, and execution.

In 1934 they went even further down the slippery slope when the colonels who ran the country put their faith in Hitler, which helped the Nazis along quite a bit. Five years later, they learned the folly of supping with the devil and fought heroically against Hitler's invading armies, but it was far too late. They discovered then that from Hitler's point of view, all that distinguished Polish slaves from Jewish slaves was that the Jews had to die. Whether the Poles died or not was a matter of indifference to him.

So they had an extremely unpleasant war, but Hitler took care of their Jewish problem. Then Stalin took back all the Ukrainians, gave the Poles a chunk of Germany in exchange, and—most important—chased all the Germans out first. So the end result was that Poland moved west about a hundred miles and the Poles got what they had always wished for—a 98 percent pure Polish population with no Jews and, as a bonus, a slightly nicer climate.

Of course, they had to put up with forty years of so-called Communism to get their wish. The point of the story is that when they were free, as a nation, to choose, the Poles pursued their own interests with ruthless disregard for morality or the concerns of others and reaped nothing but death and destruction. Then, when they were powerless to help themselves, they finished up with what they thought they had always wanted. It remains to be seen whether they like what they've got, a pure-white Christian nation that must be the envy of every white supremacist and Jew baiter from Alabama to Zululand.

However, none of this seems to be affecting me personally. If anyone has so far registered the possibility that I'm Jewish, it certainly hasn't been communicated to me. I can think of two reasons. One is that I'm in a part of Poland where income from tourism is important. The other is that all these distinctions and prejudices break down when you are confronted by real individuals. People are helpful to me and pleasant, and I like them. What if I were to put on the Orthodox outfit, with the curls, the black hat, and the funny walk? I wonder how helpful they would be to me then. Just thinking about it makes me quite uneasy.

I've experienced the same contradiction everywhere, between personal tolerance and group paranoia, and it has always appalled me that people are willing to take on such vicious attitudes to qualify as "patriots." Being British, I'm proud to be associated with the world's longest and most persistent effort to find a decent method for people to govern themselves. This pride is not transferable to symbolic objects like flags and royalty. It won't diminish or be tarnished, however many Union Jacks are burned, however many rude things are said about—or by—the royal family. Actually I'm in favor of flag burning, though I don't do it myself. Burning a flag seems like a reasonable comment to make on the policies that some politicians promote in the name of patriotism or liberty—whether they are criminal, as in Bosnia, or merely misguided.

As it turns out—and we now have Mr. McNamara's word for it—Americans who were burning the flag over Vietnam were serving their country better than those who were fighting the war. Tragic but true. How I wish my aunts could have dared to make a bonfire of swastikas in that square outside their house where the stormtroopers paraded. Wouldn't it be a fine thing to hear of even one Serb burning the Serbian flag?

Well, now the Germans are coming through Poland again. The last of their motorized columns, a final contingent of tour buses, is leaving the square now. It's a good thing this latest *Drang nach Osten* is moving on from here or there would be nowhere in town to sleep. As it is, finding a room is easy. At the restaurant all I have to say is "*Zimmer*" and they take me around the corner, where I get a little upstairs bedroom. The sheets are tiny and the towel is tinier, but everything's really clean, and who cares anyway? It's ten dollars, with breakfast, and my own bathroom thrown in.

I have one more curious meeting before I go to bed. At a parlor for soggy pizzas, I find myself drinking beer with some young Poles who have been working in Germany. It's almost the only way for them to make more than a subsistence wage. While they're in Germany it's hard to hold on to the money, but when they bring it back it's worth a fortune. One of them, an unusually tall fellow, has terribly knotted veins on his legs, so dramatic that I can't help asking him what's wrong with them.

He says it's from playing "hard" basketball and that anyone who plays all the time will have this problem, although expert physiotherapy can postpone it. I have never heard of this before. Is it true? Will Michael Jordan's legs look like this one day, like a wool sock that's come unraveled? He says it hurts, but the worst is when the swollen veins break through the skin. Ugh!

It's annoying me that I can't speak the language. Dealing with practical matters is no real problem and just takes a little patience. The phrase book supplies the words, and I've learned to pronounce them well enough to be understood. Conversation is another matter altogether. I have never found my language skills so inadequate before. German and English are both sometimes useful, but generally I'm down to sign and body language, so much of the time when I'm eating or resting is spent copying out lists of words and trying to memorize them. I work off restaurant menus and shop signs, and rehearse them as I walk, but it's slow going.

Today, Sunday, as I set out on the fifteen miles to Mrągowo, the countryside strikes me as being particularly beautiful. It did rain yesterday, as predicted, polishing up the greenery, and I notice that now there is more pasture, less grain. After living in California so long I have forgotten that you can have countryside without barbed wire. What a relief not to have those fences strung everywhere. The cows are staked out, and seem quite content with the arrangement, but of course you could not hold a herd of beef cattle that way. These cows are for milking. I'm still a shade nervous of animals with horns, but the knee-jerk terror is fading.

Poland is a great country for flowers. Every house and garden is ablaze with them. And the Poles love dogs, too, especially little ones with curly tails that look as though they've been stapled down to the spine. They yap at me through garden fences as I go by and call to one another in the night. Just when you think one dog is giving up, another takes up the cry, and others, more distant, can be heard carrying on the good work. I am fairly confident that during the course of every night, waves of barking travel clear across the country from border to border. My ruminations are interrupted by the sight of seventeen storks perched on a rooftop. That is a lot of storks. Twelve of them take off as I pass, circling overhead in an ascending spiral, as though they were practicing a maneuver.

Walking feels good today. As my thoughts circle around in my head like the storks above me, I have a sudden, crazy idea about Bosnia. It makes me laugh out loud, but it's too outrageous to take seriously. I'll put it away and bring it out again later.

Mrągowo, when I get to it, is a surreal spectacle. The town is throbbing with drunken rockers in every kind of gear—leather, punk, country, grunge—and every kind of attitude—sitting, standing, kneeling, crouching—but all a few degrees out of plumb. Four of them, mixed boys and girls in black with headbands, drive past in an open jeep waving big black flags. They are leaning forward, grasping their flagpoles with eager expressions, as though modeling one of those early socialist posters for "OUR HEROIC YOUTH." Given the state of the youth around them, their pose seems madly inapt.

Apparently, I have arrived at the end of a country music festival. I'm glad

I didn't arrive yesterday. There would have been no room at the inn, and I don't much care for country music, even in Polish. As it is, the inn is pretty full and expensive, and everyone working there is worn-out. Tomorrow they'll have to pick up the garbage. There's plenty.

On Monday morning I get out on the road early, before seven. Small remnants of the country crowd still litter the town, and there are others hitching along the road south. The next town is Szczytno (Sh-*chit*-no), thirty-two miles away, too far even on my better days. This is not yet one of my better days. My feet just don't want to do their stuff. I'm used to getting cooperation from my body, and it's depressing to be disobeyed like this. Whenever I've made unusual demands in the past it has always come through, after protesting vigorously of course. This time I can't get it to stop complaining.

That big toe is the leader of the mutiny. It's turning an obstinate purple color, and it hurts. It brushes only lightly against the side of the boot, and I've been reluctant to believe that could be a problem, but what if I'm wrong? I hate to think that I might have bought the wrong size boots. What if this crummy little micromisalignment should turn out to be the canker that spreads, the rotten apple in the barrel, the wormhole that sinks the ship? Is my toe the farcical counterpart of Achilles' heel? It's been organizing an uprising, telegraphing complaints all over my legs. They're tired of carrying so much weight, and I sympathize with them. I imagined that by now I would be an altogether leaner specimen of humanity, but all this beer and pork is not making me any lighter. I could cut it out, of course, but then what would be left in life?

The map shows a campground halfway to Szczytno, and that's what I am aiming at. As I walk, I think about the ads I watched on TV last night at the hotel and how familiar they were—all those little, inexpensive fancy items a poor person might buy as a treat. They remind me of my first days of adulthood and the presents we used to give one another for Christmas— scarves, gloves, handkerchief sets, but most of all, smoking accessories. We wanted so badly to taste a little luxury, to discriminate, to possess something of value. Tobacco was the high road to sophistication. We had chrome-plated cigarette lighters in little cloth covers. We packed our smokes in silver-plated cigarette cases (until king-size made them obsolete). Women sipped at amber and tortoiseshell cigarette holders. Men were given shiny clippers to cut notches into the ends of cigars they couldn't afford.

Pipes were a favorite gift, whether you liked them or not, and had their own vast range of accoutrements. Ashtrays proliferated.

Cigarettes were gift-packed in fifties and hundreds, with brand names that spoke directly to our social ambitions—like Three Castles, State Express, Pall Mall—or to our wistful longings, like Passing Clouds, Gold Flake, and Balkan Sobranie. One popular brand, Senior Service, claimed in small print to be "THE PRODUCT OF THE MASTER MIND," but my choice was a black cigarette with a gold tip, called Russian Sobranie. Filters were unknown. Even though King George VI, a heavy smoker, died very publicly of lung cancer, we were not informed that smoking gave you anything worse than a cough.

Poland today is going through those same early beginnings. Pointless to advertise automobiles. Who can afford to buy one? The screen is a bazaar of little things, and here tobacco rules.

The traffic on this road is heavier than before—perhaps because it's Monday or because it's farther south. The more cars pass, the harder it is to maintain my conviction, especially when my body is being so rebellious. How will I ever be able to explain why I am doing this? "What is the point?" I hear them ask—I hear *myself* ask. If I want to find out about Romania, to learn more about my father, why don't I go straight there? The trains are cheap. I could be in my father's birthplace, at little cost, in two or three days. Instead, I propose to tramp for weeks through Poland and Ukraine.

It's not as if I ever really used to *like* walking for its own sake. When someone asked me to "come for a walk," a churlish little boy's voice inside me said, "Don't want to." It sounded boring. What is there to do on a walk? Is it exercise? How dreary. Will we see anything? Nothing I haven't seen a hundred times. Yet I would usually go. To be asked to come for a walk is, I think, the sincerest flattery. It would be too ungracious to refuse.

All the German aunts in my family loved walking. *Spazieren gehen* was their joy—especially on the Lüneberger Heide, a nature reserve south of Harburg. It filled their hearts with rapture. You would think that having to walk all over the frozen streets of Hamburg to deliver that pompous religious rag, they would have had enough of walking. Not at all. They did it all their lives, and lived long on it. Striding through the heather, singing their jolly songs as they went, they felt healthy and strong and virtuous. Another twenty-five miles down the road was the Belsen concentration camp.

*Why do I have to bring that up again?*

Just to remind myself, as I stride among the fields and lakes of Poland, that even when I feel fine and it's a beautiful day and God is presumably in His Heaven, everything may not, after all, be right with the world. In fact, it very obviously is not. Something not very different from Belsen is happening down the road today. In a sense it may be worse, because this time the whole world is watching; there's no hiding from it, as my aunts hid from the truth. We all condemn it and *still* we are helpless to stop it.

The frustration I feel encourages fantasies. The crazy idea that first occurred to me two days ago won't go away. I treat it as a joke, but it won't be laughed off. I know it's absurd to the point of insanity, but then ethnic cleansing is itself so mad, so outrageous, that it seems right to oppose it with something of equal and opposite extravagance. It stems, I suppose, from this idea of walking as an act of humility, allied to sanctity. "What if," I hear this pestiferous little voice demand, "what if half a million people were to walk into Bosnia? . . ." Ridiculous. Pay no attention. But in the upper-left-hand corner of my brain, the little demon is already working out the details.

The air is more humid today and the slightly diffused sunlight is more tiring. The back of my cotton vest quickly became sodden with perspiration, so I have taken it off and spread it over the backpack to dry out. To ease the sore spots where my toes rub on each other I have put on Band-Aids, but they only ease the discomfort a little. There should be a restaurant soon, at Piecki (P-*yetch*-ki), and I am dying for breakfast and a rest. Piecki comes, but no restaurant. When I ask, they nod and send me down the road. I've been chasing it for miles now. At last, at a dry and dusty crossroads I see it. The Mazurska. It's quite capacious and has some of the appearance of an American diner but, being empty with hot sun pouring in, there's also a strong feeling of Spanish indolence about it.

The waitress, when she appears in her yellow frock, is far from indolent. She's a thin, sharp-tongued, no-nonsense woman, but she gets friendlier as we go along. She has exactly what I want—eggs, sausage, bread, and tea— mainly because I've taught myself to want what I think she's got. The place is empty but for me, so I'm free to attempt some foot surgery, a sort of UN intervention to damp down the battle for boot room. These last ten miles have felt like twenty, but I force myself out on the road again.

I wish I could get off this highway, but the map shows no footpaths. I take a chance on a cart track that runs parallel to the road for a while behind a screen of trees, but I'm soon forced out into the traffic again. Finally, at

Babięta (Ba-*byeng*-ta), arrows lead me into the woods for a mile or two. I'm so weary that I miss the campground in the trees and plod on unnecessarily for half a mile before discovering my error. But here it is, it's on a lake, even though the map doesn't show it.

This is no piece of rough ground with a hose and a soda machine. Here are good bathrooms, and laundry facilities. I carve out a little piece of heaven for myself in the shape of a tiny A-frame houselet and repair to the big restaurant with a set meal at a very easy price. There I meet a friendly fellow camper, who explains that there's more water in this part of the world than I guessed. The lakes and rivers are so well connected that he and his party have been canoeing for two weeks, spending every night at a different campsite. It sounds idyllic. One day, I promise myself, I'll try it. I tell my new friend, whose name is Wojciech (*Voy*-chek), how surprised I am by the clean beauty of the countryside. Where I come from, the word has been how filthy and polluted everything is east of the Oder-Neisse line. He reassures me. The pollution is there, all right, but it's in the south. Then he gives me the name of a hotel, the Forum, in Warsaw, which he thinks would be a good one to try. Not too expensive, he says.

Next stop Szczytno, seventeen miles. I've swallowed my pride and given up on the boots. The big bad toe has turned from purple to black and resigned from the expedition. In the shoes it's bearable, but they are lightly made and probably won't last very long. After that, I'm down to thongs unless I buy some footwear, and that I won't be able to do before Warsaw. It grieves me to abandon the boots, but I should have done so long ago. I am now an even stranger sight than usual. As well as having my vest over my pack, I have rigged up a laundry line to dry my socks, which are flapping behind me like the exotic insignia of a wandering shaman. I should be beating a drum as I go.

At a crossroads I fall in with two Austrians on a cycling holiday. We have stopped at the same small shop to buy food. They look so clean, fresh, and athletic in their sportswear, you'd think they'd want nothing to do with a dusty old tramp like me. Nevertheless, they seem quite content to keep me company, and we settle on the grassy shoulder to eat our lunch. Like the hero of many a fairy tale, who invariably meets soothsayers along the road in unlikely garb, it turns out that I have met two men with information that bears directly on my mission. They are teachers from Linz, but their passion is to play klezmer music, traditional Jewish folk music, from which I infer that they are Jewish. They have traveled widely with their band, in Romania and elsewhere. Their names are Thomas and Herwig, and as I share out the last of Vova's *Speck*, I tell them where I'm going. Both of them mourn the loss of Jewish culture in Romania.

"There's nothing left of it," says Herwig, "but the cemeteries. And even those have been cemented over."

They talk about films they have seen reconstructing the pattern of Jewish life in Bukovina, the province where my father was born. Bukovina lies along the other side of the Carpathian mountain range that I will skirt when I leave Ukraine. Brilliant images draw me to this distant place, but the glow emanates from the bright colors of early Christian art on the walls of the famous painted monasteries I have seen in pictures. Of Jewish life there I know nothing, other than that it was apparently the cradle of the ultra-Orthodox Hasidic sect.

"The Jews in Bukovina were exterminated," Thomas adds flatly, blasting any lingering hopes I had of finding some remnant of my family. It was the Romanian dictatorship, he says, that wiped them out. I have a growing awareness of how easy it was for Hitler to pursue his policies in this part of Europe and how difficult it may be for me to reconnect with my father's world.

They leave me with their cards (how organized they are) and ask me to call if I ever pass through Linz. Then they cycle neatly away to the north, and I tramp on south. My damaged foot is still more comfortable in the shoe, and I pray that the improvement will last, but it is hot and humid today as I circle around yet another lake. Although I feel quite settled in my pace, my outward appearance tells a different story, and excites the sympathy of a woman in a passing car. She persuades her husband to stop ahead of me, and I see her, a figure with short blond hair, standing beside the car waiting for me to catch up.

Once we have found a common language, in this case English, she offers a lift for the last five miles to Szczytno.

"What gave you the idea to stop?" I ask. "Nobody stops—not that I want them to . . ."

"People are afraid," she says, "but you looked tired—and okay."

Her husband is a dark, bearded man, a photographer who sells pictures of the region for postcards, calendars, brochures, and newspapers. He speaks no English but contributes unmistakable goodwill. Such spontaneous kindness should never be refused. I sit next to their baby in the back of their little family car, crowded with domestic knickknacks. If I wanted they would take me to Olsztyn, where they live, and feed me and, no doubt, house me too, but I thank them profusely. With their parting gift of an ice cream in my hand (the third Polish passion after flowers and poodles), I wave them good-bye.

On a blank wall on the side of a house in Szczytno is a sign with a big arrow pointing to the Hotel Krystyna. When I find it, some distance down the high street, I find a rather opulent affair geared to German tourists. The ground floor is a restaurant in the bourgeois manner, with high-backed chairs and flowers on the tables. Many elderly Germans are finishing their lunch. Even the young Germans look elderly. A harassed waitress comes out of the dining room to the lobby to attend to me, rather impatiently. I don't think I fit her profile of a suitable customer.

As it is there is no room at the hotel, or I might have succumbed and paid the price just to prove I could. As I wonder what to do, a tall, overtanned, and overdressed German Rambo bursts in demanding a room. The waitress sends him off in a taxi to the Hotel Lesz. It crosses my mind to offer to share the taxi, but he is so obnoxious that I let him bustle away alone.

"Oh, the Lesz is too expensive," the waitress tells me. After dealing with Rambo, she finds me suddenly quite sympathetic. "You should go to the Chinese hotel by the railway station," and she gives me directions.

A Chinese hotel in the heart of Poland? Well, here I am at the Pofajdok Hotel, alongside the shunting yards. Maybe there are Chinese here somewhere, but I haven't seen them. Still, there is something about it that reminds me of Penang and my favorite hotel on Rope Walk: dark, crooked passages, and room doors left carelessly open on scenes of mild decadence. But my room, when I find it, is as bright and clean and comfortable as it is cheap. So, having saved money on the room, what do I do? Blow it on a dinner at the Krystyna, where the bilingual menu helps me brush up on my culinary Polish.

The printed menus in formerly Communist countries remain unchanged, and are complicated, because every item has to be weighed as well as priced. Tonight I am having 130 grams of herring, 200 grams of soup, 240 grams of fried chicken, with 100 grams of tomato salad, 200 grams of potatoes, 150 grams of bread, and 50 grams of butter, each listed and charged separately. I have the same problem here that I have with nutritional statistics in America; accountancy, I find, takes a lot of the pleasure out of eating. No, sir, that's no chicken—that's 170 grams of protein, 70 grams of fat, and 133 percent of your cholesterol RDA, *per serving!* All consumed to the seamless sound of eighties rock 'n' roll.

The next day is more difficult. The main road south is a bigger highway, but I can follow a minor road for the first fifteen miles. Before I leave, the sky hosts a spectacular thunderstorm, and at first the road is cool. It passes through a forest of pines, with rain droplets still clinging to the needles. There are people in the forest, gathering mushrooms, picking up sticks. They all look furtive, and glower at me as though caught doing something criminal. My cheerful cries of *"Dzień dobry"* whistle through the trees unanswered.

For a while I walk alongside a big wired enclosure on my right, guarded by soldiers in watchtowers—the usual army setup, with parallel fences and a plowed no-man's-land in the middle, all very businesslike and threatening. Then at the southern end, on the shore of a lake, an open unguarded gate gapes its invitation to the world, making all the precautions and stern military postures seem ridiculous.

Unhappily, the rebellious toe is acting up again. It looks as though the nail is going to come off, but not before causing the maximum embarrassment. A cramp has developed in my left leg, no doubt by way of compensation. This is very depressing news. I find these long periods of walking so rewarding for both the physical challenge and the ideas that flow through my mind.

Eventually I come out onto the main highway, two miles short of Wielbark, where there is a railway station marked. I hope there will be somewhere to stay there, but I am disappointed. And I'm told there will be nothing at the next town, Chorzele, either. The bus stop beckons me. Everything hurts too much. I won't be a martyr. I ride the bus to Przasnysz. I deserve it—after all, I know how to pronounce it now—"P-*jash*-neesh."

Most of the seats on the bus are taken by middle-aged countrywomen with careworn faces, staring straight ahead. What they are staring toward, if not at, is the partition that separates the passengers from the driver, and on the partition is a large, colored poster. Out of this poster, aiming her gifts straight at us, is a voluptuous young woman in cutoff jeans and big, beautiful, bare breasts. Presumably, she is selling something. I can't believe she is succeeding. What on earth do all these devout Catholic mothers make of it? The only person on the bus likely to be stimulated rather than offended is the driver, but he can't see her. In any case he has surrounded himself with prophylactic pictures of his family, some horses, and the pope. What does this mean? I have no idea.

From the bus I see that industry is closing in on the countryside. At Chorzele comes the first big smokestack, belching black fumes. Przasnysz, for all its size, seems to have only one hotel, some way from the center. Pointed in the right direction, I begin to walk down a busy street. Two rascally looking Russians in a very beaten up automobile make the mistake of asking me for directions in German. I cadge a lift off them and after a bit catch sight of a sign by the roadside depicting a bed. I yell at them to stop, and when all the different parts of the car have come to rest, I get out, thankfully, and follow the arrow.

The word associated with the drawing is *noclegi.* It is nowhere in my phrase book, but *noc* means "night," so I guess I'm on the right track. The sign appears again outside a two-story villa with iron railings and the statutory yapping dog. A bell push produces a tinkling sound inside, and a plump, motherly woman in a floral halter and shorts comes out to examine me, followed by a chunky husband close behind. They engage me in preliminary chat through the iron bars until I pass their test. I'm allowed into the citadel, and from then on, they can't do enough for me.

The price is very reasonable. First, though, they are required to record my name in a register. Owing to the peculiar handwriting of a clerk in my Los Angeles consulate, my name is usually read in Poland as "Goward." If it were not such an ugly name, I wouldn't object. Edward is bad enough. Goward is out of the question. I am *not* Goward. My host is delighted, because he too is an Edward.

After I have seen my room, we go into the garden, which is an Eden of fruits and vegetables, and I am fed enormous quantities of wonderful greengage plums. Even the dog thinks they are wonderful, because she eats them, too. I have never before seen a dog eat fruit.

My ability to communicate in the Polish language is definitely improving. I am able to ask Edward about some piles of building materials alongside the house. He tells me that it is useless to put money in the bank. Whenever he gets any money, he buys wood and bricks. When he has enough, he builds something. He built his own house. Now he is building another one nearby. It is the only way, he says, to protect his savings. Indeed, looking around, it is obvious that many people are following the same plan. Poland is in the grip of the do-it-yourself fever that gripped England after the war. Everybody is desperate for bargains, and the slogan of the day is "HUR-TOWNY." Every other store and enterprise screams HURTOWNY at me. It's the Polish equivalent of SALE, but it really means wholesale, dirt-cheap, a bargain.

The one thing Edward's wife won't do for me is cook, so he takes me and the dog out for a walk to the military garrison nearby, a massive building, more on the lines of a monastery. The restaurant, he says, is in there. Mystified, I wander through the great halls and up the stone steps. I open the wrong door and am almost deafened by an off-duty soldier practicing a drum riff with a small rock band. Just a few doors away is a huge, empty salon with tables and a self-service counter. So solid is the masonry that the rock music is inaudible in here. Taking potluck with some unfamiliar items on the menu, I end up with two kinds of pork and fried potatoes, but very tasty. What a remarkable coun,ry this is, where dogs eat plums and the army runs hotels and restaurants.

More great thunderstorms rumble through the night, and in the morning it rains. I'm trying everything I can to get my calf muscles back to work—massage, rest, heat, light exercise—but the result so far is dismal, and I'm in despair. One more night here, and I'll try again. More thunder and lightning and another trip to the army canteen. It really is a splendid room, with coffered ceilings and paneled walls. It's pre-world war, of course, and demonstrates the prestige the army had in Poland under the regime of its hidebound and blinkered aristocrats.

After a sleepless night with more storms, I have got to get going again. The next town is Ciechanów (Tchye-*kahn*-off), another fifteen miles, but on country roads, thank heavens. Edward is insistent that I visit a church on the way at Rostkowo. For him it has enormous significance, something to do with the life of a certain Saint Zładiław (but the little crosses on the *l*'s make them sound like *w*'s—Zwadiwaff!). Anyway, Edward's church gives me something to aim for, and maybe I'll be overwhelmed by some transcendent marvel. So I make my farewells, and with a few more plums in my pack I limp away on the four miles to Rostkowo, hoping for a sign.

As I leave the outskirts of Przasnysz, one thing is clear. The superficial gloss of prosperity that surprised me earlier on my way south has faded. This is not a tourist destination. The streets are undeniably shabby, and there are signs of deprivation. Later, on my way through the country, I meet an aged man leading a tired horse, pulling a small cart. They appear to have come directly out of the Middle Ages. Toothless, wrinkled, and bleary-eyed, he gapes up at me with a grin that is both shy and pathetic, taps on his throat with a horny forefinger, and makes a hoarse, questioning sound, which I interpret as "Vodka?" He doesn't believe my regretful "*nie,*" and repeats the performance several times, before plodding slowly and despondently on. The cart is shaped like a square box with four high sides. In it sits an old woman holding on to a calf. She neither moves nor looks up. It somehow occurs to me that the old woman and the calf are of equal importance in the man's life. I wonder which he would save first.

Perhaps it is this somber thought that inspires me to joke with a young woman in a village store. I can't find the word for "cheese," and flip frustratedly through the phrase book until finally I ask her, "Shall we go dancing?"

She looks astonished, then bursts into laughter with squeals of "*Nie. Nie!*" That cheers me up.

At Rostkowo the only sign I can read is the name of the saint, which I already know. The church itself is small and nice enough, but nothing special. Anyway, it's locked up. I sit on the church wall, massaging my painful muscles, squeezing stale arnica jelly on them and between my toes. Some more toes have now joined the protest movement. I'm wondering what to do. If I push these physical problems too far, maybe I'll lose all chance of recovering in time to walk later. From here I have to follow a gravel cart track for a few miles that will take me on to a bigger road. As a last resort I decide to walk it in flip-flops. It helps the toes, but the muscles like this even less. By the time I get to the road, I know I'm beaten. I've walked 130 miles from Kaliningrad, but I'll have to arrive in Warsaw on wheels. Maybe there I can find a way to recover from these aggravating problems.

# Chapter 17

*I* took the bus to Ciechanów and spent two nights in a modern hotel on the outskirts of town hoping for a miracle recovery, but it didn't happen. Wondering what to do while I was there, I talked to a Welsh engineer, a resident at the hotel, who was designing a factory to make seat covers for Ford. He told me that the only action in town was a strip joint. He had heard you could get a Russian stripper for two hundred dollars. There was a premium on Russians. He didn't say what you could do with her, but I suppose it was obvious. It made me sad.

The next day, feeling rather defeated, I walked to the station. The train to Warsaw was busy, and all the second-class seats were taken, but curiously the bar car was almost empty. There was a burly man with a bushy black beard who was buried in a voluminous newspaper, like an anarchist trying to escape notice and, at the other end of the carriage, a young man of dark complexion. The barman stared vacantly through the window at a flat landscape full of wheat, cows, and scattered buildings under a gray sky.

The buildings got closer as we went south. The train clattered over iron bridges spanning tributaries to the Vistula. Later, on the edge of Warsaw, we passed a bus depot, absolutely vast and crammed with buses. There must have been a thousand of them, at least. How could so many buses be parked out of commission in the middle of the day? I wondered whether some tremendous event had occurred while I was walking that I had simply not heard about; a countercoup, revolution, or catastrophe maybe.

It happened to me once in Peru. There had been a revolution, and I found out about it only when I tried to order wine with my lunch. During revolutions, wine is off. Another time I was up in a light plane when, unknown to me of course, a big earthquake shook California below me. The sense of there being something inexplicably wrong with everyone when I landed was quite dramatic. In this case, though, the more reasonable explanation would be that there were no spare parts.

A few minutes before we pulled into Warsaw, the young man came down to my end of the coach and we got to talking. He was a Moroccan student of pharmacy at Ciechanów, named Aziz, and he spoke French. He was very friendly, and immediately gave me two pieces of priceless information. One was the address of a student hostel, where, he said, I could get a room for $2.50 a night. The other was, at first, even more astounding. He said that if I first dialed the numbers 867, I could make free phone calls to anywhere in the world. As soon as we got onto the station platform, he proved it by calling his family in Tangier from the pay phone, and making me talk to them. He told me his family was "diplomate," and I guessed that meant that in Morocco they would be pretty well off. He wasn't dressed like a man who lacked the price of a phone call.

He said he had stumbled on the formula by accident, and was very proud of it. I could understand his pride. What a dramatic difference it would make if long-distance calls were free. That would be a political program I could get behind. Later in Warsaw I did try his magic numbers, but it was not easy. They only worked on certain pay phones, which were rare. I managed once to get through to California, but the person at the other end couldn't hear me. After that I gave up.

The other gift, though it was less exotic, produced more solid benefits. On the map of Warsaw I had bought in Ciechanów, Aziz showed me the street, Zamenhofa, and then took me out of the station. I knew nothing of modern Warsaw when I arrived; my images and associations were all from the past, and inevitably related to warfare and atrocities. I knew the city had been largely destroyed in the war, but it had not occurred to me to wonder what might have been built there since. My first impressions were not encouraging. We emerged from a long tunnel onto Warsaw's main boulevard, Jerolimskie. Across the street was one of those dreary open spaces that probably looked fine on the architect's drawings but, in practice, end up being sterile or abused. This one was being abused, by fly-by-night vendors of cheap clothing, jewelry, gadgets, and the kinds of things we used to say, rather quaintly, had "fallen off the back of the truck." But at least it was alive.

Above it loomed an immense building that was not only incredibly ugly but was also obviously dead. I looked on my map and saw that it occupied an area of about a square mile. Even in plan view on the map it looked horrible—a giant four-legged bug from outer space that had fastened its claws into Warsaw's heart before expiring.

This, I learned, was the Palace of Culture, Stalin's gift to the heroic people of Warsaw. A week in the city did not change my opinion that the city will not recover until the palace is gone. We walked half a block to the next big crossroads, a bewildering maze of traffic lanes, underpasses, and intersecting tram lines. Aziz pointed to a tram stop far away in the middle of the road, told me the number of the tram to take, the number of stops to go, gave me two tickets, and disappeared, waving, into the crowd.

The problem was how to get there from here. You could move only by tunnel, but there were several of these platforms marooned out there. How would you know whether you had come up at the right one? It was a bit like an upside-down version of bobbing for apples. I had a feeling that the view from there would not be at all familiar. I tried to map it in my mind, held my breath, and dived. When I came up, I found I had overshot my mark and was on the opposite side of the crossing. Directly in front of me was the Forum Hotel, recommended by my friend in Babięta. I went in, learned that rooms began at $135 a night, and came out again rapidly. I did not think that Wojciech could ever have stayed there. I dived underground again and came up to see a tram with the right number just getting ready to leave, so I hopped on.

It took me into an older part of town, which must have survived the war, and the sense of relief I felt was so marked that I was caught up in my own reflections. These older buildings were not particularly beautiful in themselves. In fact, taken one by one, they ranged from ordinary to grotesque, but they dated from a period when facades were lavishly decorated, and the overall effect was of a busy, intricate, and mysterious world of many layers and possibilities. And that, I realized, was my idea of what a city should be—not the cheapskate concrete and curtain-walled catastrophes that dehumanize our twentieth-century townscapes and are fit to be viewed only from automobiles.

The tram was taking me down Marszałkowska, a busy commercial street, and when we came to a six-spoked traffic circle called Zbawiciela, I found that I was going the wrong way. Not that it mattered. I still had another ticket, and tram rides are fun. I changed to the right tram, and we rattled back up the street, past Stalin's curse, alongside some pretty public gardens, and a hotel and restaurant called Saski that looked appealing. Zamenhofa was in a quieter area of residential buildings arranged in haphazard fashion among odd-shaped fragments of dessicated lawn and shrubbery. The idea, I guess, was to relieve monotony, which it certainly did. For casual visitors like me, though, it was quite bewildering, since the buildings all looked identical. It took several days before I could find the hostel without losing my bearings and blundering out into the street again. A compass would have been useful.

The entrance was in the middle of the building, dividing it into two wings, and the concierge lived and slept in a tiny wooden lodge facing the door. I presented myself as best I could, but she quickly gave up trying to understand me and summoned a young law student, Andrej, to translate. He told me that it was, indeed, true that during the summer months traveling academics like myself (oh, sure!) could take a room. Normally the rent would be a hundred thousand zlotys a day, but the price was reduced to fifty thousand because at the moment there was no hot water in the bathrooms. Very soon, he added, there would be no bathrooms at all, at least not on my side of the building, because they were tearing them out. I could expect a certain amount of noise and dust. On the other hand, it cost one fiftieth of the price at the Forum. I had no difficulty deciding to stay. I got a dark, depressing room on the ground floor, with three beds, a table tattooed with cigarette burns, and a dingy, threadbare carpet, but it was home and I slept there for five nights.

Warsaw was an elusive city. There was something ghostly about it. I went back to the Saski that night and ate there. The dining room was quite grand, in the old style, its huge windows draped with velvet curtains in red to match the carpet, and a high plastered and decorated ceiling above it all. A small polished floor and a dais at one end of the salon evoked visions of tea dances for the gentility of old Warsaw. Our "Bob" would have been happy here. Nostalgia for those better days—however misplaced—helped mask the present shabbiness, but it could not disguise the fact that all those eating there that day were hopeless interlopers. It was made for the members of a vanished society. Unfortunately, judging by the mediocrity of the cuisine, they had taken their chef with them.

The oldest parts of the city, by the river, were the most hospitable, and it was there that I spent most of my time, limping in and out of churches, monuments, cafés, and restaurants. These ancient sections around and within the old city walls have been lovingly rebuilt and refurbished, and they constitute a small oasis in a city that otherwise seems oddly vacant.

When I finally made contact with the oboist, Jerzy, it was my bad luck that he had that day begun his vacation, but he took the trouble to come into the old town from the suburbs with his daughter, just to talk with me. We met at the Literacki, one of the cafés that come close to reviving their former glory, and I told him of the strange feeling I had about the city. He said that what I had observed, without realizing it, was that the people in Warsaw did not really belong there. The original inhabitants had been either driven out or killed decades ago. It was, in a sense, a squatters' city, and it would take a while for a new culture to grow.

In pursuit of the remains of the Warsaw ghetto, I came upon the Pawiak prison museum, where countless thousands of Poles killed by the Nazis are memorialized. Using letters, documents, clothing, implements, toys, all the little things that were part of their everyday existence, an effort has been made to reconstruct hundreds of lives. They look out at us from their photographs, smiling, brightly confident of their future; they make Jerzy's point in the most poignant way. What has happened is indescribably sad. From being a city that grew through history, richly layered with the legacies of every phase of its evolution, Warsaw appears reduced to the status of a village surrounded by a wasteland where rootless people scurry about like ants in the shadow of Stalin's giant, fossilized ego.

As to the ghetto, after looking for it everywhere, I found I was living in it—or, rather, where it had been. Not a brick is left standing, just a few gardens and monuments.

Despite these terrible losses, Warsaw is still a major city, with an infinite amount in it to see and understand, and I did what I could. I took the bus out to the palace at Wilanów only to find it closed; I explored the Russian flea market in Warsaw's immense stadium across the river, keeping my hand on my wallet like a good boy. But it was all secondary to the main purpose, which was recovering the use of my legs. Then I made a stupendous discovery. All this time I had been religiously devoted to the special high-tech socks with their patented wicking action that I was given to wear with my boots. But on the third day, I found that if I wore cheap cotton socks instead, it made the crucial difference to my toe.

Perhaps this was not to be the first time success or failure of an expedition was decided by so trivial a margin as an eighth of an inch of cotton, but to me it was another miracle. I offered generalized thanks to whatever patron saint had interceded, stopped thinking about Warsaw, and began planning for Ukraine. Additional motivation was provided the next morning at seven by the jackhammers that began ripping out the bathrooms. As I clambered over mountains of rubble to pee, I knew it was time to move on.

What I needed to continue my journey were a visa, a seat on the train to Lvov, a map, and some rudimentary information about the country. Being in the capital of the country next door, I didn't anticipate much trouble. However, there were difficulties. Obviously, the visa had to come first, and here the main problem was finding the consulate. Apparently it had been moving around from house to house, like Nathan's floating crap game.

I pinned it down in the end. It was set up like a sting operation in the front room of a house on the other side of town, and I got my visa, after several visits and much waiting around, for a hefty fifty-dollar fee. Unfortunately, that was all I got. I would have liked to know a few simple things about traveling in the Ukraine, but everyone was too busy or couldn't understand. I asked what currency was in use there and what it was worth, and it seemed to me that they didn't know. Obviously, that was ridiculous. How could they not know about their own money? I must have heard wrong.

I phoned the British embassy and asked the press attaché there. He sounded like a pleasant chap. His name was Tim. He knew absolutely nothing about Ukraine, let alone what currency was used. He promised to bring it up at a meeting later if I cared to call back, but when I did, it transpired that nobody else had anything to offer about Ukraine, either. I don't know if they asked the ambassador, but it did seem strange that among all those diplomats not one had the slightest curiosity about the place next door. Did they know something I didn't know? Did Ukraine exist at all? Maybe the

Ukrainian consulate really was a brilliant fraud, a Ponzi scheme that collected fifty dollars a head and skipped town.

The question became even more serious when I tried to find a map. At first I was quite casual about it. Across from the Saski Hotel was a shop of many windows, devoted to maps and such. But they had nothing on Ukraine. Neither did the two other stores I had stumbled upon around the station. Increasingly desperate, I wandered the city. There were maps of Fiji and Mali, and Burundi and Bali, and a street map of Kathmandu, but no map of Ukraine. How was I going to walk through Ukraine without a map? I'll get one when I arrive, I said, but I didn't believe it.

The ticket was relatively simple. Warsaw-Central, the station I had arrived in, was the obvious place to start. It is a four-story den of thieves and vagabonds, an urban guerrilla's dream and a tourist's nightmare—in other words, an exciting, unpredictable adventure or a colossal waste of time, depending on your objective. I had already enjoyed it as a spectacle. Now I wanted to buy a ticket. I guessed my train would leave from there because it was the most southerly station. I was wrong, but had to stand in line for an hour to find out that my train actually left from a rather quiet station called Warsaw-Gdańsk, just around the corner from the hostel where I was staying.

How convenient, I thought, and took a tram there to buy a ticket. Wrong again. All international tickets have to be bought at Warsaw-Central. I took the tram back. At an office on the fourth floor, the clerks, like all others, resolutely refuse to speak or understand anything but Polish. However, another hour of standing in line gave me time to perfect my strategy. I found paper and pen, learned the words for "write," "how much," "date," and "time," and when I got to the counter, pushed my paper and pen at the clerk and got her to write it all down. I was rather proud of myself. The young American ahead of me had failed to deal with this challenge. He, too, wanted a ticket, and he was outraged when the clerk refused to understand him. Red in the face and blustering, he was ejected from the queue without mercy and is probably now lying in some Warsaw gutter, a broken man.

The train, I learned, would leave at six in the morning on Thursday. As Wednesday passed into memory and I still could not find a single word, picture, or drawing to do with Ukraine, it began to dawn upon me that I would be taking the train to Lvov even less prepared than I had been for Kaliningrad. I had a few harsh words to say to myself, and then, to ease my frustration, I went to a department store and bought an umbrella.

When I got on the train, the man with the seat next to mine was still asleep in the bunk over my head. Seated across from me was a motherly woman with a great many large parcels. Where she or the train had come from I never found out. At first I was quite optimistic about talking with her, as she seemed very willing to respond, but it was like making bricks without straw. There seemed to be no common threads of understanding with which to bind together the few little bits of information I was able to elicit. If she had tried to question me, we might have made progress, but my efforts drowned in her passivity. In the whole fourteen hours we shared, I learned only that she was going home to Lvov, that her mother would meet her, and that she knew nothing about the hotels in the city. She tried to tell me about the money, but it made no sense. All I heard was something about coupons.

The other passenger, when he eventually slid down off his bunk, was even less communicative. He was youngish and dark-haired, in a black leather bomber jacket, brown polyester trousers, and cheap shoes. He had a sullen look and sat reading a tabloid paper in the determined fashion of someone who wants to keep to himself. I guessed that he was one of the army of "guest workers" that migrated constantly across Europe between rich countries and poor ones.

Three quarters of the journey was in Poland, and looking out, I was treated to a reverse pageant of agriculture through the ages; from combine harvesters to tractors to horse-drawn reapers to handheld scythes. I saw wheat tied in sheafs and stood up, three or four at a time, in the stooks that I remembered from the English countryside of my childhood. A man sat on a stool milking his cow into a bucket in the middle of a field. Another plowed his field with horses. A man and woman worked together pitchforking their mown hay into small, round-topped stacks.

Rolling through a rural station, I was strangely attracted by the elfin features of a female stationmaster, so cutely uniformed with her peaked cap and the short stick with the red disk at the end, her lollipop wand of office.

At Przeworsk we passed among big industrial plants, apparently idle, their smokestacks lifeless. At Przemyśl, the farthest south we would go, there were more dead factories, but over the rooftops were clusters of

Byzantine domes repeating the shapes of the little haystacks, reminders of the long departed Ottoman empire.

Then something entirely unexpected and magical happened. We stopped and, slowly, the entire train of many coaches was raised several feet into the air. If the train had taken flight, I would not have been more surprised. It had something to do with the wheels, or rather the bogies. I presumed it was to accommodate the broader gauge of track used to the east, but it didn't make sense, because the train came down on the same track as before.

Almost immediately after we began moving again, the border officials came on the train. A short, sharp-looking Polish guard stamped my passport and that of the woman opposite. He looked at the man's papers and uttered something that had all the finality of a guilty verdict. The blood drained from the young man's face. He launched into a frenzy of protest, becoming more and more angry. The guard shrugged and left the compartment. The man followed him, and reappeared later, haggard and forlorn. He threw his pass down in disgust, slumped on the seat, and buried his face in his hands, making spluttering sounds of despair.

It was strange to sit alongside such a powerful display of emotion, knowing nothing of what had caused it or of the fate he was contemplating. Even stranger was the fact that three hours later, as we came to Lvov, he was still sitting there, but cheerful and composed and reading his paper as though nothing untoward had ever occurred to disturb his expectations.

# Chapter 18

*I*f my performance in Kaliningrad was a pretty fair demonstration of the art of arrival, my showing in Lvov (L-*voff*) was closer to a fiasco. The difference was due entirely to my state of mind. For one thing, I felt particularly stupid, having sat opposite that sweet, placid woman for fourteen hours without being able to coax a single piece of useful information from her. For another thing, it was late in the day. I allowed myself to think I was in a hurry.

When the train drew into the station, I helped my companion get her seven huge bags of booty out of the compartment and down to the platform. I wasn't being entirely altruistic. I thought there was a faint chance that whoever came to meet her might, in some way, help ease my passage into this city, but when I saw the frail little lady who greeted her and registered an older version of the same insipid smile, I abandoned all hope in that direction and joined the human tide that swept into the station building and swirled around inside it. There was not a calm spot anywhere. Almost every arriving passenger had brought huge bales, boxes, and baskets, and they were bobbing about in the confusion as though two columns of porters on safari had met in a head-on collision.

I searched the station walls in vain for any sign of a language I understood or a map that might tell me where to go. Outside the station, to my disoriented eye, all was frantic chaos. There were buses and trams, but I could not know where they were going, and the competition to get on them was fierce. I should have been patient, followed my own rules, sat it out quietly somewhere until the crowd dispersed and I could get some kind of grip on the situation. Instead, anxious for a quick resolution before it turned dark, I asked a policeman.

Two of them were moving through the crowd. They wore pale blue uniforms, and I swear it was the color that seduced me. I confused them subliminally with officers of the United Nations, and equated them with peace and security. I walked up to them and said, "Hotel?" One of them turned to me, and I saw immediately that I had made a mistake. He had the kind of face I personally detest—a lean, jocular, ass-kicking face. He managed to grin and bark simultaneously.

"Passport!"

I showed it to him. He scanned it, marched me briskly out of the station, and yelled at a crowd of disreputable-looking men gathered around some vehicles that even a wrecker's yard might have refused. The call was answered by a burly man of villainous appearance wearing the standard black leather jacket. The cop addressed him with an offhand, joking remark. To me it sounded something like:

"Here's a little gift for you, Georgi. Don't forget to cut me in on it later."

Georgi, if that was his name, ushered me to his taxi, if that's what it was. There was not really enough of it left to tell. We were able to squeeze in at the front somehow. A comrade of his already occupied the remains of the backseat. I had just enough of my wits about me to remember the Russian for "How much?" so I said, "*Skolko stoit?*"

He raised both hands.

"*Desiat' dollar.* Ten," he said.

Outrageous as I knew this must be, I felt like paying a penalty for my own stupidity and let it go. The contraption ground into motion and we set off. Georgi spoke about ten words of English and the same number in German. He quickly came to the point, and I understood him a lot better than I let on.

He did not want to take me to a hotel. Hotels are expensive. He had a room. It was somewhere called Ternopil'. He would take me to the room. Hotel bad. Room good. Ternopil'. He wanted to imprison me in a room, take all my dollars, and then sell me to a laboratory for radiation experiments.

Reasonably enough, I refused.

"Hotel," I kept insisting. In frustration he slammed his fist on the steering wheel, which I thought a risky thing to do. He held frantic conference with his mate, then started all over again. Actually, as I watched him perform, I began to warm to him. Scurrilous and unshaven as he appeared, there was a soul in that bulky body, and it strained to bursting with resentment over my thickheaded obstinacy. I could sympathize, having endured hours on the train with much the same emotion, and I had to admit he expressed it much better than I had. Fuming with impatience, slapping at everything near him, he tried again and again to get me to surrender to his plan, and we seemed to drive around forever, while I wondered whether he really needed my permission.

So I was quite pleased at last to find myself outside the Grand Hotel in the heart of town. It was too grand for me, but at least the clerk spoke English. With sorrowful disdain he spoke of another, cheaper, establishment and sent us and our jalopy a few hundred yards farther along the road. It was called, curiously, the George'a Hotel. What the apostrophe-*a* meant, I tried later to discover, but it dated back to Polish times, and nobody seemed to know. The name was up there, in stucco, on the facade, and that was almost all that could be seen of the hotel, for the rest of it, including the main entrance, was obscured by scaffolding.

The side door, the only way in, was like the entrance to a jail. People entering and leaving had to run the gauntlet of a bunch of tough-looking men who were gathered around it, laughing and smoking, while watching them from the side street was an even bigger crowd of soldiers or police with a military vehicle. There should have been an air of crisis, or at least some tension around this unusual scene, and it was puzzling that all the players were evidently treating it as a normal everyday occurrence.

It struck me, not for the first time, that I had spent the greater part of the day being mystified by one thing or another. The explanations I gave myself were pure speculation. Without language, passing through societies in catharsis, I was no better able to account for the phenomena around me than an illiterate peasant resorting to magic and superstition. I was schooled to be forever explaining things, and to be miserable unless I could understand and interpret what was happening around me . . . and yet, the kaleidoscopic images I had witnessed that day were all the more fascinating for being inexplicable. Ignorance might be more hair-raising than blissful, but I had survived, and there was a certain joy in simply recording *how* things were rather than forever asking *why.*

Feeling unduly magnanimous, I gave an extra five dollars to the rogue who had brought me there. He wanted more, and I laughed and squeezed through the hotel door. The receptionist was just as haughty and abrupt as I had expected. It would have been more correct to call her the interventionist, but I already had a sense of the local style, and laughed it off. The price of the room was fourteen dollars, with no bathroom and a suggestion of occasional hot water. She made it clear that only a fool would not know that the restaurant was open until eleven, and she thought me stupid for asking whether I could call Germany from my room. Then her phone rang and she had no more time for me.

I climbed a fine staircase with elegant curving banisters to the first floor, where the rooms were arranged around a central well with a broad-domed skylight above it. Tall carved doors opened onto big rooms with lofty molded ceilings and high windows. Clearly this hotel had once had a lot of class, and maybe one day would again. Meanwhile, it was a disaster. I managed to squeeze a meal of sorts out of the restaurant and walked out into the night.

The tough guys around the doorway wanted to buy dollars, and from them I discovered that the unit of currency, for want of a better name, was actually called *kupón.* One mystery resolved. The hotel was close to an intersection of several big and busy streets. The statue of a local hero, Shevchenko, stood in the middle of the road. Beyond it, in the direction from which I had been driven, I saw that the street broadened out into a great open area, about a hundred yards wide and very long. Down the middle of it ran a broad, cobbled carriageway and at the far end stood a fine, ornate building that looked like, and was, an opera house.

On each of the four days and nights I stayed in Lvov, I spent some time walking around this splendid esplanade. I joined the enthusiastic audiences that gathered to watch chess players with time clocks, hurling joyful insults at each other as they slammed their pieces across the board and their palms on the clocks at breakneck speed.

On the afternoon of Saturday, the big market day, the benches were packed with peasants resting under the bright sun. There were many stout women, past their youth, firmly seated on the benches with their legs apart, skirts smoothed tight over stockinged knees, in blouses and wool cardigans, with scarves around their heads, weathered faces fixed in expressions of satisfaction. Done with the market, it was their chance to claim the freedom of the city for an hour or two before the long road back to their farms. Some of them had a man alongside, bucolic, slightly tipsy, and grinning like a jester.

Other older men, pensioners maybe, in faded nondescript suits with stiffly pressed pants like the postwar clothing of my parents' generation, walked carefully with canes, upholding their dignity. Farther along, toward the opera house, the crowd became younger. The racing chess virtuosi were there that day, too, and a dense knot of men watched and listened to their good-humored taunts, but many other, quieter games were in progress, attracting less attention, but creating pools of tangible reflection alongside the mainstream of people ambling to and fro.

I was there on Sunday, August 14, too, which happened to be Ukraine's National Independence Day. Up and down the esplanade, fiery impromptu orators drew small crowds into loud and lusty argument, while ancient veterans paraded in pale blue uniforms and little boxy caps, larded with operatic piping and medals.

Overlooking the scene from all sides were the great ornamental buildings of the nineteenth century. In this vast precinct from a bygone era there was a peaceful atmosphere, which I thought would be impossible to reproduce among modern buildings, however carefully designed or placed they might be. Those massive old stone blocks, dinosaurs from the age of czars and emperors, were once as potent and aggressive as the concrete power structures of today. They had housed the great corporations and institutions of empire, and must have been hot in the pursuit of profit and the prosecution of control. They had been raised up over the labors of millions. In their time they were overbearing symbols of the powers that ruled the throng, that chained armies of clerks to their desks, laborers to their gangs, and soldiers to their battalions.

The polished black cobblestones I walked on, like the billions of others that paved Europe during that century, were laid by hand, and cleverly, too, to form a pleasing fan-shaped pattern. Rich men in carriages could look down and see their superiority illustrated in stone beneath their horses' hooves. But that was all in the past. Today, the pattern in stone was just that—a pattern. The big buildings had taken their toll, and were paid for long ago. The heat had gone out of these monoliths of a hundred years ago, their force was spent, and a cool serenity remained. The art survived the loss of power and became benign. In Lvov, where the war passed them by undisturbed, they now shed their benevolence over the newly liberated population. Time matters. Time changes things. Time can't be faked.

That was the best of Lvov (which I learned to think of as L'viv and pronounce L-*veev*, as the Ukrainians do). The rest was hardscrabble. I began immediately to look for a map to guide me between L'viv and the Romanian frontier at Chernivtsi, but without success. The hotel clerk told me categorically that there was no such thing as a map of Ukraine. Of course I didn't believe her, but proving it was another matter. I spent Friday in fruitless efforts, and gave up. All I could think of doing was to find an atlas of some kind and make a copy or tracing. At least I would know the names of some towns along the way and have a rough idea of the distances between them.

The main library, as it turned out, was nearby and close to the market, and I went there on Saturday morning after looking around the stalls and buying a few odd things I hoped would keep until I was on the road. It was a modest library, with very little on open display, but the woman (Why always women? What do the men do?) at the reference desk was nice, and helpful. She found a school atlas. The two hundred miles I intended to walk were shown on three inches of map, but still it was a lot better than nothing. I tore a page out of my notebook, did a rough tracing of the roads south, and began to make dots for the towns. The Cyrillic script was printed so small that I had difficulty reading the names. It was an old atlas, and the roads were indistinct and undifferentiated as to importance or condition. I foresaw having a great deal of trouble.

It was then that the usual miracle intervened. A chubby, balding little man in his sixties bustled into the reading room and stood next to me at the counter where I was working. As he was talking to the librarian, I saw his eyes wander my way, and then he asked if I spoke German. So I began to explain what I was up to, and he said he could help.

"Come and sit at the table," he said. "You see, I am a geography professor, retired actually, but I have surveyed every bit of this territory you are going through, between here and Chernivtsi."

He gave me the names of the towns were it would be best to stay, where he thought there were hotels, and he knew from memory how far they were from each other.

"But why don't you get a map?" he asked.

I laughed. "That's what I was trying to do, all of yesterday. It's impossible. There aren't any."

"Come," he said. "I'll show you."

We went out together, and he walked me to the very first and most obvious shop I had gone to, just a hundred yards from the hotel. Within minutes he had procured a road map of Ukraine. I was astonished and a little humiliated.

"How is that possible?" I asked. "Why didn't they give it to me yesterday?"

"Ach, don't blame them," he replied. "They only came in today. By Monday they will be all gone. Do you want a small-scale ordinance survey map? They have those here, too."

But the flow of miracles had dried up. They had maps of everything but the area that interested me. And as for dictionaries, phrase books, or guides, there were none. Still, I pushed my luck.

"Do you know anyone in the English department of the university?" I asked. "It would be a great help to talk with someone there."

My cherubic factotum, whose name I wrote down, lost, and later couldn't remember, was more than willing. We walked the streets behind the hotel for fifteen minutes, to arrive at a classic example of a nineteenth-century temple of learning, not very different from my own alma mater in London, lavish with brown marble and granite, echoing flagstones and neo-Gothic windows, where thoughts fly heavenward while the feet freeze. L'viv has a typical Continental climate of hot summers and long, freezing winters. During the summer months, when the building is largely empty, the architectural environment is ideal. It was pleasantly cool and breezy as we clattered up the long flights of steps and down the galleries to the small rooms where the English department was tucked away. Luckily, a secretary was working there to tell us that one of the professors was probably in town. She phoned his home, and then told me to call him later when he would be back.

I thanked my guide profusely—he seemed not to want anything else—and, buoyed up by my good fortune, I went to the post office, thinking I would write to William. I had sent letters from Russia and postcards from Poland, but I didn't know how long they would take or whether they would get there at all.

It was an intimidating challenge to write something comprehensible to him about my experience. A vast chasm separated it from anything he could have known. I wasn't sure how to make the bridge, and thinking about it made me uneasy. Even though we lived a rather simple life by American standards, it distressed me to see him already taking for granted so many things in the way of food, leisure, and entertainment that I regarded as luxuries. It made me equally uncomfortable to watch his growing addiction to electronic imagery, junk movies, and cool clothes. At home in California, I used all the cliché arguments on myself to restrain my objections:

The world has changed out of recognition since I was a boy.

Obviously, I can't impose the culture of my childhood on my son.

Remember how insufferable you found your teachers saying, "When I was your age, *we* only got threepence a month pocket money. *We* walked to school barefoot . . ." and so on and on.

But being in Europe reminded me how much more is demanded there by schools, how excessive those three-month American summer vacations are, how much higher are European expectations in general. And being in Ukraine made the consumption patterns of American teenagers seem positively obscene. Thinking about it, I felt deeply anxious that I might have failed him and delivered him up to Mammon, as it were, without the spiritual equipment to survive.

Would it have been better to bring him along with me? I had considered the idea, but it seemed too long and arduous a trip for a twelve-year-old. And when I thought of what might have happened if the two of us had been in that field with the bull, I shuddered.

So I wrote down a few anecdotes I hoped would amuse him and returned to the George'a. I found the hotel full of bicycles. That is to say, the hall was packed with them—some assembled, some in parts, big bikes, little bikes, baby bikes, flowing up the staircase and through the doors. Accompanying them were a number of men who resembled the cop at the station. By now the receptionist was talking to me—as I found in Szczecin and later, it takes time to develop a relationship—and she told me that the bicycles belonged to a party of Serbs. Their buses were waiting outside and would be leaving soon. They came twice a week to buy bicycles. Two years before, it had been the Poles. Last year, it was the Romanians. This year, it's the Serbs.

It was revealing to observe how conventions give way to necessity. This once luxurious hotel condescending to act as a biweekly goods depot brought home how close to the bone the knife of austerity had cut. Yet people behaved with dignity and spirit, where the Russians, I thought, were more stoically enduring. I supposed that Ukranians were feeding off the joys of liberation, while Russians viewed their new freedom as a mixed blessing.

As for the Serbs, I could not restrain the foolish reflection that one should not be dealing in bicycles while one's compatriots were out raping and torturing. Of all people, I should know that, war or peace, life goes on in all its trivial detail. Wasn't I the one who, at the age of thirteen, looted the bombed ruins of a block of flats down the road from my school and came away with a caged canary?

I had hoped to get the English professor to have dinner with me that evening, and on the phone he said he would be pleased to meet me, but not until tomorrow, at lunchtime. It seemed worth spending another day. On my walk back from the university—more correctly, the Polytechnic Institute—I had passed a restaurant with huge plate-glass windows and majestic purple velvet curtains drawn inside them, so I thought I'd try it out.

At first the headwaiter wouldn't let me past the lobby. It was not for foreigners, he said. The menu was only in Ukrainian. How I understood him I don't know, but I took the menu from him and read out some items I recognized, like *kotlet, salat z pomidorio,* and *kartoflia.*

"*Dobre,*" he said, half convinced, and let me through. It was an enormous space, two stories high, with pillars, dim wall lighting, and chandeliers. Carved wooden partitions discreetly separated the tables, visible through the gloom only by their small table lamps. They covered most of the floor, but there was a curtained stage on the left and a small dance floor in front of it. The atmosphere was one I love, of mysterious shadow and suggestion. I was halfway through a pretty good meal when the lights went down even further and a hilariously bad cabaret struck up on the stage, consisting mainly of girls writhing, in swaths of chiffon, without the benefit of choreography or dressmakers. Colored spotlights wandered about looking for something worth lighting, and I think the music was being poured out of oil drums.

It was an evocative, if unintended, throwback to the improvised nightclub scenes of the forties, and I enjoyed it immensely. Back on the esplanade, though, something of a much superior quality was being offered that night. A slim young man with refined features sat with a guitar in front of the opera house, singing songs of great dramatic range and depth. Behind him, in the deep embrasure of the main entrance, a girl danced. She was also wrapped in long black chiffon, but hers was consummately well designed to follow every nuance of movement. What had been ridiculous in the restaurant was made sublime. A crowd of hundreds stood around them in a large arc of silence. It was clear that the words matched the music in importance, but even without them this was a performance of great merit. His songs had the force and delivery of Jacques Brel's but were distinctly his own, and her inventive improvisations kept fresh and alive what might easily have become tedious. Like everybody present, I felt a great joy at being surprised with such a wonderful gift. People were generous with their coins, and surrounded the couple with congratulations.

When I came back to the hotel and walked under the scaffolding, my happy mood was abruptly broken. A sinister figure was lurking in my path, hiding stock-still in the shadows. At the other end of the scaffolded tunnel a small girl was crying out for her mother:

"*De ye Mama? De ye Mama?*"

At her feet a little poodle was scurrying around in a panic. Then the hiding figure burst into peals of laughter and stepped out from her hiding place. A horrifying kidnap in progress was transformed into an innocent game. They had wanted to see if the poodle could find Mama.

On Sunday I took the professor, whose name was Yuri, to lunch at the Grand Hotel. It was a cheap gesture. I was getting a very good rate for my dollars from the tough guys outside the hotel, and I could easily afford it. For him, as he admitted, it represented a small fortune. I was beginning to realize that the modest amount I carried with me in dollars made me a plutocrat by Ukrainian standards, a heady but disturbing phenomenon. I told Yuri of my incredulousness when I discovered a loaf of bread cost only a small fraction of an American cent. He interjected a sobering thought. I might be a *kupón* millionaire, he said, but by the time I left Ukraine I could also be a dollar pauper. He warned me that outside L'viv I would be forced to pay my hotel bills in dollars. This was the exact opposite of what the receptionist had told me, and so I was inclined to believe him.

I would not be able to get dollars for them, he said, and there would be nothing to spend my *kupóns* on unless I intended to invest in bread. We calculated that I had enough *kupóns* to buy fifty thousand loaves. I said that although I had the highest regard for Ukrainian bread, it would be difficult to get so many loaves out of the country while they were still edible. But we agreed that if they could be dried in the right conditions, they would make excellent bricks—light, strong, durable, with a high insulation factor, and of course a valuable resource in the event of a siege.

The silliness, I must admit, was mostly mine. Yuri was a rather settled family man in his forties, and more cautious than I, as befits an academic. He apologized for not inviting me to his home. He said he would be embarrassed, things being so very difficult for everyone at the moment. I told him about my visit to the Fursovs, to let him know I was accustomed to hard times, but he didn't elaborate on his own situation. However, he did tell me an interesting story that added piquancy to the meal.

It was about the hotel we were sitting in. Obviously, a great deal of money had been spent on it, to make it so incongruously luxurious. Apparently, the money had come from a wealthy Philadelphia matron who had gone into partnership with the owner of the place after privatization began. Unfortunately for her, the owner turned out not to be the owner after all, and the real owner, whose claim dated back to prerevolutionary times, appeared. She lost her investment, but strangely enough, the phony owner was doing very well.

The main course was a Ukrainian speciality with meatballs, which he pronounced quite good, but as always in these situations, there was an underlying suspicion that he was thinking about what he could have done with the money. I got a little practical help, however, by asking him to write out for me some phrases in Ukrainian that I might need, such as: "Can I sleep in your field? I have a tent." Or, "Is the water good to drink?"

In the afternoon I spent a good deal of time looking at the map. It was not a good map. There are maps that reveal information at a glance—like most Michelin maps, for example. Other maps are very confusing and deceitful to the eye, and this was one of them. Most of the place names were printed in faint orange, often overlaid by other detail. The roads were in various colors, but some were almost invisible. The rough texture of the paper didn't help, and my unfamiliarity with the Ukrainian alphabet, which differs from the Russian, made it worse.

My geographical genie had instructed me to take the number 5 bus out of town. That would get me on the road to Bibrka, a village about thirty kilometers away, where there was a small hotel. The next stage he recommended was a little longer, and would take me to Rohatyn. Two stages beyond that was the provincial capital, Ivano-Frankivs'k. Two more days of walking would get me to Kolomyia, and another two days to Chernivtsi. Then I would be one day from the border. So after nine or ten days' walking—in theory—I could be in Romania.

My feet seemed at last to be in good shape. Wearing thin socks had really made the difference. Although the nail of the unruly big toe was black and evidently planning to secede, the toe itself, for the first time in weeks, was not inflamed. I felt fairly well prepared but for the lack of any kind of dictionary or phrase book.

That evening I went out for my last visit to the esplanade and found, to my delight, that the singer and dancer were performing again. I watched and listened to the end, and this time went up to them to express my appreciation. The man was extravagantly pleased by my praise, coming as it did from a foreigner when all things foreign were deemed to be better, and he responded eagerly. They were Russians, a married couple in their twenties, called Sergei and Veronica. They had come from Saint Petersburg for the summer and were staying at a nearby hotel. He spoke enough English for us to get by on.

I said I would be interested to see what their hotel was like, and he asked if I would like to meet some of his friends. It turned into one of the most extraordinary evenings of my life. The hotel was a grim building farther down the Svobody Prospekt, which flanked the esplanade. I would have guessed it to be an abandoned office block or department store, with its dismal and featureless gray exterior of identical floors. The hall was so dimly lit that from the street it looked quite dark, but once inside the big, dank foyer, I could see, framed by a distant doorway, brightly lit men in clouds of tobacco smoke whose faces and movements were into the listless phase of drinking.

Sergei and I went to the fifth floor, where Veronica, who had gone ahead, was changing. The room was in a terrible mess, but quite recognizably a theatrical mess, there being many signed photographs, shoes, dresses, mirrors, articles of makeup, and accessories scattered over the bureau and the unmade bed. Veronica was looking pale and harried in the light of the naked bulb and didn't want to go anywhere or do anything. Sergei asked me if I would wait outside for a while, and later came to tell me that she would follow us. I doubted that she would.

Russian English was so much better than no English, and it was wonderful to be in the company, at last, of a bright, inquiring mind. We traded biographies, and as he was explaining how they tried to make a living between Petersburg and L'viv, we walked across the esplanade to the shadowy buildings on the other side and plunged together through a gap in those imposing ramparts of empire. In the small, unlit streets beyond, after several twists and turns, we came to the front of a building that, like all the others around, appeared to be deserted. By now, I had already made the mental transition from the 1940s to the 1840s and felt I was in the world of Dickens and Dostoyevsky. We entered the house through an unlocked door and were in pitch blackness. Sergei brought out a book of matches and struck one. It revealed only a wooden plank floor leading to the foot of some stairs. We advanced, he struck another match, we walked up the first flight, he struck another match, and so we went on.

The sudden brief flare of the paper matches threw me back into a story of Robert Louis Stevenson's, called "The Master of Ballantrae," that had me biting my knuckles as boy. The hero is deceived into climbing some stairs in the dark and is saved from plunging to his death when a flash of lightning shows the steps broken away abruptly under his feet. Stories of unsuspected doom lurking at the edge of innocent pleasures were a staple of my adolescence, and it's a wonder that I ever dared put my confidence in anything or anyone. I thought how fortunate I was in the certainty of my judgment that Sergei was not plotting my downfall.

We climbed three floors and, match by match, I got occasional glimpses of a house falling apart around us. Then, somewhere at the top of this decaying structure, light shone under a door ahead of us and we went through. It took a moment to resolve the jumble that confronted me in this one small room. It was a photographic studio, an artist's loft, a poet's garret, a canteen, a bedroom, and a workshop. It would have made a wonderful stage set for *La Bohème.* There was very little room to walk. Most of the floor was occupied by variously shaped pieces of wood, metal, and fabric leading new lives in support of objects made from chipped enamel, cracked china, dented tin, punctured upholstery, and other materials that could have stocked a flea market.

A tall, rangy man in his early thirties, with a wide and irrepressible grin, was introduced to me as "Master Peter," the photographer. He was intensely interested to meet me. So, in his quiet way, was a more contained young man, Vasily, the painter. From a corner behind a partition a shorter man, with a clipped beard and fuzzy hair receding from a high forehead, gazed at me with piercing eyes and a half smile and was presented as Igor, the poet. Among this exuberant clutter we had a painter, a writer, a poet, a musician, a photographer and, eventually, because she did come, a dancer. So of course we had to have a performance, and although it was spontaneous and unscripted, Peter and Sergei between them produced and directed what could only be called a theatrical production in which I was made the object of a multimedia interrogation.

It took the outward form of a photographic session. With a mug of tea in my hand, I was pressed firmly into an ancient armchair where, I knew, hundreds had sat before me. While Peter assembled battered floodlights, unearthed a tripod, and disentangled yards of wire, he and Sergei kept up a battery of questions. Who were the writers I admired? What paintings had I seen? What was the price of Nikon in America? What did I think of this and that and the other? I racked my brains for authors, painters, and prices, trying to keep up with the demand.

Vasily was perched on a stool to my left with a sketchbook. Igor was staring at me from the back of the room with a pen in his hand.

"You see, Mister Ted," said Sergei, beaming, "Master Peter is making for you a picture. Igor is composing for you a poem. Vasily is making drawing."

Peter jumped in. "We are make big publicity. We are send you picture. Now, here you must choose. Which you like?" A sheaf of prints was thrust into my hand. There were some remarkable things. A bizarre yet triumphant picture of a cheerful peasant dwarf leaning crookedly on a stick in front of a tumbledown building, all tilted on the paper so that only the dwarf's torso and head are upright, while the rest appears to be sliding away into chaos. There was a subtly colored photograph of a painting by Vasily, an assemblage of the broken toys of civilization grotesquely mired in a swamp. Landscapes, superimpositions of Veronica dancing, pictures of the city, all photographed on old stock, printed on damaged paper. The camera looked ancient. Everything was improvised. How they even got electricity into this room was a mystery.

It was an indictment in its way of the Western way of life, where easy access to every possible resource can make the very idea of improvisation seem foolish. All the time, I could not forget that this bright oasis of light and intellectual hunger and excitement was marooned like a capsule high in the black, decrepit space of a broken and deserted building. The eagerness of these people to express themselves was inspiring, and eventually I stumbled out of there clutching the prizes I could not refuse, feeling half drunk with the attention and enthusiasm that had been pressed upon me.

I brought out with me a picture of Igor with his poem written on the back, which I have yet to understand, and several of Peter's wilder photographs. A more immediately useful gift was a pocket book of useful phrases in both Russian and Ukrainian, translated into English. It was given to me by Peter, over my protests, for I knew it was a true sacrifice. So the last of my three wishes was magically granted, and I could continue my quest with functioning feet, a map to guide me, and words to be understood.

But the most valuable, though most uncomfortable, prize was the drawing that Vasily had made. It came as a shock to me. It was a good portrait, but it was not the person that I liked to imagine myself as being. He had given me a generously broad forehead, curlier hair, a rounder face, a more prominent nose, a fussier mouth and, beneath my chin, a pair of eloquently gesticulating hands. If there was a Jew in Ted Simon, this, I thought, was him. With extraordinary intuition, Vasily had focused directly on the purpose of my journey. I was forced to recognize the decades of evasion, tinged with distaste, that I had adopted for my protection, and to wonder again what price I had paid for the immunity I had sought. It was only later I learned that the building in which this cell, cabal, convulsion of talent had convened was in the old, abandoned Jewish ghetto of L'viv.

# Chapter 19

Although I am far from being the drinker that W. C. Fields was, I do seem subconsciously to share his fear of having to survive on "food and water alone." How else should I explain why I so often find myself thirsty and without water in arid situations? I managed to do it in the middle of a Sudanese desert. I did it in Russia. Now I've done it again.

It was that same old distrust of hotel tap water that I blame.

I'll get a bottle downstairs, I had thought as I left this morning, but the restaurant was deserted. It was too early. I was on my way and didn't want to backtrack to my room.

I'll find a shop somewhere, I told myself.

There were none—not before I took the bus; not when I got off it at the edge of town. Now I'm already halfway to Bibrka, I've been walking for three hours, it's hot, I'm thirsty as a sinner in hell, and my bottle is dry.

Looking over to my right, down a few gently sloping acres, I see a number of vegetable gardens laid out, and in one of them, a headscarf is bobbing up and down. A woman is watering her vegetables. I approach her gently and, with bottle in outstretched hand, utter my rehearsed plea.

*"Daite meni bud' laska vody."*

It sounds like gibberish to me. I have developed no affinity for Slavic languages, and the words carry absolutely no conviction. If I were her, I wouldn't understand a word I said, but she has received the message all right. She turns to me with a wailing and pitiful cry.

"*Ya ne main vod-y-y*," she howls. That final stressed syllable lingers over the dusty gardens like a siren. If it were blood she was refusing me and I dying for the lack of it, she could not sound more stricken and torn. It is obvious to me, in that instant, that there is no water nearby. How could that be? No one would lay out vegetable gardens in Europe without a shallow well or a stream. Something must have broken or dried up unexpectedly. She must be having to carry every drop from some other source, poor woman. And no doubt the garden is what keeps her family alive.

I retire to the road in confusion, but not without hope. The gardens could not be far from a village. And soon enough I am in Vidnyk, a very small community along the way. In one of the cottage gardens a woman sits in the shade of a fruit tree. I repeat my incantation, and she points resentfully at a curious construction close to where she is sitting. Slowly I figure out that it must be a well, but I can't see how it works. The woman is disgusted. She has to get up and show me, a grown man, how to do this simplest of all things, something a small child would do without thinking—draw water from a well.

She shows me a green-painted flywheel, whose connection with this unfamiliar apparatus I hadn't grasped. I turn it, and having taken the lid off the concrete blocks, I see a pail come up from a dark hole. The well is not appetizing. It looks dirty and the pail appears stained, but I see the stains are fused into the tin. The water that comes out is clear, cool, and delicious. It sustains me for another two hours on the road. The countryside is pleasant, though nothing very special—just fields and mixed deciduous trees, rather small to my eye, which is now accustomed to the giant firs, oaks, and redwoods of California.

According to the map, I have just crossed from one watershed into another. Everything north of here drains into the Dnieper basin, an immense, rambling river system that finally feeds a series of massive dams and reservoirs around Kiev before finding the Black Sea. From here on south, the water belongs to the Dniester, which skirts the Carpathian range and follows roughly the same route I intend to take, at least as far as Chernivtsi. Without the map, though, I would not have known. There are no peaks and passes, not even any substantial hills. The watershed seems quite arbitrary. I am having a good time walking, not least because for once my feet are getting no more tired than the rest of me, but all the same, by the time I get to Bibrka I'm glad to stop.

The map says Bibrka is a town with anything from two to ten thousand inhabitants. From the look of it, two would be more likely than ten, but unlike Vidnyk it has edges and a middle. Peter's phrase book offers a number of hotel-related questions in Ukrainian, all a bit too elaborate. "Where" is *de*. "Hotel" appears to be *gotel*.

"*De gotel?*" I ask a few times. People look at me strangely. They seem surprised, even disconcerted, as though I were questioning their faith or their potency. Too late I realize that the elaborations I'm leaving out are probably essential, some form of courtesy without which the question strikes them as unbearably rude. But they point me along until I come to the edge of a small square, well off the main road, with trees, unwatered shrubs, paths, and broken benches. In front of me is an unmarked three-story building. One door leads into a bakery. The other, according to a woman in the bakery, is the door of the *gotel*. It appears very unpromising, but I open it. Inside is only a bare and dirty wooden staircase. I walk up the stairs a way, calling out, but there is no answer and I see only closed doors above. I have been in many kinds of peculiar hotels around the world, and this is yet another kind.

Perplexed, I descend to reflect on my next move. Fortunately, an open taproom is visible in the next building, where men are refreshing themselves with half-liter glasses of ale siphoned up from the cellar. The men, however, seem strangely solitary and unapproachable. After a glass of beer, I go back to the bakery, hoping this time to break through. Obviously the ritual has worked, because I strike lucky. There at the counter is the town's French teacher, buying bread. She is a petite dark-haired woman with an anxious manner. In the ordinary way, I think she would have avoided me, but she cannot resist the opportunity to speak French with me. Merely a chance to hear the language spoken is incentive enough for her to overcome her shyness.

She tells me that the woman who has the hotel will be back soon, and she will wait with me. She is so eager to talk that we sit down on one of the few good benches and spend fifteen minutes or so together. She has never been to France, of course, and wants me to comment on her pronunciation, which is actually quite good. I realize, as I hear her talk about school, that people here place great importance on teaching the European languages. The school in this tiny town offers English, French, and German, and according to her this is standard throughout the country, putting to shame most schools in California, which can barely even offer Spanish.

We have not forgotten the matter of the hotel, but there is a touch of mystery about the subject, something she herself does not understand or can't communicate to me. In any event, the person we are expecting does not come and the teacher can wait no longer. Instead, she says, she will take me to the police station. This is an alarming turn of events.

"Why?" I ask with a faint laugh. "What have I done?"

"You will have to register," she says. "Then they will help you."

In some doubt I follow her, but the policeman, to my relief, is as elusive as the hotelkeeper and cannot be found. Meanwhile my new friend has come to a weighty decision, and leads me to another part of town. We are going to church, she says.

The church is Russian Orthodox and there is a service in progress, judging by the singing. She asks me to wait, goes inside, and soon, when the singing stops, asks me in. The church is full of clothing, in boxes, crates, and mountainous heaps. Many women are busying themselves with it, under the direction of a young priest. I suppose it is a consignment of aid from overseas. My friend introduces me to Nadia, an attractive, I would even say sexy, woman somewhere around forty, with red hair and bright lipstick over a creamy complexion. She wears strikingly colorful clothes and looks quite defiantly secular among the shawled and scarved church ladies, and she speaks English moderately well.

My nervous friend hurries off, hardly managing to say good-bye. Soon, when Nadia is done with whatever she's doing, she walks me back to her house, and for the first time since I arrived in Bibrka, I am given some clear and welcome information about my fate. I have been invited to spend the night with Nadia.

She knows I am a writer and tells me she is an electrical engineer. She is obviously a very energetic woman, with her own electricity, and tells me very quickly that she has two daughters, far apart in age, and is "divorcée."

"You also?" she asks. "You are divorcé?" as though it were a question about my education.

"Absolutely," I reply. How did she know? All kinds of possibilities race through my mind. Is this some kind of invitation? But she seems deliberately impersonal. I ask her what kind of work she is doing, but she says she is unemployed. There is no work for her now in Ukraine. I wonder how she manages this expensive look she has, but I'm afraid to offend her accidentally.

Her home is well away from the main road, down a lane, among gardens and cottages. She has an apartment in a small complex, rather like a scaled-down California condo. What makes it even more exceptional is that everything in it seems to work. Even the refrigerator. Where did I last see a refrigerator? In Gdańsk, I think. The Fursovs didn't have one, I'm almost certain. Come to that, I don't think they even had milk or butter. There's much excitement in Nadia's home because her older daughter, a flowering teenager, is about to leave on a long trip with friends.

Nadia takes me into the living room, converts the couch into a very acceptable bed, and tells me that she will have to be out for most of the evening because of her daughter's departure. She will take me to the restaurant, and I will be able to find my way back.

The restaurant turns out to be above the bar where I drank the beer. It's a big room with twenty or so tables, all unoccupied. Translucent curtains cover the big windows facing on the square. I sit in solitary splendor, waited on by a number of people, who bring me more beer and good food. Every now and again the kitchen door opens a crack, and a new face peers through to examine me. How different this is from Medovoje. There nobody was interested. Here I am a phenomenon. Already, I am sure, half the town knows that Nadia has a foreign lodger. From being an object of suspicion, I have perhaps become a figure of romantic speculation. Well, it won't last.

While eating, I give some thought to Nadia. She seems remarkably confident, to leave me alone in her house knowing so little about me. Perhaps, like me, she trusts her intuition.

There's nobody home when I return, so I settle down to write some notes. Then I put a little present to her daughter in an envelope and leave it where it can be found the next day. I'm asleep before she comes home. She gives me breakfast in the morning but is too busy to sit with me and talk. She may even be glad to see me go, an unneeded complication in her life. Yes, I say, I know the road to take. Yes, thank you, I had a good night's sleep. Good-bye, and thank you very much. It was kind of you. Good-bye.

I walk up to the crossroads, where there are people waiting for the bus, and follow the main road out of town. I wonder what the story was about the hotel and the police. I wish there had been more time to talk, but I guess sooner or later I'll find out. I have a long walk ahead of me—almost twenty-two miles to Rohatyn. But today I have water, it's lovely weather, and now that I'm farther away from L'viv, the countryside is opening up again with gently swelling hills of verdant pasture dotted with sheep. Here for the first time I see geese on a distant hillside, patrolling in long lines like white embroidered stitches on green cloth.

I am taking extreme pleasure in my feet. If anyone had tried to tell me earlier that I would one day develop a relationship with my feet, I think I would have taken it as an insult, but now that we have traveled the bumpy road of love together and I have been forced finally to accord them the respect and attention they have lacked all our lives, a new affection is blossoming and they are rewarding me, at last, with true service. So it is with a light heart and even lighter feet that I arrive at the first sign of human habitation since leaving Bibrka, a hamlet with a railway station. It's a little puzzling. I wasn't expecting to cross a railway track at this point, but the map is so vaguely drawn that I don't worry, and press on. The road rises gradually now into those green hills, and after a few miles I can't resist the impulse to lie down on this soft green grass and munch on the usual bread, cheese, and sausage I have brought with me.

As I lie back admiring the little white clouds wandering above, a shepherd comes slowly toward me from a distance. He approaches very courteously (or is it cautiously), as one would a lamb, and we exchange greetings. He sits down near me and I am able to put a few words of explanation together, including "English" and "walking" and "Rohatyn." When I mention Rohatyn, he looks a little more intently at me and repeats the name as a question. Then he delivers the bad news. This is not the way to Rohatyn. "That way," he says, pointing the way I came.

I have only to look at the map more carefully to see immediately that he is right. What I took to be the main road from Bibrka was in fact a minor road going west. It's extremely embarrassing to realize that I could have made such a fool of myself and that I didn't even notice where the sun was. And to have crossed that railway line without question was unforgivable.

There is no way to correct my mistake on foot without walking the nine miles back to Bibrka. I won't do it. Even if I *could* walk thirty miles today, I wouldn't do it. I hate going back over the same ground, and already I have an idea. There's no way to avoid going back to the station, but the railway line runs south to a town called Khodoriv, fifteen miles west of Rohatyn. Between these two there is both a road and a railway. So I decide to play at trains.

When I get back down to the railway track I see a signal box to the left of the crossing, with flowers around it and wooden steps up to a door. A knock on the door brings a cheerful Germanic-looking fellow, who immediately beckons me inside, as though he were expecting me. He seems very pleased that I've come, and finds my attempts to explain my predicament quite absorbing. Our relationship quickly becomes a great deal richer and more interesting than our conversation, which is of course quite primitive, since it is entirely in Ukrainian.

There certainly is a train I can take to Khodoriv. It will arrive in a couple of hours. There I'm lucky, because I gather they are quite rare. From Khodoriv, he says, I can take a bus. Meanwhile the best thing to do is to take a beer, or even two. We walk out across the track and north to the station. It's small and deserted. The beer comes from a tap next door. He buys a round. Then I buy one. Then he hears someone turn up at the ticket counter, an inscrutable semicircular hole in the wall with bars. He asks about the bus. Alas, there is no bus from Khodoriv to Rohatyn.

So we go back to the signal box, and now three more men arrive, a wonderfully diverse crew. Most impressive of them is a powerfully built man of Mongolian extraction. He has green eyes that glitter through the narrowest of slits and gold teeth set in a jaw that could trap a bear. Fortunately, he seems to be in great good humor. Then there is a slim auburn-haired man with Slavic good looks and luminous brown eyes, who would be handsome but for the fact that half his teeth are missing and his gums are cherry-red. The third man is stunted, a shade lopsided, and older, with fading red hair and a gap-toothed grin. Suddenly I am aware of how often teeth, or their absence, are among the first things I notice in this part of the world. Maybe the fuss Western dentists make is not all self-serving hype, as I tend to think. Or maybe the people here open their mouths more.

Anyway, they all gather around, this marvelous group of character actors, a grin on every face, and the five of us are having a genuinely merry time dealing with my problem. The amount of actual information that passes between us is negligible—hardly a byte on the Internet—but what a rich flow of feeling there is bouncing around in this old wooden signal box.

I am reminded irresistibly of scenes from Dublin pubs, and it only goes to show, in my view, that you don't have to be Irish to be Irish.

But it seems, after all, that out of this broth of conviviality a solution has emerged, if only I could get the hang of it. I have already been told about the train to Khodoriv, though I can't say quite what words were used to tell me. Now, apparently, they have agreed that between Khodoriv and Rohatyn there is some other kind of conveyance. It's called a *dizel' poyizd*. But what is it? The way they talk about it, I get a romantic notion that maybe they're going to smuggle me onto a freight locomotive, or maybe it's one of those row-yourself contraptions from the age of Buster Keaton. Who hasn't wanted to try out one of those?

My phrase book is open at the page on trains, but there is no *poyizd* on it anywhere. Again and again the signalman labors to convey the meaning of *poyizd*. He draws wheels and tracks. He is laughing in frustration. But Peter's booklet says trains are called *potiah*. If a *poyizd* isn't a train, what can it be? Well, whatever it is, I'm going to get it. It's funny how well we communicate in general, and how blocked we can get on just one simple thing. I have no difficulty explaining that I want him to write a note I can show anyone in Khodoriv to tell me where the *dizel' poyizd* is. And what a moment of glorious revelation that will be when the beast appears before me!

The train is due soon. We shake hands all around, I hoist my pack off the floor and, armed with my precious piece of paper, I cross over to the station to buy my ticket. The train, when it comes, is long and surprisingly important and busy, and must have come a long way. All the passengers look weary; the men are unshaven, and the compartments look as though they've been lived in for a week. I was expecting a small commuter train, but suddenly I am plunged into Russian long-distance rail culture, which I've read about but never experienced, where each carriage is a community watched over by a guardian with his own little compartment, where the samovar is always bubbling. And, yes, there is a guardian in this carriage, but she is a fierce, elderly dragon lady. She seizes me and draws me into her private world, from where she conducts her life; it has a bed, a sink, and a teapot. She tells me a story about her hard times and extorts a dollar bill from me, not unwillingly given. The few miles to Khodoriv are quickly eaten up. At the station I show my piece of paper, and fingers point down the platform to a train, on the right.

"*Dizel' poyizd?*" I ask, mystified.

*"Da. Dizel' poyizd."*

You mean it *is* a train? Damn. Whatever happened to *potiah*? A thought strikes me as I sit down, waiting for it to start. At the back of Peter's book are the translations from the Russian. And there it is. They were using the Russian word for train—*poyizd*. Why? I'll never know.

The *poyizd* is a smaller, slower train, but the journey to Rohatyn is soon over. As I gaze around me, I can't bring myself to feel bad about the way things turned out. I know I was supposed to be walking, but it's important to be where life is, too, and I wouldn't have missed today's encounters for anything. The main thing is to move through this world slowly, and make contact, and walk when I can. And after all, I did put in twelve miles this morning, even if they were all in the wrong direction.

At Rohatyn a bunch of people get off and most of them turn left outside the station and walk up a slow incline, so I follow them. The houses come closer together. Now there's a small shop or two, and eventually, at the top of the hill, is a square, several tin.es bigger than the one at Bibrka, with various roads leading off. It's still only early afternoon. Plenty of time to get into my hotel room, wash a little, change my socks maybe, and then come out and look around. The hotel is easy to find, on the other side of the square. This time it's a real hotel, with a lobby and a dour receptionist behind a partition with a counter. Or maybe she's the owner. Despite her sour look, I'm glad to see her, glad to be here. I put down my bag, advance with a smile on my face, and ask for a room.

*"Meni potribnyi nomer,"* I say. *"Odnomisnyi."*

*"Ni."* She shakes her head, the way you would to dislodge a fly.

There is no denying the sudden sinking feeling inside of me. I want to believe it's a misunderstanding. The hotel can't be full. If it were, she would not be looking at me with this implacable go-to-hell look. It's me. I'm not wanted. Using every conversational trick I can muster, I try to break through. Look, I have dollars. Or I can pay in *kupóns*. Just one night. What's the problem? Where else can I go?

I can't make a dent. The sense of deprivation is extreme. I had a lot invested in the idea of staying here. Never in my life have I been turned away from a hotel. The mixture of anger and resentment that wells up in me is hard to control.

She tells me I must go to a hotel in Ivano-Frankivs'k, a hotel for foreigners. That's halfway to Romania. To hell with that. I shake my head at her, and she just turns away to her accounts, removes herself behind her partition. Finally I admit I'm beaten, and shuffle off to join the ranks of the persecuted minorities. Outside in the square, I walk around slowly, trying to simmer down. My pride is definitely engaged here, not really so much by being refused a room as by being refused consideration. How could that woman look at me, listen to me, and still behave with such steely indifference?

Obviously, she's obeying orders. Obviously, there's something going on here about hotels and foreigners and police registration that I don't know, that's going to affect me considerably. Aside from the fact that they're nuts to be still doing this, hanging on to some completely obsolete regulation from a paranoid past, aside from that, I find the woman's soulless obedience to the rules chilling. She's the kind of person who reminds me that the toughest guards in the concentration camps were Ukrainian women. I picture her doing the triage at Auschwitz. It's not what you expect in the hospitality business.

All right. Enough of this venom. Where does it say I should be comfortable and stay in hotels? The question now is how to make contact. I miss the bike. If I were on the old Triumph, rolling into this square, people would be making contact with me. It never failed. People only had to look at us, the battered boxes with their maps and logos, the leather bags from Argentina, the scarred paintwork, the clothes I wore, to know that I had come a long, long way. Maybe I didn't feel like a hero, but I looked like one.

Now I'm just a middle-aged gent of suspect origins with a gray backpack. Suspect motives, too. Since all Westerners are rich, why am I pretending to be poor? There must be something wrong with me. Keep away.

The answer to my problem comes to mind quite quickly. It's obvious, really. It has been since Bibrka. It just hadn't surfaced. Find the language teachers, stupid! To do that, I need to find the school. It should be easy to spot a school building. Even though it's the summer vacation, I have a feeling that someone will be there for sure. I start walking around more purposefully, and before long, in an open grassy area, I see an institutional building that must be a school. Through the open door I see a woman cleaning the passage.

"*Zdrastuyte,*" I say. "*Vy govorite movoyu Angliskoyu?*"

Straight from the book. Of course she doesn't speak English, but she can smile. Flustered, she leads me into an office, where another woman sits, looking serious. The first few minutes will decide. If she doesn't kick me out straightaway, I'm sure something will come of it.

Peter's booklet has a list of professions—engineer, scientist, doctor, journalist, farmer, businessman—but no teachers. Obviously, teachers are not expected to travel. Not a high-status profession, I guess. Foiled again. All I can come up with is *professor.* That's a pretty universal word.

*"Professor Angliski?"* I say in my most winsome manner. Maybe she'll think *I'm* an English professor. Well, either way, if she's smart, she'll put two and two together, but just to broaden my chances, I throw in, *"Ili Tedeski, ili Franzia."*

This is wild. I think *Tedeski* means "German," or is that the Spanish word? As for *Franzia,* that's pure guesswork. *"Ili,"* believe it or not, means "or," and how I know that, I cannot say. The word does not occur in Peter's booklet. It's not a word tourists are supposed to need.

She's thinking. We struggle through some phrases together. I try to convey my problem with the hotel. I don't know if she's got it, though. There's a funny expression on her face, half sympathy, half despair. It could go either way. But she looks like a decent person, dark soft eyes, graying hair, very responsible. She calls the woman in from the passage and they confer. It looks bad. She doesn't know what to do. Then she picks up the phone, talks for a minute, says, *"Moment,"* talks to the other woman again, makes another call, has another brief conversation. It's looking better. I don't think she'll abandon me now.

She says something that sounds like "Wait for a while," and takes me to another room, where I can sit comfortably. I'm content. I have no idea what's going to happen, but I'm sure now it's going to work out. About twenty minutes later the phone rings, and the cleaning woman comes to get me. A man is on the phone and he says, in English:

"Hello. My name is Michael. I will help you."

# Chapter 20

*M*ichael, whose name was really Mihail, walked into the building a little while later. He told me that it was not a school at all that I had found but a communal institute affiliated to the church. All the same, the plan had worked perfectly. They had known whom to call, but it had taken some time to track him down.

Michael was an English teacher at the high school. So was his wife. And they would like me to come and stay with them.

"I was able to assist two German people before in a similar way," he told me. "I know the problems."

He was a lean, active man in his thirties, tall, light-skinned, and fair-haired, with rather neutral good looks and a kind but slightly formal manner. We walked briskly together out of the town, down a number of dirt roads between low houses, then over a small bridge and alongside a stream for a while. Rohatyn had a few buildings at its center to justify its status as a town, but the urban pretense quickly faded within yards of the square. It was really just a sprawling agricultural village, with the country still deep inside it, untroubled by traffic or officious boundaries and restrictions—much more like the small towns of Africa or Latin America than of Europe.

Michael lived near the apex of a large triangular grassy commons. Staked out on the succulent grass were cows of every size, color, and breed, and wandering among them were many flotillas of geese, some errant chickens, and an occasional goat, all looking like farm toys brought to life against the intense green background. Along the far side of the triangle a railroad track ran, raised on a high embankment. Another side was formed by the main road to Ivano-Frankivs'k. The third side was a dirt road flanked by private lots with houses.

Michael came from a peasant family named Nepijvoda, an unlucky name for peasants, you would think, since it translates to mean "without water." They owned one of the pieces of ground alongside the dirt road. It was really a fenced compound, including a main house, a smaller two-room cottage, a dog, a yard and, in defiance of their name, a good productive well.

Since Michael was married, with two young children, he had taken over the main house. The older members of the family—parents or relations, I wasn't quite sure which—were tucked into smaller spaces, where it seemed they were quite content to be. The dog commanded the yard from a chain and had a good bark. I was careful not to test the bite.

Michael's wife, Leda, was a lovely woman with mesmerizing light blue eyes and a steady gaze, which seemed to come directly from her heart and melted mine every time it was turned in my direction. It became apparent very quickly that they had no intention of letting me spend just one night and disappear. Leda immediately rearranged their lives to accommodate me. The space they occupied was modest and all on one floor. There was a living room with a small room attached, divided off by double doors. The living room was also Michael and Leda's bedroom. The children, a boy and a girl, slept in the smaller annex, but while I was there the girl slept with her parents.

The kitchen was small and primitive, as was the bathroom. There was no sewage or septic system, and normally the toilet would have been an outhouse, but Michael had brought in a chemical toilet, which was, relatively speaking, the height of modernity. I found it disagreeably smelly and tried to hold my breath while I used it. Later, when I was obliged to use the older facilities of other houses, I learned to appreciate Michael's innovation better. The only other room in the house, opposite the kitchen, was where Michael's mother slept.

I stayed there four nights, never intending to, but always cajoled into remaining a little longer, for one good reason or another. It was easy to submit when I was being made so welcome, and I justified my stay by the amount I was learning about the state of the country. The Nepijvodas, along with many others, were suspended at a fascinating time of transition. Their roots were undeniably deep in peasant agriculture and customs. Their house was essentially a peasant cottage, which they, as teachers, had upgraded a little. If the Ukrainian economy had been anything but moribund, they would have quickly moved up into a quite different lifestyle.

Already they had bought a plot of land and built the brick shell of a new house on it, but as their house went up, their real income dwindled to the point where every new board, every doorknob and roof tile, even if it could be located, became a major expense. With their extended family around them, they knew how to live a peasant existence at very little cost. They had enough to eat, and their children were healthy and well educated, but the slightest increment of luxury imposed a crippling penalty. The family car in the driveway may as well have housed rabbits for all the good it was as a conveyance, since gasoline was virtually unattainable and unaffordable.

They walked everywhere, and maybe would have done so anyway, but there were times when they longed for the choice. Trains were cheap, but when Leda made a trip to L'viv to find a plumbing fixture, for example, she took a day, beginning at dawn and ending when we met her at the station at midnight and walked back, along the tracks under the stars, to the house.

One of the plums Leda dangled to keep me there was the prospect of solving all my overnight problems at one blow. In two days' time, she told me, their school would convene a conference of all the foreign-language teachers of the province, English, French, and German speakers from every town between Rohatyn and Chernivtsi. Without doubt, she said, they would be delighted to meet me and, above all, to hear me. It certainly sounded like a good idea, so I settled in and walked around, visited their new house, and embroiled myself in another great postal adventure as I attempted to send yet another parcel to Germany to lighten my load.

Leda took every opportunity to tell me that I was foolish to walk alone through the country. According to her, crime was raging over the countryside like a plague, and there were dastardly villains everywhere just itching to crack my skull. No doubt the sharp rise in acts of criminal violence in her world in recent years was very shocking. I could not convince her that by comparison with the United States, Ukraine's criminal fraternity was still in kindergarten.

I told her how much safer I felt walking around Eastern Europe. I gave her the comparative figures for deaths by shooting between America and European countries, but she seemed as impervious to them as the average American citizen. I don't think that Michael and Leda, unlike many big-city folk in Eastern Europe, would care to move to America. They might be glad to go there and make a bundle, but they are too much in love with their own country—meaning the soil, the grass, the trees, the rivers—to want to leave it. Because of those feelings, tough as the circumstances of their life were, I was not made constantly aware of aggravation, frustration, and envy. Like the artists of L'viv, they had other resources to depend on.

I tried hard to make myself useful, but it was difficult not to be more trouble than my efforts were worth. One of my ideas was to cook a meal. Since meat was generally too expensive for them to buy, it gave me an opportunity to spend my restless *kupóns*. I planned a rather elaborate kind of stew, and the meat was not hard to come by. I found one shop with one kind of meat that just happened to be more or less what I wanted. I took a kilo, which was half of their total supply.

Buying vegetables was a more depressing experience. It is usually harder to find good vegetables on sale in an agricultural area, since people generally grow their own, but in Rohatyn the problem was exaggerated. I mourned over the bruised and wilted greens, the withered flaccid roots, the split and rotting tomatoes. I could find none of the herbs or spices I wanted. At the last moment, after I had bought most of the ingredients, the enterprise was almost wrecked when I found that all the onions were rotten.

The pots were the wrong size, and so were the dishes. The knives were made for purposes that were strange to me. I didn't know what to fry the meat in or what to use for flour or where to put the compost. The kitchen, too small to begin with, overflowed with my misguided attempts to bring this foreign recipe to the table. Everyone became involved in trying to extricate me from my own mess. With the energy they expended they could have produced three meals. And when all was done, I served up only a pitifully small amount of a rather dull dish, which the family ate rapidly with a brave pretense of enjoyment. It was a learning experience I was not encouraged to repeat.

The meeting with the teachers was more successful. Leda took me to the school and showed me around first. It was in a three-story building, much bigger and more impressive than I had expected. Leda was so innocently proud of what she and the other teachers had done to overcome shortages, and particularly a frustrating lack of textbooks. There were some stunning displays on the walls, clever learning devices, and much that was aesthetically pleasing.

She may have expected me to be rather condescending about her school, coming as I did from a culture that was so much more successful materially than hers. Actually, I was thrown into great confusion. In the first place, I was ashamed of myself for falling victim to an elementary trap. I had been judging a society's sophistication by what was in the shops. Because the shop windows were bare and life was austere, I had assumed the school would be inferior, and was shocked by my own mental laziness. Also, as it happened, my own twelve-year-old son was in a public school in California at the time, soon to move up to high school. Along with some other parents, I was disenchanted with California's public school system, which seemed to have lost its way.

My inclination was to tell Leda that her school compared very favorably with my son's. I wished he were in an environment that put more value on schoolwork and taught languages. I thought her building did a much better job of emphasizing the communal aspects of the school. The sprawling, disjointed campuses at home, with their prefabricated units, felt so ephemeral. Even the obvious absence of electronic technology was a recommendation to me, as I was beginning to feel that computers had no place in schools. Yet how could I know, without speaking the language, without hearing the teachers teach, that the most awful, archaic travesties weren't being transmitted in these bright and pleasant classrooms? Invidious comparisons come so easily. The grass in the fields of Ukraine was most definitely greener, but whether it was greener in the classrooms, I could not be sure.

There were about thirty teachers gathered in one of the classrooms to meet me, and all of them seemed genuinely friendly and eager to hear me. I wish I had been able to reward them better. I gave the same little speech in the three languages they taught, saying how valuable I thought it was to be able to speak other languages, telling them a little of what my adventure was about, and passing on some of my observations of Ukraine, including jokes about my plan to corner the bread market, which may have been ill judged. They were all enthusiastic and forgiving, and I was sure I had secured beds and breakfast all the way down the line if I wanted them, but it didn't quite work out like that.

Rohatyn had one magnificent treasure from the past, and I was lucky to see it. Michael persuaded the curator, a priest, to unlock it for me, and we went to visit it one afternoon. It was in the woods alongside the stream I had passed when I first walked with Michael to his house, but I probably wouldn't have noticed it on my own. It was a little wooden church, dedicated to the Holy Ghost, and built four hundred years earlier, in 1598, to replace an even older one from the twelfth century. It boasts a rare five-tiered icon made in the seventeenth century during the Ukrainian War of Liberation, with a highly militant theme involving the exploits of St. Michael, the patron saint of the cossacks. There is also a portrait of the head priest of Kiev disguised as Melchisadek, a series of representations of the holy days of the church, and some books, all from the same time.

We had never spoken about religion. I don't belong to any church, and unless the subject is raised by others, I am not inclined to discuss it, since it is not usually a fit subject for debate. Yet I can be deeply moved by the evidence of faith and devotion in cathedrals, churches, mosques, and temples, and this small but exquisitely built oak church from the Middle Ages, with its brilliant icons, affected me as much as any.

Perhaps Michael, realizing this, said something to Leda. On Friday she asked if I would like to come with her to her Orthodox church for a harvest thanksgiving service, and I said I would be glad to. The church was a simple building of massive stone, with an undivided interior. Two rows of columns ran longitudinally to support the roof. Judging by their appearance, the congregation consisted mostly of people who worked on the land, and they packed the church, leaving only the center aisle free. The women, in skirts or dresses, wore scarves over their heads. The men looked a little awkward in their suits. They stood throughout the service, which was very long, lasting well over an hour. Only a few older or infirm celebrants had seats against the walls.

The service had a more conversational tone than I had witnessed before. The priest, a big, swarthy man with a black mustache, spoke to his flock often, between songs and ritualistic acts, and his voice was firm and strong, but he used the sounds of everyday speech rather than intoning a liturgy. This simple, colloquial style seemed to give the people more power over the flow of events, and they seized it with enthusiasm, responding vigorously, with ever greater ardor. Despite the length of the service, there was none of the boredom and distracted behavior I remembered from the church services I have attended in England and elsewhere. These people took an intense interest, they were joyfully committed, their faces clearly showing the good it was doing them to open their hearts.

The service took many twists and turns, and because I could not follow the spoken words, I afterward made notes of as much detail as I could recall, but sadly they were later lost in an accident. However, the spiritual content remains indelible. At one point, some members of the congregation raised a series of flags on poles and formed two columns in the center aisle, women on the left and men, I think, on the right. They looked very stern. The emotional temperature rose to new heights as there was more singing, chanting, and ritual. Packed in among the happy devotees, with Leda nearby, I could not resist the heartwarming effect of so much feeling, but for me the climax, when it came, was as staggering as it was unexpected.

The priest was talking again, with added emphasis it seemed, and his eyes were roving over the church and reaching down to the end where I stood. Leda leaned over to me and whispered:

"The father is talking about how you have come to our church from far away to be our guest. Now the people will sing a song of welcome to you."

All the passion with which they had worshiped their God was suddenly turned on me. The intensity of it was unbearable. I stood in the spotlight of their emotions as they turned toward me, singing lustily with shining faces, and I was almost vaporized by the heat. It was out of all proportion to my significance, and far from feeling glorified by it, I was humbled.

Possibly others in my shoes might have resented being made the object of such concentrated attention, but I realized I was only standing in as a symbol for mankind in general. I took for myself as much as I dared of what was offered, and was filled with an overwhelming sense of gratitude. A wizened little lady next to me turned and placed a small paper bag of apples in my hands. I would have kissed her if her head hadn't been so far below mine, but tears came to my eyes.

The bond among Michael, Leda, and myself became remarkably strong in those four days, but even so I did not suspect the lengths to which Leda would go to protect me from what she thought was my dangerous behavior. Although she lobbied her teachers for a place for me to stay between Rohatyn and Ivano-Frankivs'k, she said there were problems. The best idea, she thought, was for me to go with the teachers in the bus to Ivano-Frankivs'k. Then she could come with me, we would be able to stay at her uncle's house, and she could show me around.

"But what about the children?" I asked.

"Michael will look after them," she said. "He has to stay because he has work to do." And as was her habit, she looked into my eyes as though there were something behind them she could not quite read.

So early the next morning I said my heartfelt good-byes to Michael, and we took the bus. As we traveled, I collected names and addresses for Kosiv, Halych, and Burshtyn, all towns along the way, which would have been very useful if Leda had not had other ideas. We spent a pleasant day in the provincial capital, which was her hometown. The fuel crisis was extreme, buses were rare and undependable, taxis virtually nonexistent, so we were limited in what we could see. She took me to the university where she had studied, an ugly glass-and-concrete building with some broken windows, but we were unable to get in. Then to the park, where she had spent so many of her leisure hours. Much of the time she had a sad and dreamy expression, as though she were looking back regretfully on much happier, more optimistic years, and indeed that would hardly be surprising.

The park had obviously seen better days, and was somewhat disfigured by work being done on a stadium, which was the center of a current political scandal. We saw another statue to Shevchenko, and then a pavilion where there was a tourist office. We went inside to see if there might be anything of value or interest to me. The walls were decorated with posters advertising holidays in various parts of the former Soviet bloc. Strangely, it had never occurred to me before that a tourist industry had been functioning behind the Iron Curtain. It was rather like a mirror image of ours, and extended over such a vast area of the globe that they had all their own versions of our favorite destinations, such as the Mediterranean, the new world, Asia, and the Middle East. It created an entirely novel perspective on lives that I had always envisaged as fixed in one place, with transportation to a gulag as the only opportunity for travel.

Leda interrogated a tourist official on my behalf, and he became very friendly. He telephoned his friend, a former Intourist guide in Chernivtsi, who spoke French and who offered to help me when I arrived there. Then we waited interminably for a bus to take us back to Leda's uncle's house.

The house was large, and built on solid, old-fashioned lines, with many staircases and passages. It housed a large family, which gathered for dinner around a big table in the kitchen, strategically placed near the boilers in the basement of the house. It was a huge meal of meat, salad, and carbohydrates in every form known to man, or so I thought.

Uncle Viktor was a tall, strong man in his seventies, who seemed destined to live forever.

"Our family lives for a long time," said Leda. "One of them is over a hundred."

Opposite Viktor sat his son, an oil engineer who spoke some English and taught at the city's Oil Institute. He was even taller than his father, but slim and much milder in character, with curiously babyish lips. Every morning of the year, Leda told me, come rain or shine, he ran to a nearby lake and swam. The women, who listened and laughed and put food on the table, included Leda's aunt and her cousin's wife, but it was the uncle who spoke most of the time, with Leda translating for me. She was so transparently proud of him, it was a pleasure to watch her.

Until his recent retirement he had been the director of a collective farm. It was not something he had chosen to do, he said. He was forced to take the job, in 1955, and this was not unusual. In many cases, men who had been kicked out of higher positions were made to manage collectives as a form of punishment. They were entirely unqualified for the work, and their motivation was questionable, to say the least.

He, at any rate, had some knowledge of farming. When he took over the collective, it was in a terrible state.

"The pigs were all up on their hind legs screaming for food," he said, through Leda, "and the cattle were skin and bones. Nobody wanted to work there—they only turned up in the hope of stealing something."

He worked night and day to turn it around. Every evening he went out to visit one or another of the families who were employed there, explaining to them why they should come to work. And eventually they came, although it obviously had more to do with their respect for his tireless efforts than any patriotic motive.

The collective did become successful, one of the very few that did. It specialized in producing seed for wheat, and was able to reach a yield of almost two and half tons per acre, which for seed is a pretty good standard. Unsuccessful collectives nearby were amalgamated with it, until it grew to twenty-five thousand acres. Since his retirement, though, production had dropped back to only a third of what it was. If he felt any satisfaction at this proof of his ability, he disguised it very well. He explained that since it was now possible for people to own their own land again, nobody wanted to work for the collectives anymore.

It was during the course of the dinner that I learned what plans had been made for me. It appeared that there was yet another branch of the family farther south, in the foothills of the Carpathians. It would be very interesting to visit them, said Leda. We could take the train to Kolomyia next day, look around that city, and then later take the train to Yaryemcha, where we would spend the night with her cousins. It would have been mad to refuse.

"They don't make it easy in the Ukraine."

That's what I wrote in my notebook the next day, underlined, in a spirit of disgruntlement. I was being a little ungrateful, perhaps. Actually, it was made easy for us to get to the station. Leda's cousin, the oil engineer, not only had a fine car but he even had gasoline in his tank—such a rarity that I wondered whether he had a secret oil well of his own. He took us to the station in style, but then we couldn't find the train. We stood on the platform where it should have been, and saw nothing. Leda was lucky to find someone who knew. About half a mile down the platform, hidden from view behind the station building, was another rail head. When we got close enough to see the train, it taunted us by blowing steam and grunting, although it was not due to leave for ten minutes. Everybody began to run. Evidently, trains were known to leave when they felt like it, but this one was only fooling. We found a half-empty carriage, settled down comfortably, and began to talk. I was asking Leda about Kolomyia.

"Are you going to Kolomyia?" a voice asked. "Because if you are, you are in the wrong carriage. You need to go two up."

When we got there, it was packed solid. The seats were arranged as in a bus, and we stood crushed in the aisle between them. It was obvious, too, that most of the passengers were in a foul temper, miserable about going to work on a Sunday to earn money that wouldn't buy anything. At the next stop, two seats became free in different rows. Leda asked the man next to her, who was reading a paper, if he would mind switching with me.

"Go jump in a lake," he said, or words to that effect, and he sat tight, obstinately indifferent, for forty-five minutes until we arrived.

The station at Kolomyia had lockers. I wanted to leave my pack there, and the lockers apparently worked perfectly well, but it was impossible to use them. They were coin-operated, but hyperinflation had long ago driven the coins out of circulation.

So it was, at every turn, that some shortage or malfunction or irritating regulation could stifle any initiative you had in mind. Making progress, as we understand it in the West, was harder than swimming through treacle, and didn't seem worth the effort. The only sane approach would be to reduce expectations to the lowest possible level, stay within the confines of what was familiar, and survive until times improved. But for many, even that was impossible, as inflation made it imperative to find new resources. Crime was one answer—whether economic or violent. Although I had no fear for myself, I could understand why Leda would see me as a ripe target for those who had become desperate.

We walked into town down a tree-lined boulevard and found a small hotel, where I was able to leave my pack for the day. Kolomyia is a sizable town with a few hundred thousand inhabitants, tucked up against the side of the Carpathians. It is pleasantly laid out, with avenues, parks, and monuments, including the inevitable statue of Shevchenko. In prosperous times it might be good place to live, with the mountains close by.

A demonstration that had something to do with the coming elections was under way when we arrived, with music and speeches in the central square, and there was an enjoyable feeling of fiesta in the air. We lingered for a while, but the novelty wore off soon enough, and Leda took me somewhere where language was less of an impediment. Kolomyia has a fine museum devoted to the art and culture of a Carpathian hill tribe known as the Houdsul, who still preserve their traditions. We wandered for an hour or two among their richly beaded and embroidered costumes, their spectacular headdresses, the reconstructions of their domestic interiors, and glorious displays of their wedding dresses and rituals. All of it was evidence of a highly developed and coherent culture, and it appealed very strongly to Leda, comforting her with evidence that people can survive with their beliefs and customs intact, even through the worst of times.

With these elevated concepts in mind and with the beauty of the Houdsul designs still before my eyes, we stepped back into the streets of Kolomyia, where, quite soon, I needed to find a toilet for the most minimal purpose. I already had plenty of evidence that attitudes to these matters were very different from what I have become used to in Europe and America, so I was not expecting to find gleaming porcelain and a deodorized atmosphere. In fact it occurred to me that if I was to simply pee up against the nearest wall, hardly an eyebrow would be raised, and but for Leda's presence that is probably what I would have done.

Even so, what I eventually found, after an inquiry or two, amazed me. Traveling for years through Latin America and Asia, I thought I had seen just about every variation on the theme that was possible. I think of myself as being quite amenable and undemanding in the face of strange situations. I have even adjusted my own habits considerably, since I find that European customs are far from being the most practical or hygienic. Nor have I forgotten the dread with which I used to visit *"Les Toilettes"* in the cafés of Paris when I first lived there in the fifties.

So it was, in its way, quite an exciting event to come across what I would like to nominate as the Most Disgusting Latrine in the World. It was on a street near the market and stood alone on the sidewalk. It was just a large wooden box, stood on end, with one of the sides removed, the open side facing toward the houses. Perhaps there was a hole in the bottom. If so, it led nowhere and was full. Because of the smell, I couldn't get close enough to examine it in detail. The inside of the box was smothered in heaps of every color and consistency of feces, and it looked as though someone had been using the material to conduct a class in plastering techniques for rather slaphappy students.

It was quite impossible for me to imagine anyone crouching in there and yet, quite clearly, several people must have done so recently. Why were there no footprints leading away from it? What did the people think in the houses opposite? Did they enjoy the spectacle? These and other questions remain unanswered. I didn't stay long to admire my discovery, but went off to find a suitable wall instead.

There is, I suppose, something quite admirable about this indifference to a natural function. Western sensibilities, at the other extreme, often strike me as absurdly fastidious. There must be some practical middle way between upended wooden crates and marble palaces connected by tube to distant and dying lakes. Plenty of good solutions exist, but they all meet the same difficulty that countries like Ukraine are now experiencing. In the transition from a peasant to an industrial culture, we seem to sever our animal connections with the earth instead of refining them. We seem to exchange old superstitions for new myths and taboos, which throw our entire relationship to the environment out of balance. The best of the old is lost. The worst of the new is terribly destructive, but I still see no way out of the dilemma.

The train to Yaryemcha followed the River Prut almost to its source, the same small river that, farther south, became the great river defining the frontier of Romania and that emptied into the Danube delta, so close to where my father spent his youth. We climbed slowly into the hills, arriving at the station just before dusk. Then we climbed a mile or more on foot until we reached the small cluster of houses known as Staryi Hvizdets', where Michael's sister, Hanna, lived with her husband, Dmytro. The house was probably one that had grown in an organic fashion for hundreds of years. It was not as big as the house we had left that morning, but it sprawled even more, and was surrounded by a fine collection of animals.

The welcome was on a grand scale. Once again, the house swarmed with people determined to fill us with food and drink and to extract from me every fact and opinion I had ever stored or conceived. Dmytro was a railroad engineer, not too different in appearance from the signalman near Bibrka. Immensely convivial, he and his brother plied me with vodka and made up in energy and goodwill for what we lacked in language. Halfway through this marathon, Leda left us to talk with her cousin and to sleep. Just as in the signal box, I felt that between us we had accomplished a great deal, with almost nothing to show for it.

The experience was a haunting one, mainly because I slept on a bed made up in the dining room, had quite eventful dreams, and was woken long before dawn to be offered for breakfast exactly the same delicious but overfamiliar dishes that I had failed to conquer the night before. The entire visit took place after dark and had a seamless quality, as though I had never slept at all. We washed in bowls, as there was no running water, used an outhouse that made me nostalgic for Michael's bathroom, and walked with the engineer through the chill air down to the station. It was still dark when we boarded the train to Kolomyia.

Leda became agitated about leaving me. I assured her that from Kolomyia I would be able to look after myself perfectly well. She looked more frequently than ever into my eyes, to divine whether it was really safe to abandon me to my fate, and I had to exclaim several times that I knew what I was doing. It was hard for me to understand her anxiety. She knew that I had traveled a great deal before. What kind of an impression can I possibly be making now, I asked myself, for her to see me as so defenseless?

But she did let me go. At Kolomyia, her train left very soon after we arrived. It was a difficult parting. I felt sure we would meet again. Then impatience overcame my sadness. It was time to move on. Romania, with the mysteries I hoped against hope to resolve, was very close.

# Chapter 21

As a younger man out in the world, I had always been at pains to detach myself as best I could from habits of thought and behavior. I imagined it would be preferable to be a self-created individual, owing nothing to any one race or culture and equally at home with all of them. Clearly, I fell very far short of this impossible ideal, and it is as well that I did. Nevertheless, I scarcely ever gave any conscious thought to my origins, and for much of the time was quite oblivious to my appearance.

It now seems to me that this impulse toward a total neutrality may have come from an early distaste for the person I thought I was, and that would have to include my Jewish side. So it is only natural that, given the object of this journey, I would swing rather to the opposite extreme. I was unusually sensitive to my own Jewishness, and always looking for ways in which it might be affecting the people I encountered. Yet I never had a sense of it arising in the minds of others. Although I was traveling among people who were preponderantly of a much lighter complexion, I never noticed, either by word or glance, a hint of an unfavorable judgment in my regard. Except when I raised the subject myself, by reference to my father, it was never mentioned, and with the possible exception of that woman in the hotel at

Rohatyn, I had been treated normally and decently throughout my journey.

The matter of racial characteristics is a very delicate one. It would be absurd, and hysterical, to insist that Jews can always be spotted by their appearance. Equally ridiculous is the pretense that differences of appearance do not exist between broad ethnic groups. All those heartbreaking photographs in the old Pawiak prison show rather clearly that some Jews do share certain recognizable features and some don't. Why should this be a problem? Presumably, Chinese people are not unhappy to be identified as such by their appearance. The coyness that one encounters about being able to "tell a Jew" must itself arise from a veiled anti-Semitism, and I know this from having been able to detect it in myself at an early age.

When I was about fifteen, I answered the door to a youngish man with blond wavy hair, pale blue eyes, and a noticeably fresh complexion. He was vigorous and handsome, with the regular Nordic features sported by the models in cigarette advertisements whose appearance I admired so much at the time. He asked for my mother, who knew him, and afterward she told me that he was a recently demobilized army captain, and hence—in my eyes—a war hero. He had come to gather signatures for a petition on behalf of a new state of Israel, and he was of course Jewish. The shock and wonderment this information produced in me have survived half a century, and though I did not analyze it at the time, I know there was a good deal of pain and envy, too.

Most teenagers are unhappy with their appearance, but it is clear to me now, if it wasn't then, that I did not want to be identified as Jewish. Presumably, the infection was in the air and I caught it. Actually, according to a recently conducted private poll, I do not look so much Jewish as just plain foreign. From the English point of view, at the time I probably appeared more exotic than Jewish. It may well be, for all my heightened awareness as I crossed Poland and Ukraine, that I was seen in much the same way there.

For my part, since Szczecin I could not recall having seen a single person whom I would have readily identified as Jewish. Hardly surprising. For all that time I had been passing through ethnically cleansed territory. If the Poles had been the worst offenders against the Jews, the Ukrainians had been close behind and the Russians had certainly been bad enough. Now there were almost no Jews left in this entire part of Europe. Of those whom Hitler had failed to exterminate, most had since left under pressure of anti-Semitic policies. The few who had attempted to return and settle were made unwelcome. As I saw it the consequence, paradoxically, was that Jews, and probably members of any race on earth, could travel quite comfortably across this landscape—as long as they kept moving on.

Only when they form substantial groups, large enough to embody a culture, do they seem to arouse the paranoia and venom of racial hatred, and even then, maybe, only when the culture is expressed with a force that seems to obscure individuality. I was quite comfortable in that church in Rohatyn, and I was able to take part in the universal elements of a faith that clearly inspired the parishioners with great zeal. Yet if I had been there as a Hasidic Jew, in black hat and ringlets, surely my presence would have been intolerable to both sides.

I remember a time when black skin was a remarkable rarity in England. Until American soldiers came to prepare for D-day, I don't think I had ever seen a black man in the street. Visiting cricket teams from India, Pakistan, and the West Indies were given tremendous respect, and the occasional African dignitary was pictured on newsreels being received at Buckingham Palace. Beyond the traditional and rather comical British xenophobia that regarded all foreigners as "wogs," there was no prejudice against blacks. How could there be? We had nothing to fear from them. Only when waves of immigrants from the West Indies, Pakistan, and East Africa flooded in and formed their own communities did some of us turn ugly about the horrors of curry, *pujas*, peculiar bathroom habits, or black sexual potency.

For all the jolts of revulsion I received on my journey, from Colonel Fursov's staircase to that disgusting cloaca on the street in Kolomyia, it never crossed my mind to think of the people I met as "dirty Russians" or "dirty Ukrainians." The thought came up only as a result of Ukrainians asking me, rather impatiently, why I would want to go to Romania. Romanians, they said, were dirty, as well as being thieves. I became interested in this phenomenon of pots calling kettles black, and of course, with my father's origins on my mind, I could not forget that the words *dirty Jews* have been howled through the ages.

Only once in my life have I been called a "dirty Yid" to my face. It happened in London in 1954. A stranger muttered the insult as he passed me in the doorway of a restaurant. By then Jewishness was no longer a conscious issue for me, and I looked around to see whom he could be aiming it at. By the time I realized he had meant it for me, he had disappeared. I was shocked but unhurt, as though some madman had fired a pistol at me and missed.

The words themselves I gave no thought to, supposing *dirty* to be just a slanderous epithet with no particular significance. I was surprised to learn, quite recently, that Jews used to be characterized as actually dirty. A good example is provided by the American journalist John Reed, who glorified the Russian revolution in *Ten Days that Shook the World.* Reporting on the war in Eastern Europe in 1915, he visited a Jewish community at Rovno, a city not far from Lvov, which was within the Pale—that is to say, it was in the area where Jews were legally permitted to live. His description is larded with revolting images—"evil smelling," "slimy puddles," "bloated flies," "glaring signs," "greasy proprietors," "reeking doorways," "unhealthy faces," "people who smiled deprecatingly and hatefully."*

With his companion, Reed entered a Jewish bar and drank kvass. A Russian officer came in, "sniffed the air, bowed to us, and staring malevolently at the frightened girls who served, said distinctly: 'The dirty Jews! I detest them,' and walked out."

Near the city of Czernowitz, Reed crossed the front line at Novoselitsa, on the Prut River, to find himself between "blocks of tiny Jewish shops, swarming with squealing, whining, bargaining people, and emitting that stale stench that we know from New York's lower East Side. Old Jews in long overcoats, derby hats resting on their ears, scraggly beards, elbows and hands gesticulating—the comedy Jew in a burlesque show—filthy babies crawling in the lamplight, rows of women in Mother Hubbards and brown wigs, nursing their babies and gossiping shrill Yiddish on the door-step."

If Reed had been observing a colony of cockroaches he could hardly have made it sound more disagreeable. Was this the culture that my two Austrian acquaintances in Poland—those two very neat and clean Jewish musicians—had held in such esteem and mourned over? Hardly.

Naturally, it interested me to know whether my father was once part of the same scene that Reed described with such loathing. Could he have jumped such a broad cultural abyss? At first I thought he must indeed have done so. Even as late as 1938, the scene had barely changed. In that year Sacheverell Sitwell wrote about visiting Khotin, another Jewish town in the same region, and what he saw there, or rather the way he saw it, was hardly

---

*The War in Eastern Europe* (New York: Scribners, 1916).

any different. But Czernowitz, which by then had become Romanian, he described very differently. This was a thriving city of a hundred thousand people, run entirely by Jews, but he emphasized how well the women were dressed and that the children were often beautiful.

"The benefit of this Jewish hegemony is a noticeable quickness of brains. Shopping takes up a tenth of the time that it consumes in other towns. And any foreigner who has the good fortune to be mistaken for an American can depend upon a rapturous welcome, for the U.S.A. is the land of opportunity where everybody has a brother or cousin who has made money. . . .

"But the genius of the town is for the theatre . . . it is, indeed, *the* town from which theatrical talent will come."

Cernăuți (Cher-no-*oots*), as it was named in my father's time, is at the northern tip of a historic mountainous region called Bukovina. Although it has always been disputed territory, Bukovina has its own cultural coherence. Much of it is still in Romania today. My father's birthplace, Botoşani (Bo-to-*shahn*), was an important town in Bukovina, and probably had more in common with Cernăuți than with those squalid Russian slums on the Prut.

The general area of Bukovina is referred to as the cradle of the Hasidic sect, the ultra-Orthodox Jewish community. I had known them only from the outward appearances of the men, with their black hats and coats, their ringlets and pale skin. As Sitwell described them, in Bukovina in 1938 they were more exotic still. He talked of their "long, black gowns" and "wide black hats trimmed with red fox's fur," which he said "were forced upon them in the middle ages. . . . the red fox was a metaphor for duplicity and cunning; when the fox was about, the farmer shut up his geese and chickens . . .

"In the Bucovina, also, the Jews are often redhaired and redbearded. . . . The square of some small town may have twenty or thirty Jews strolling in it, and a Rabbi will come past, in a caftan of purple silk. This curious assembly is like the reality from some mediaeval country or kingdom, that never existed. For these are the Jewish lands, or at least the Jewish towns. They are conscious of their nationality. . . . They regard themselves as a race apart, and it is in this light that they are looked upon by the people among whom they are dwelling."

Sitwell went on to mention towns and provinces that were mainly, or even entirely, Jewish, where "they cling to their old customs and have not moved with the times. . . . What is to become of this population? They cannot emigrate, and no one wants them, elsewhere in Roumania. It would be true to describe them as the most implacably mediaeval population in Europe. The backward and conservative Jews are ever the same."

He talked about the Jews of the Kraków ghetto, where married women still had their heads shaved; of Lublin, which was to Jews almost what Rome is to Catholics; of the five million Jews distributed between Poland and Romania; and said: "This Jewish population has begun to swarm, and it is difficult to see what form of emigration can be of help to it."

To begin with a characterization of certain Jewish communities as backward, medieval, and inward-looking and to extend that description automatically to a "swarming" population of five million was one of those terrible generalizations that certainly helped the Holocaust along.

"The question of the Jews in Eastern Europe," he concluded in 1938, "would seem, in fact, to be insoluble. But it is a problem which becomes, yearly, of increasing importance and, soon, it will have to be faced, resolutely."

As we now know, it very soon was, and in the most horrific of resolute ways. It is heartbreaking to read his remarks with hindsight. Although Sitwell was one of those Englishmen who had conceived a certain admiration for Hitler, Hitler's solution to the Jewish question was probably not the one he would have chosen. Even so, the alienation that Sitwell felt for these people, who seemed to him so determined to stand apart from the rest of the human race, was obvious. It troubles me a good deal to recognize that in his shoes, I might have shared his feeling.

From my earliest days, when I would occasionally see Hasidic men in some parts of London, like Golders Green, I assumed that I could have nothing in common with people who chose to set themselves apart in this way. I regarded them just as I did policemen, stationmasters, or anyone else in uniform—as people you would only approach if you needed them to perform their official function. I knew less about what went on in Hasidic homes than I knew about the back rooms of police stations, and my mother, I think, knew even less than I did. However, my mother was able to tell me that my father had come from an Orthodox—though she did not say Hasidic—Jewish background and that he had attempted to distance himself from it.

I should like to deal with the difficulties of my parents in a formal, digni-fied manner without breaching the rules of discretion, but my mind slips immediately, like a detective camera, to an image of my father—well, not my father, but my father's trousers as my mother turns out the pockets be-fore cleaning and pressing them, and finds a note, carelessly left, confirm-ing by implication my mother's suspicion of the existence of "another woman."

So uncharacteristic was this carelessness that I believe the note was de-signed to burst the thunderclouds that hung over these two sadly mis-aligned people, and of course over me, too, in my fifth year. Surely my father, who every morning refurled his umbrella so carefully, folded his *Daily Telegraph* to the regulation baton length, and set off, precisely on time, in his overcoat and bowler hat, both carefully brushed by Mother according to his instructions, to join the brigade of City employees streaming toward London Bridge—surely he would not have ignored the presence of such a potent scrap of paper. As a model of discretion, he must have prided himself most of all on his far-reaching control over every circumstance of his life. How otherwise could a Romanian Jew, born on the eastern slopes of the Carpathian Mountains, hardly in Europe at all, have so expertly acquired the language, manners, accomplishments, and even the nationality of that stereotypical British figure, the City gent?

For most of my life I knew nothing about him or his family, until I ob-tained those naturalization papers. In 1933, when he applied for British na-tionality, the police carrried out a routine yet thorough investigation, as was normal in those days, and I learned something about how he had made such a brilliant transformation. The report read:

> With reference to the application for a certificate of naturalization by Haim Sin Simha;
> Applicant's full and correct name in his country of origin was as shown; in 1914, however, he commenced to use the name Simon in-stead of Simha, and later, Henry instead of Haim, and documents have been produced to show that from 1919 and during the whole of the time he has been in this country, he has been known by and used the name of Henry Simon for all purposes. He resides at 2, Sidewood Road, Eltham, S.E.9 and is correctly registered with Police under ser-ial No. EZ 56759.

Applicant was born on the 16th. June, 1897, at Botosani, Rumania, and he is in possession of a copy birth certificate, No. 7/5681, issued at Botosani on 24.11.1919, in his correct name. The certificate shows that Haim Sin Simha was the son of Simha Sin Leizer, and applicant states that 'Sin' is the equivalent of 'son of', and that at his birthplace the local custom is for a son to be given his father's first name as a surname; he was therefore named Haim Sin Simha and not Haim Leizer, and he has never used the surname Leizer.

He is of Rumanian nationality, but has no passport. After leaving Rumania he went to Egypt, and Police records show that he came to this country from Egypt and in 1922 was in possession of a laissez-passer, No. N.P.137, issued by the Ministry of Interior, Egypt, on 27.4.1920. He states that he afterwards sent this document to a friend in Egypt for the latter to obtain a renewal for him, but it was retained by the local authorities who stated that if Simha wished to obtain a fresh document he must return to Rumania. He has produced correspondence showing that he afterwards applied to the Rumanian Consul in London for a passport, but received the reply that a passport could only be issued to him on condition that he returned to Rumania to perform military service.

Applicant is employed as foreign correspondent and as clerk in charge of the export department of Messrs. John Loudon and Company, produce merchants, London Bridge House, S.E., and has been with the same firm since July, 1928. He receives a salary of £312 per year, and appears to live within his income. In July, 1930, he purchased, for £800, the freehold house in which he resides. . . .

As shown above, applicant's father is Simha Sin Leizer, and his mother is Miniha Leizer, née Jacobsohn, Rumanian subjects; both are still alive and are residing at Braila, Rumania.

On 10th. August, 1930, applicant was married at the Register Office, Islington, to Augusta Lina Bertha Flugge, a German subject, who is still alive and residing with him. . . . There is one child of the marriage, Edward John, registered in the surname of Simon; born 1st. May, 1931, at Harburg, Hanover, Germany, during a visit paid by applicant's wife to her relatives. . . .

The total length of applicant's residence within the United Kingdom is about 12 years. He first came here in 1913 with a relative, and remained here for almost a year, and then returned to Rumania. He again came here in March, 1919, and was here until August, 1919, when he went to Sudan to take up employment there. In 1920 he spent two months holiday here, and on 16.5.1922 he returned here to take up permanent residence. . . .

Applicant speaks, reads and writes the English language well. He acts as foreign correspondent for his firm in English, French, German and Italian . . . appears to be a respectable man. Metropolitan Police records have been searched but nothing to his detriment has been traced. As far as can be found he has never been associated in any way with subversive movements, and nothing is known against him by M.I.5. . . .

Before leaving Rumania applicant received a good education, and was employed as a general clerk and foreign correspondent. In 1919 he obtained a situation with the Sudan Construction Company, as foreign correspondent and general clerk, and was sent to the Sudan to be employed there on the irrigation scheme. He remained there until April 1922, and was then discharged owing to the closing down of the works. He then returned to England. . . .

He had an exemplary record. He seems to have known what he wanted from the age of sixteen, when he first came to England. But how did he come? How could he afford to? And what was all that about military service? The report is quite clear:

"Applicant has never performed any military service."

What was he doing in Romania during the war, between the ages of eighteen and twenty-one, the prime age for cannon fodder? How did he avoid conscription? I could hardly blame him for trying. The ranks of the Romanian army have never been fun, and even less so for a Jew. He skipped the country without a passport at the age of twenty-two, obviously a draft dodger, because they wanted him back. All in all, he seems to have taken a lot of initiative for someone from such a closed, inbred background as the one I imagined. He made really adventurous choices, and yet all in pursuit of a most respectable, undramatic—one might even say humdrum—life. The more I knew, the more enigmatic he became.

What kind of an education could he have had, I wondered, in Romania during the First World War? And how did he pick up all those languages? The police report continues with glowing references from four respectable

City gentlemen who knew him through work. Their names were White, Lynn, Moat, and Savage, all carefully chosen, good old Anglo-Saxon names. If even one of them was Jewish, it would be astonishing. They knew that for all my father's exotic looks, he had become virtually one of them. He observed no odd religious customs, had no funny food fetishes, remained calm and contained, and, as far I know, did *not* gesticulate.

My father's first jobs in London were with grain brokers in the City. One firm merged into another. Then the bigger one went broke in 1928. By then my father had made his mark, and quickly got another good job. His referees all knew more about what he did during the day than he ever told my mother . . . but then, she knew things about him that they and the police didn't know. She knew that, try as he would to keep up the neutral, pragmatic, no-nonsense exterior, memories planted in him in childhood were hatching out and working their way to the surface. He placed odd restrictions on diet at home, and was extraordinarily secretive about his activities outside the house. She had no idea how much he earned. He was authoritarian and kept her on a tight budget. These things offended her. She had not escaped from one form of oppression to be crushed by another.

The most dramatic thing she knew, that the old boys didn't know, was that on the day after their wedding night, when the marriage was consummated, he told her that there would be no more kissing, because it was an unhygienic practice. To my mother, that was an outrageous stipulation and a betrayal of their relationship. To him it was perhaps a fairly mild concession to his childhood conditioning. After all, he could have asked her to shave her head and wear a brown wig. The marriage must have been doomed from that moment.

At the end of the Second World War, because Romania was on the wrong side that time, Cernăuți became Russian and was called Chernovtsy. By the time I got there it was Ukrainian and called Chernivtsi, and it was my last stop before Romania. Anatoly, the tourist official I had spoken to from Ivano-Frankivs'k, was not at home when I got off the train. Left to my own devices I found a number of hotels, but none of them would take me, and slowly but surely I was captured by the Ukrainian bureaucracy and forced into its expensive five-star cash-cow hotel at the edge of town.

Anatoly turned up later, and at mid-afternoon came with a car, took me into the city, and walked me around. There was an intriguing resemblance between Anatoly and the English professor in L'viv. They both wore the same medium-gray suits, both had the same flat, expressionless faces and the same agreeable manner that betrayed little emotion. Both struck me as men who had traveled through life as passengers rather than drivers. Of course, these were facile generalizations to make. They had worked within a bureaucracy, and would naturally have some of the outward characteristics of the apparatchik. Anatoly, however, was making a serious effort to break out of the mold and set up on his own. Something was coming to life for him.

He told a rather moving story about the demolition of Lenin. Inevitably, there had been a statue of Lenin, standing sixteen feet tall with his arm outstretched, on a very handsome pedestal. When the USSR collapsed, the crowd came to demolish it. Anatoly watched as the statue was carted away on its back in ignominy. All he could see was the arm sticking up out of the truck, in reproach, seeming to him to be crying out, "What have you done?" He had a vivid flashback to the mass graves of his childhood, when bodies, still in rigor mortis, were flung into pits. The rigid limbs often stuck up through the dirt.

"I thought, This is tragic to do this. Why should we destroy our history? And the pedestal was a fine piece of work. It would have served another purpose very well, but they tore it to pieces."

Instead of removing Lenin, it would have been better, in his view, to remove some of the bureaucrats who were clogging up the system. He told a sidesplitting tale about an Italian businessman called Carlo, who arrived in Chernivtsi one morning after a long and exhausting train ride. Coming from Belarus, he had not needed a visa, but my five-star hotel refused to admit him without one. The story then proceeded from one absurdity to another, during which the poor Carlo was forced to stand outside a series of empty offices throughout the day, in a state of collapse, not daring to move in case the one *specialista* who could adjust his papers should condescend to appear for a moment. Meanwhile Anatoly was all over town seeking the absent bureaucrat.

Shortly before six in the evening, the *specialista* was tracked down in his cousin's garage. Anatoly was given twenty minutes to get to the other end of town, pay a tax, get a clearance, and bring it back to the *specialista* to sign. With a minute to spare, Carlo got his paper and was admitted to the hotel, a total wreck. He went to his room and asked for a coffee, but they said it was too late, and anyway they didn't do room service.

Chernivtsi appeared to me like a somewhat reduced and lifeless version of L'viv, and utterly changed from the bustling Jewish community Sitwell described so vividly. When I explained the purpose of my journey to Romania, Anatoly told me what he knew about the history of Jews in his city, and I began to appreciate how wildly inconsistent the treatment of Jews had been. Apparently, many Jews had survived quite well in Chernivtsi through the war, when it was part of Romania. Anatoly remembered the important role they had played in the city of his youth.

"Most of the doctors were Jewish," he said. "And the best teachers in the university. In fact, the Jews really made this city work, but they were gradually driven out by the anti-Semitism."

They left a kind of emptiness, he thought, a barren feeling. He seemed almost embarrassed to admit it.

"Maybe we lost a lot when we lost the Jewish culture."

Efficiency was lost, too. Ironically, the city was not as clean as it used to be, and he regretted that most of all. At the apartment block where he lived, his neighbors gave him the good-humored nickname of "concierge" or "janitor." He was the only one who bothered to keep the public areas, like the paths and steps, clean. He laughed. "When they see me at work they call out, 'Look, the concierge is here.' "

I wondered whether in Romania I would find the same "cleansed" towns, the same faintly melancholic regret. Would every trace of Jewish life have been eradicated, as Herwig and Thomas predicted? I suspected that things would not be so cut-and-dried. Romania did not strike me as a very "thorough" country. I knew that terrible pogroms had been carried out there at the beginning of the war, but only in specific places. I knew that Jews had been encouraged to emigrate, but not all went. And there was another factor—the Gypsies. There could be no hope of an ethnically cleansed Romania with such a startlingly distinct minority everywhere in evidence, as I had been promised. No, Romania would be different.

I could not afford to stay in Chernivtsi more than one night, and had to decide what to do. I was about twenty miles from the border, and on the other side, about the same distance away, was the first big town, Suceava (Sou-*cha*-va). The road to Suceava was a major highway, and did not look like an interesting route to walk. From Suceava to Botoşani was another twenty-five miles, but that road ran due east, away from the mountains. And I very much wanted to walk into the mountains.

The beauty of the Carpathians is not so well appreciated in the West. With the legend of Dracula as the only point of reference, most Westerners must think of the Carpathian mountain range as a remote and faintly dangerous setting for Ruritanian fairy tales. It does pretty much define the eastern edge of Europe and, given what has been going on around there for the last sixty years or more, relatively few travelers have been enterprising enough to go out and see for themselves.

It is an unusual mountain range because of its wonderfully graphic shape—a shape that, on the map, resembles nothing so much as a huge nose pointing east, complete with a blob for the nostril. Within this hook lies Transylvania. The upper bridge of the nose, alongside which I had been traveling, cuts off a corner of Ukraine. The rest of it lies within Romania, and around the outside of this noble profile are the three ancient kingdoms that were brought together in the last century to create the Romanian nation. They are Bukovina, where I was now; then Moldavia, reaching down to the tip of the nose; below that, stretching across to where the upper lip would be, are the rich plains of Walachia and the Danube basin. At the end of the First World War, Transylvania was taken from Hungary and added to Romania as a prize for having been on the winning side, making the country a fully rounded entity for the first time.

The language is Latin-based, dating back to a time when Romania was conquered by the Romans. As a province called Dacia, it was at the outer edge of the Roman empire. When Romanians are promoting their own glory, they like to refer to themselves as descendants of the Romans, and many Romanians do have features typical of Italians today. When their critics are looking for a way to insult them, they usually point out that Dacia was populated by slaves, implying that things have not changed much since. My own observation, which seems just as valid as the other two, is that the Carpathian nose looks unmistakably Jewish.

But the Carpathians conceal jewels that are most definitely Christian. In the folds of these green hills lie the fabulous painted monasteries of Bukovina that I had waited so long to see, and several of them were within reach of Suceava. Walking to them would give me a chance to learn a little of the language and the customs of the country before I got to Botoșani. So I chose to take the bus to Suceava.

Although the bus station was only a mile from the hotel, Anatoly insisted on coming out in the morning to drive me there. Buses are cheaper and more popular than trains. On that dry, sunny morning a whirling crowd animated the bus station with strings and clusters of people queueing for tickets, waiting for buses, and besieging food stalls. Anatoly made sure I got the right ticket for the right money, and as an extra kindness he surreptitiously bought bread and fruit for the journey and pressed it upon me at the last moment.

The bus was in better condition than I had expected, but it was old and there were no extra conveniences, such as fans or air-conditioning. To be sure of my seat, I had to sit in it, and every inch of the bus was packed long before it was due to leave. The aisle was crammed with standing passengers. There was no room inside for luggage, and all my possessions were piled on my lap. The seats were narrow, the sun beat down on the metal roof, and as we sat there, immobile for twenty minutes, not a breath of air moved in or out of the bus. Beads of sweat became fountains. Squeezed into my seat like a punctured and overripe peach spurting juice at the slightest movement, I tried to keep absolutely still. The prospect of the hours ahead was too awful to contemplate, until the bus at last began to move.

Almost immediately a draft of cool air washed over me, and I came to life and looked around. It was the first time since I'd left Hamburg that I found myself in an ethnically diverse crowd. Many of them had darker skins than mine, indicating that they were mainly returning Romanians. What had brought them here? If they were here to buy things they couldn't get at home, then life in Romania must be tough indeed.

The men standing in the aisle, with baskets at their feet, were surely peasants. That was clear, from their fingernails to their quiet, engraved faces. Within a few miles of Chernivtsi they left the bus, sometimes in the middle of nowhere, and I realized that the bus was offering an unofficial service to the local peasantry. Soon I was able to set my pack on the floor between the seats, and with the cool air now flowing through the bus, the ride became a happy experience.

At the border, progress was slow and unpredictable. A police barrier held us up for a while. Then we passed through into an area where long columns of transcontinental trucks waited. The drivers had tables set out alongside their cabs and were eating lunch and playing trictrac, cards, and chess. Obviously, they had no hope of getting through anytime soon. The bus seemed to have some priority, though, and found a way to weave around and through the stalled juggernauts, only to be confronted by a mass of people, on foot or with horses and small carts, pressing up against a high chain-link fence. We were marooned there too for a while, but then again we took precedence and were let through to the customs building. There the trouble began.

Two uniformed men, one in white, one in blue, came on the bus and made us produce our tickets. Then they verbally attacked the driver. Though I couldn't understand the words, they sounded blistering. They took him away to a nearby table, and the arguments continued, with new contestants being brought on. It sounded bad. Then the man in blue came back and delivered a stern lecture to us all. He sounded so grim that I thought this must be the end of the road. Nobody near me spoke any language I understood, and it was impossible to know what the crisis was about. Then, after all, we were allowed off the bus, and once we were off I found an older woman who taught French.

"It is nothing," she said, disgusted by the fuss. "*Rien du tout.* We have a bus with forty-seven passengers when it is supposed to carry only forty. And of the forty-seven, only twenty-eight have tickets. The driver has been forced to buy tickets for all those who don't have them. He is not very happy."

The customs arrangements were peculiar. We were assembled at one end of the building. From there a flight of cement steps led up to an open landing one floor above, where the officials conducted their business. On the other side of the landing, another flight of steps led down to what was presumably our escape hatch. Old people and parents with children had to struggle up these steps with their heavy baggage, baby carriages, and whatever else they might be bringing. It could be done, of course—especially with help from others, which was freely given—but it was such a gratuitous imposition, and so symbolic of the power and indifference of officialdom, that I thought it quite humiliating. What could be the point of it? And what was beneath that platform? There must be some bureaucratic rationale. I stood up there before the arbiters of my fate, wondering whether a trapdoor would suddenly spring open beneath my feet, snatching me from sight forever.

But the trapdoor remained unsprung. The driver paid for his tickets. We eventually shuffled out into the open air again, to be met by Romanian immigration. They were more than usually interested in me. I had to go to a different place to talk to a rather fat man about my intentions.

"Do you have any drugs or guns?" he asked, in an interested sort of way.

Of all the possible answers to this question I chose "No."

"Really?" he said, with a knowing smile. "Then you can go."

By now I had had time to study my companions, and I saw that, as usual, they had been assembled by central casting to act out a melodrama of espionage, terrorism, and tortured romance. A tall, bent, and pockmarked man in a camouflage suit was moving around the company in the most absurdly furtive manner, flashing bundles of dollars. Two young men with crude and greedy expressions were behaving as though they were engaged in some kind of conspiracy. A very attractive blond woman, with a haunted and exhausted look, cast anxious, imploring glances around her, while a very corpulent youth, who earned ten dollars a month as a dental assistant, admitted that he was training to be a currency hustler.

The French teacher winked and flashed a gold tooth at me, meaning, I suppose, that she was undercover CIA or KGB, or both, while the most dangerous person on the bus (other than myself) was probably the septuagenarian with the bicycle. As for the driver, I had no doubt that he would soon hijack his own bus and hold us ransom for the money he had lost.

In the four years since the death of Ceaușescu nothing good had come out of Romania. First there were the grim scenes of battle with the Securitate—the secret police—then the sordid executions, the never-ending revelations of monstrous outrages, state-sponsored vandalism, euthanasia, repression, and poverty, until Romania sounded synonymous with hell on earth. But from all my experience of traveling to countries with dismal reputations, I knew that life in general could never be as bad as it appeared from a distance, even though particular aspects could be unexpectedly worse.

I was glad I had taken two months to reach Romania. Although it wasn't planned for that reason, I knew that I was much better prepared now to distinguish between what was merely inconvenient and frustrating and what was true misery. In the time I had spent walking and thinking, I had cut myself free again from many of the dependencies and expectations that our overheated culture fosters. I hoped to have a calmer perspective on this society that was supposedly in ruins.

As the bus rolled and bounced over country roads for an hour, I looked out for evidence of dirty, thieving, mischievous-looking Romanians and for signs of the destruction of rural life but saw neither. We were traveling over fairly flat land, well away from the Carpathians. The countryside was not unlike the south of France in an earlier, less developed era. The agriculture had a casual appearance, and there was little equipment to be seen. Shade trees lined the roads, and we passed through a few villages where the buildings seemed too old to have been disturbed. Eventually, at the edge of Suceava, came the first signs of industrialization, but nothing that would have seemed out of place in France or England forty years earlier. The streets of the town seemed to be in no worse shape than those of Chernivtsi, and rather more interesting to look at.

Fortunately, the bus driver must have lost his nerve, because there were no further incidents and we arrived safely at the bus station, near the center of town, shortly before noon.

# Chapter 22

*T*he language was making a fool of me. Through all my struggles with Polish and Russian, I had consoled myself that in the end, I would be back with something familiar—a Romance language. I spoke French, Spanish, and some Italian. Once I had even been taught a little Latin. Romanian should be easy to grasp, but it wasn't, and I felt deceived, frustrated, and depressed.

Take the expression *please.* There is *s'il vous plaît,* or *prego,* or *por favor,* all pleasant-sounding entreaties. What did my newly acquired dictionary tell me to say to this waitress? *Vă rog*! Where is the Latin in that? How can you say *vă rog* and mean "please"? To me it sounds like "go to hell."

I looked up at her, getting ready to plead. She seemed softer and more receptive than the others I had encountered. The place was friendlier, too. I was in the restaurant of a roadside inn, fifteen miles from Suceava, at a hamlet called Ilişişte (I-li-*sheest*). The dining room was large and nicely proportioned and had many tables laid with fairly white linen. Windows looked out over a terrace, where there were more tables. Beyond that, some distance off, was the road and then a forest. I had walked here from Suceava the day before, and this was my second night. I liked the place a lot.

The restaurant had all the cupboards, buffets and counters, crockery and glassware to provide for a good crowd. In prosperous times it would certainly have had a great ambience. Tonight I was the only person eating. Only one other table was occupied, by a couple drinking beer. The TV was showing episode 263 of *Dallas*, dubbed in Romanian.

In my hand I held a sheet of paper headed MENIU. Below the heading was a long list of dishes, knocked out through four carbons on the old Underwood machine I had seen on the desk outside. I pointed to an item.

"*Achesta,*" I said diffidently, "*vă rog.*"

Her features expressed some sympathy. Her mouth drooped a little, and her lashes dipped over sorrowful brown eyes. This was unexpected. In my experience so far, gathered from several restaurants over three days, when they turned you down, they did it with blank incomprehension; sometimes indifferent, sometimes irritated, but always incredulous that I could have supposed something on the menu would be available. I couldn't blame them. Imagine having to tell people day in, day out that there was nothing on the menu. It might have been going on for years. It would definitely harden you. It was nice of this girl to care.

"*Nu meniu,*" she said. "*Cotelet?*"

I had known from her expression what was coming, but still my heart sank. I had not realized how much I had been looking forward to something different. There was nothing really wrong with *cotelet*. It was a piece of pork hammered flat and grilled, but I had had it at every meal, bar one, for three days. The exception was at this very restaurant, where, expecting *cotelet*, I had been given something like kebabs by mistake. The meat was the same, just cut up and skewered, but it made a change and it was what I had hoped to get again.

I nodded in defeat and thought back to the other places where I had eaten *cotelet*. There was the restaurant at the Hotel Suceava, where, at Anatoly's recommendation, I stayed the first night. The hotel was fine, apart from the restaurant. I first sat there for lunch on the day of my arrival. The tough ladies who came through the swinging doors from the kitchen, like cops going out on the beat, had my number from the start. They were not interested in diners who asked questions and made choices. They left me to stew in my unrealistic expectations for an hour, until I was ready and grateful for *cotelet*.

At the deserted flyblown restaurant above the patisserie in Gura, on my way to the monastery, she (the waitress as archetype) took the offensive, advanced on me with one eyebrow slightly raised, and said, *"Cotelet."* The words *or nothing* were silent. I submitted without question.

At the Suceviţa (Soo-che-*vi*-tsa) monastery there was an overnight lodge with a restaurant. Again I was the only diner, and determined to hold out for something different. She said I could have potatoes. Very well then, I said, bring me two servings of potatoes. She brought one. I ate it, and asked for another, but by then there were no more potatoes, so I had *cotelet*.

It might seem absurd to say that this was the saddest thing about Romania, and yet these experiences, in their joylessness, evoked the miserable state of the country very well. These restaurants were so obviously intended to be packed with enthusiastic diners, laughing, chattering, flourishing their wineglasses, flushed and merry with good talk, all conspiring to create the inimitable atmosphere of well-being that Latin cultures do so well. I didn't think it unfair to make the restaurant a metaphor for Romania. As melancholy as a restaurant is without food, so is a culture that has lost its heart, and it was this sense of hollowness, of just an ache where the heart should have been, that pursued me throughout the country. In that respect it was very different from the other struggling Eastern nations.

Romania, with its great fertile plains north of Bucharest, once used to revel in an abundance of food of every description. In the novels and histories of Romania, the literate members of the population lived the life of restaurants, cafés, and boulevards. They pretended to be in Paris, puffed themselves up with speeches, ceremonies, and swank uniforms, determined to have a good time as long as there was time at all. "Eat, drink, and be merry, for tomorrow we may become Hungary . . . or Russia . . . or Bulgaria." They indulged in more than the usual amounts of cynicism, corruption, folly, and exploitation, but there was also an expansive longing to be greater and better, frustrated constantly by the powerful forces ranged around them.

A wonderfully poignant account of the end of this era was left to us by Rosie Goldschmidt (writing under the name E. G. Waldeck). Apparently a woman of beauty, wit, and exalted connections, she was the daughter of a rich and influential German Jewish banking family that had sought refuge from Hitler in the United States. She had the sangfroid—or was it *chutzpah?*—to return to Europe before Pearl Harbor and to set up in Bucharest's most elegant hotel, while the Nazis gradually infiltrated and absorbed Romania. Even more extraordinary, she cultivated an intimate relationship with a fanatically committed member of the Nazi elite, a young German count who considered himself violently anti-Semitic, although on intellectual rather than emotional grounds. They had known each other for years, and he was very well aware that she was, as she herself put it, "non-Aryan." In fact she worried, at the time, that her associating with him might harm his career. Their discussions of the "Jewish question" make fascinating and bizarre reading today.*

Her descriptions of the effete and bankrupt aristocrats who haunted the marbled halls of the Athene Palace Hotel are priceless. Two of them, whom she nicknamed with sad affection the Old Excellencies, embodied all the tired cynicism of their class. She asked them what they thought were the prospects of Jews in Romania under Nazi hegemony.

"The Jews, they said, were too important in the economic life of Rumania to be liquidated in a hurry. Moreover, they said: 'Though we are antisemites we are somehow unable to live without Jews. A Rumanian never trusts another Rumanian. Only in the Jew can he confide his sordid little affairs.' "

In that last twilight time before an endless night settled on Romania, she described the goods in the shops—the lace, the silk, the embroidered blouses, and the last of the perfumes from Paris. The food, she says, was sensational, including "parts of animals you never thought of eating, such as cow's udders done in red wine sauce, or a special delicacy—the testicles of ram . . . done in a sauce with everything in it. And you polished off your meal by very sweet confitures of fruit with a touch of maraschino. From all this you put on two pounds every day and got the gout. Every respectable Rumanian had the gout; that is, the few hundred thousand who could afford such meals."

While the "respectable" Romanians ate, drank, schemed, and dreamed, a huge, illiterate peasant population provisioned the kitchens while frequently starving themselves. If Ceaușescu ever had an ideal—and according to the biographies, that seems doubtful—it was to turn the tables on Romania's restaurant-goers. Instead, the sum effect of his efforts was

---

*She writes: "The Count once told me that it was a painful discovery for a pure Aryan not to be able to tell a non-Aryan when he saw one."

to take the joie de vivre out of everyone's life and shut the joint down.

But that night in Ilişişte it was much too soon to make grand generalizations. I was simply rather bewildered, because in most other respects Romania, thus far, had been a pleasant surprise. The first shock had been delivered almost as soon as I got off the bus. I was only a short distance from the hotel, and on that short walk I had to admit that I liked the look of the place. This was a startling admission, because it had all been rebuilt, and most of it consisted of five- and six-story concrete buildings, which I usually abominate.

I had to concede that these were the first I'd seen in a long while that were interesting, even elegant, with their clever changes of angle and the intelligent way that the balconies had been designed to break up the severity of the facades. There were imaginative terraces at ground level. Best of all, the buildings were clean and undamaged. This was quite disconcerting, and I didn't know what to make of it. I had been certain that everything built under Ceauşescu's regime would be awful.

I checked in at the Suceava Hotel, and went to the market to change money. The entrance was a crowded passage where people sold roasted sunflower seeds, tiny grilled sausages, sandwiches, cakes, and other curious and enticing snacks. Behind the covered market for vegetables, meat, and dairy products was a flea market with many rows of covered stalls displaying every kind of used object that penurious householders might have dug up to see them through bad times. Business was brisk; there were hundreds of people crowding the aisles. Among these traders were many who bought dollars.

My difficulty was that while I knew this was now the established way to change money, I was not sure of its legality. Police, in pairs, patrolled the market, and I was unnecessarily wary of them. After I had asked a few traders what they paid—they all had calculators and showed me their prices on the LCD screens—I produced two twenty-dollar bills for a hard-bitten man presiding over a collection of machine parts and gadgets. He was not impressed by my dirty notes. He ran his fingers over the creases, held them up to the light, examined the serial numbers carefully, and rejected the one dated 1977. He was sure it was a forgery.

"No gut," he said. "Problema Russkie."

I pictured the Wells Fargo teller in California being told that she was handing out Russian forgeries, but I substituted another bill, with the right date, and got my money without difficulty—a stack of red and purple notes worth just over 44,000 lei.

I found a good dictionary, but it was little help with the grammar, and apart from my difficulty with the words themselves, I noticed that peculiar things could happen to them. Sometimes a train was *tren,* but sometimes it was *trenul,* and sometimes even *trenului.* This habit of sticking bits on the ends of words was hard to acquire. Figuring that they must be prepositions—postpositions, really—I worked out one or two examples, but it was tough going, since the conjugations and declensions seemed quite obscure. Then there was an unusual sound, too, an *i* with a hat over it that sounded like a French *u* spoken through lemon juice, and it cropped up in the most common words, like *pîine,* for "bread."

The women behind the hotel desk seemed to have a natural inclination to be helpful, a quality I had not noticed much lately. Between them they spoke smatterings of French, English, and German. They translated for me and gave me accurate directions and useful information; in fact, they did what hotel employees are supposed to do, and I was flabbergasted. They gave me a map—entitled "A Proficient Guide of the Municipality"—and I learned that the nearest monasteries were Humor and Voroneţ (Vo-ro-*nets*). To get to them I should go to Gura Humorului, which translates literally as Mouth Humor-the-of. Even the news that I planned to walk there didn't cause them to spurn me. They told me about this inn at Ilişişte, phoned for a room, and said they would be glad to keep some of my things until I got back.

I walked out the following morning on a cool, gray day, past a sprawling brewery and a ball-bearing factory, and up into the Carpathian hills. What I saw during those two days of wandering around the countryside contradicted more of my expectations. Instead of ruin and dislocation, I found a rural peasant culture that looked well defined and intact. Its problem, from the national point of view, was probably that it simply served itself. Judging from the fields and gardens, the livestock, the clucking of hens, and the honking of geese, the peasants would have had no trouble stocking their larders, but not much of it was getting out onto the market—and none of it, in my experience, was getting into the restaurants.

As usual, it was the houses that made the first and strongest impressions on me. This was obviously an area where rainfall at times was extreme. I saw the same storm drains spanned by little footbridges that John Reed described outside Czernowitz seventy-eight years before me, but where he saw them awash with filth and sewage, I saw only rainwater. The villages were clean, and the wooden houses very nicely built, in a strong, traditional style. What was most pleasing about them was the effort that had been made to decorate and embellish them. The outer walls were covered with small painted shingles cut to a sort of fleur-de-lis pattern that interlocked and made for a rich and distinctive texture. All the openings were framed with generous moldings. Doors, windows, shutters, and gates were all built with an eye to beauty as well as function. The fences were capped with little tin roofs of their own, cut to a pretty pattern. These recurring patterns and ways of doing things gave the villages the same satisfying coherence that, say, stone and Roman tiles give a village in Provence.

Most of the farm traffic was by horse and cart, and it was rare to be on a road where one at least was not in sight. Usually they followed one another in trains, moving only a little faster than I could walk, and that was particularly true on the road out of Suceava. The carts were unlike any I had seen in Europe, Asia, or Africa. They were very long and narrow, looking more like troughs on wheels, and they traveled silently on car tires. Occasionally, one would come off a field with a huge load of hay, and I saw how ingeniously the stack had been built, with outriggers to three or four times the width of the cart.

The horses were small and dark, some hardly bigger than ponies, and were almost always driven by men, if driven is the word. Generally the man simply sat, half asleep. The horse knew where to go, and traveled at its own pace. Many carried lumber; some carried produce or milk churns. Others were returning empty from the city. Once or twice I accepted a lift simply for the pleasure of moving at such a pleasant dawdle through the hills and villages.

The men wore jaunty little trilbylike hats with narrow brims, but otherwise I found the clothes drab and undistinguished. Although I could never suppose that a peasant's life would be easy, it seemed to me that these people at least had a sustainable existence, and there was no sign of forced collectivization or of their villages having been interfered with in any way. The only machines I saw were a sawmill and some smaller tractors used for hauling. Whatever had happened in the rest of Romania, this part of Bukovina, at least, appeared undisturbed.

Of the monasteries at Voroneţ, Humor, and Suceviţa it is hard to say enough to convey the wonder and awe they evoke. With their brilliantly painted walls and their womblike interiors, they touch the soul at every level. The art that entirely covers the exteriors of these buildings tells, in comic-strip form, the fundamental stories of the Orthodox faith, while at the same time making powerful propaganda against the enemies of Byzantium, with Turks and Catholics cast as the devils. Their fascination is as potent as the mystery of how their colors lasted through four centuries of exposure to sun and rain.

Sacheverell Sitwell, a famous aesthete of his time, also saw them and marveled at their survival. He pointed out that the fronts of some houses in Venice were once decorated with frescoes by some of her most famous artists yet they lasted for only a few years. He believed the persistence of the Bukovina works could only be explained if they were done "with all the mediaeval care and attention that was devoted to miniature painting"—an immense labor, considering the area covered.

They are altogether extraordinary, and if I had made the journey simply to see them, the effort would have been more than justified. But I did have another purpose, and it was time to be getting on. A pity, really. I had become quite attached to Ilişişte. It was cheap and comfortable, the country around was lovely and calming, and they served a good wine, which helped to make up for the *cotelet*. I was also saddened by the realization that I could no longer afford to walk very far. Now, too late, my feet were performing wonderfully. It would have been no hardship to walk any distance, but if I was to unravel the mysteries of my father's family, there was no time left for anything else. Reluctantly, I accepted that from here on I would have to stay on buses and trains. Altogether I had walked about three hundred miles, not as many as I had hoped, and yet I felt they had served their purpose. In those hundred hours of tramping across Europe I had covered an awful lot of emotional and mental ground.

In the morning I left to take the bus to Suceava, change some more money, collect my things, and leave for Botoşani in the afternoon. The bus stop was directly in front of the inn, but I waited in vain. After a while I began to thumb the drivers of infrequently passing cars, but none showed any interest. Thinking that an offer of money might help, I brought out my last three hundred-lei notes, limp and ragged as they were, and waved them at the next vehicle, a white van. The van came to a screeching stop.

Two young men were in the cab, and one leaped out and opened a sliding door in the van for me. Glad to have learned the secret of hitching in Romania, I thrust the money at him, but he was not at all interested in it. Somewhat bemused, I sat on the wheel arch inside and hung on grimly as they drove at reckless speed to Suceava, covering in fifteen minutes what had taken me five hours to walk. There they put me down, very courteously, still refusing the money, and drove off.

Remembering the money changer's aversion to dirty money, I took a crisp new hundred-dollar bill to the market, but my previous connection had disappeared. This time I dealt with a loquacious, bearded rascal and a sidekick who reminded me of Molotov. They didn't like big bills at all. Big bills, they said, were probably forgeries. I managed to scrape fifty dollars together in tens, fives, and ones, all of them filthy, and that pleased them very much. Then I got my things from the hotel and took the bus to Botoşani.

For no obvious reason, I was beginning to feel excited. The chances of my finding out anything significant about my father now were really remote. Neither he nor his family had been in Botoşani for at least eighty years, and even if there were someone alive who could remember the Leizer family, he or she would be in Israel, New York, Timbuktu—anywhere but in Botoşani. Still, I couldn't repress the sense of anticipation.

It is easy to speculate on the processes of the subconscious, and impossible to know them. Why, after eradicating him from my life for so many years, was I now in a fever of impatience to find out something about my father? His leaving must have hurt me, of course. But other children have gone through divorce without banishing one parent from their thoughts. The rift between mine must have been terrible to have created such a trauma. Was it a clash between people or between cultures? My mother never took it out on the Jews. On the contrary, she helped many, and for a while sent me to a Jewish school. Yet she must have been implacable with him.

Was it from loyalty to my mother that I cast him out? Or did he really abandon me? There were meetings between us, three that I recall. At the first I must have been very young, maybe six or seven. We were in bed wearing pajamas and making jokes about farting under the covers. When I was about ten, he took me to Schmidt's, a German restaurant on Charlotte Street, and introduced me to chicken liver pâté. I remember the food, but I don't remember him. The third meeting was a stiff encounter in the park at Marble Arch when I was thirteen. I cannot picture him, either there or at any other time. I recall only that I had nothing to say to him. I never saw him again.

Somehow, during the war, I learned that the ten shillings a week he was supposed to send my mother rarely appeared. Then I heard that he had remarried, to a Jewish woman, had two daughters, lived in Oxfordshire, and worked for the BBC in the foreign-language department. Although I don't remember my mother saying anything to me about him that was overtly hostile, I never made the slightest attempt to find him or to know more about him. He did not appear in my conscious mind until his death, and even then it was just a walk-on part. Only after my mother's death, thirty years later, did the curiosity stir in me. It hurts to think what must have lain frozen beneath the surface for so many decades.

Now, as I was coming closer to his origins, to places that he had known, maybe even things he had seen and touched as a child, the need to discover him for myself welled up with great force. Hopeless though it might be, I was going to make a serious attempt to learn more about this man Henry Simon, aka Haim Sin Simha, to whom I owed my existence and whose face I knew only from one small faded print of a tennis party, taken some time before I was born.

# Chapter 23

The bus to Botoşani was half full of people in workaday clothing and carrying makeshift luggage. They filled the front half, and they knew what they were doing. I sat over the back axle and bounced up and down for two hours, but it was worth it. I could open the windows and let the breeze blow around me. Romanians, I learned, did not care for open windows, and thought drafts were dangerous. As soon as the bus got under way, I saw the other face of Suceava. The city sits on a high bluff on the west bank of the river, but I had come to it from the northwest and so far had known only the older part of it. Now I had to cross the river and saw that the city spread across the valley. This was where Ceauşescu's legacy was visible. The valley was carpeted on both sides of the river with smokestack industries and all their ugly accompaniments.

Through the countryside, the villages again appeared to have been left intact, but at Botoşani the same ugly industrial scene was repeated. Of course, it was no worse than what happened in Europe and America through the Industrial Revolution. The tragedy was to have that foul mess repeated long after its evolutionary function was gone. Ironically, one of the best-read works of English literature in Eastern Europe, and one sanctioned by the Communist regimes, was *Hard Times,* by Charles Dickens. Although it presents powerfully the impetus behind labor unions, it also paints a most devastating picture of industrial pollution. Indeed, it is hard even to read it without choking on the smoke from the mill chimneys, but that message seems to have been sadly ignored.

This time the bus station was far from the center, and I walked forever down one of those bleak, prefabricated avenues that modern dictators like to install, like catalog items, for their parades. It was long, broad, and filthy, and lined with monotonous concrete blocks. Here were all the eyesores and travesties I had missed in Suceava—the rubble, the pollution, and the wearying atmosphere of failure and collapse.

Here, too, Anatoly had given me the name of a hotel, the Rhapsodia, and I found it easily enough. It was more pretentious than the one in Suceava and almost twice the price, but I was lucky again with the desk clerk. She spoke some English and pointed me down the road to the Unirea.

"It is where the government and Party people used to stay," she said. Hoping it wasn't haunted, I walked a few hundred yards down a quieter street, passing on the way a small church decked out in what looked like embroidered cloths or blankets, for some ceremony. It was the first building I had seen that might have dated from an earlier century. Beyond it, a few youngsters were drinking sodas at tables on a raised concrete patio. I saw a couple of lock-up shops advertising Coca-Cola and Marlboro, and it suddenly hit me how pervasive that Marlboro logo had become. The brash red symbol was splashed over every medium—on TV, shop fronts, buses, T-shirts, posters, and magazines. The bright simplicity of it seemed to appeal directly to Eastern Europeans, mired in their drab uncertainties. In the confusion of these miserable days, ironies were a condition of life, but one of the most pungent, I thought, was that red should be the color that now symbolized carefree affluence. And kids would go broke to purchase the symbol. Marlboros cost seventeen hundred lei a pack. Decent indigenous smokes cost three hundred. Average wages were worth between ten and twenty packs of Marlboros a month, but if you wanted to look like a kid who was going places in Romania, you had to smoke Marlboros.

The Unirea was in the concrete block next to the patio. It was dark inside, cool and funereal. The desk was raised up like a reviewing stand, and the clerk spoke only Romanian, but I passed inspection and got my room upstairs for twelve dollars, complete with fan and naked lightbulb. I dropped my bag on the floor and, with my notebook and a copy of my father's birth certificate, went back to the Rhapsodia.

The address of my grandparents was written in an old cursive style, and not easy to read. It appeared to be 856 St. Sf. Ion. There was a little curlicue over the *I*, like the cedilla under the *s* in Botoșani. The receptionist had no difficulty deciphering the address. *Sf* stood for *Sfínt*, meaning "Saint." *St.* was *Strada*, meaning "Street." So they had lived at 856 St. John Street. The church of St. John, she said, was still there, but everything around it had been torn down, rebuilt, and renamed. She showed me where to go on a map and wished me luck.

The general area was easy to find, though the streets were sometimes hard to identify from the sketchy map. Of course, there was no St. John Street anymore. It surprised me a little that the churches had been left standing. Whatever else he had been, Ceaușescu clearly had not been that foolish. Meanwhile, an even more pertinent question was swimming lazily to the surface of my mind. Was it significant that an Orthodox Jewish family should be living in an area identified by one of Christ's disciples?

In London I would not have thought twice about it. St. John's Wood, for example, is home to a number of devout Jewish families. But unlike London, Botoșani once used to have a large and predominantly Jewish area, and while I still did not yet know where that had been, I felt sure it would not have included the parish of St. John. Was it possible that my grandparents, Simha and Miniha, were not quite the fanatical Jews I had supposed them to be?

I found a church that seemed to be in the right place. It was undistinguished and uncared for, and sat on a fenced plot of dry ground among weeds and ragged trees. There was no identifying sign, and I prowled around it a couple of times trying the doors, which were locked. I was startled by an angry man coming out to question me, and I asked as best I could whether this was *Sfínt Ion*. My accent immediately mollified him. Yes it was, he said, but the address meant nothing to him. He made a sweeping gesture of hopelessness to indicate that everything was gone and that he was not responsible. Then he went back inside.

I had not really expected to find much left from the time of my father's birth. Even the church, sad and worn as it was, looked as though it might have been built since then, perhaps to replace an older one. It would have been a miracle if those ninety-six tumultuous years had left anything intact, but I was hoping for a miracle. I felt as though I deserved one. I meandered back to the Rhapsodia, somewhat depressed, and the weather got through to me. The last days had been sunny, but the humidity was becoming oppressive. Banks of cumulus were climbing up the sky, and it was going to rain. I wanted to find something in this blasted city that I could say my father and I had both seen.

My friend at the Rhapsodia was off duty, and her replacement could not talk to me. I told myself that unless I got some kind of grip on this language, I would get nowhere. I went back to my room and spent three hours, with a dictionary and a newspaper, deconstructing and reconstructing sentences, trying to acquire a basic vocabulary, but I was not pleased with my progress.

There was no restaurant at the Unirea, only a lunchtime canteen, so I went back to the Rhapsodia and found, to my surprise, that it was not necessary to eat *cotelet*. I could have steak and fried potatoes for eighty cents and a bottle of Romania's best wine, Murfatlar, for under two dollars. Putting it that way helped revive my morale. Also, for once, I was not the only one dining. Eight prosperous-looking older men and women were gathered around a far table, and I heard what sounded like Hebrew. I guessed immediately that they were Israelis, and thought I might not be the only one here digging into his past. I considered talking to them, but they exuded a curiously unfriendly aura, so I decided to wait for another opportunity.

By morning, the weather had changed and the sky was leaden with intermittent rain. I had a letter to mail and went out to find the post office. The map took me past a neglected ornamental garden, through mounds of rubble, and along a narrow dirt path that skirted a deep pit where work on some foundations had apparently ceased. I came out onto an asphalt area flanked on one side by massive concrete blocks and on the other by a market square. Whoever had designed the buildings had consciously made the material his god. Everything that could be done to emphasize the concrete was done. As in the misconceived town hall of Kaliningrad, large rectangular chunks of it thrust out of the buildings in all directions to make balconies and extensions. Each individual block was bad enough, but here was a whole community of these deformed creations.

Behind the square arose another range of newly constructed cement hutches, and below it was the post office, where I watched a clerk paint glue on the back of a stamp, rub another stamp over the glued surface to take up the excess, and then paste both down on my envelope.

I returned through the flea market, a dirty, puddled area of mud and asphalt. The layout was similar to the one in Suceava but much less inviting, and the stalls had less to offer. A number of men were changing money, and I planned to return the next day. It began to rain again, and I walked into the roofed food market. Thick crowds of people in moist clothing milled around huge mounds of fresh cheese on stone slabs. In the damp air, the smell of the cheese and clothes hung heavy and fetid, like the gases of digestion. Yards, even miles, of sausage festooned other stalls. There was little variety, merely enormous quantities of cheese and sausage, and the grossness of it gave me the strange sensation of being in the bowels of some great beast. The crowd moved with a life of its own, and I let it carry me out into the street like one of a hundred turds, where in my slightly hallucinatory state I perceived what it might feel like to be a Romanian.

The buildings I had seen earlier appeared as monstrous organisms that seemed to have reared themselves up out of the limy rock by some life force as alien to flesh and blood as silicon is to carbon. With those strange protuberances, like stumpy limbs, rings of stony bone, and chunks of splintered carapace, they were bursting out of their shells. These vast creatures, either dead or simply growing at a rate imperceptible to man, loomed in no discernible pattern, as though they had broken through the earth's crust arbitrarily, like mushrooms, with all the debris of their upheaval still scattered around them.

What relevance they were intended to have to human life was quite obscure, but humans, resourceful as ever, had found ways to live in them. In among the crags and shelves of cement, in the cracks and crevices, on ledges and under overhangs, people had burrowed like Cappadocian cave dwellers, installing windows, running pipes, stringing wires, growing flowers, and even flying flags. Through the fallen scree that surrounded these mountainous growths, paths wound their way tenuously, and on the edges of stagnant pools small gardens had been started. I stared unbelieving at this nightmarish scene until the sky lifted. Walking on, I came to a smaller, older building in the Victorian style, with stucco facade, broad steps, and a portico, the only one in this Neolithic park that had been designed and built for human beings. Through a doorway that, in happier times, had been carved and embellished with thought and feeling issued a stream of happy people, led by a bridal couple carrying flowers. Enlivened by a saxophone and an accordion playing jolly, tootling music, a wedding procession set off on its winding way among the monstrous mastodons of masonry. The sun broke through, and I had to admit, as the phantasmagoria receded, that all was not yet lost.

In the lobby of the Rhapsodia, which had become my headquarters, I met one of the Israelis, a short man with a belligerent air. I introduced myself and explained why I was there, expecting him to show some interest, but he seemed to regard my approach as an intrusion. I asked if he had seen any part of the town that dated back to the old days.

"It's all gone. Everything is changed," he said abruptly, and moved away as though I were about to touch him for a loan. The girl at the counter, though, said there was one street, the Calea Naţională, that was part of the original ghetto, and there was even a synagogue there. I saw from the map that by sheer chance I had missed it, and I went out to look, turning left this time instead of right.

The Calea Naţională ran south, away from the hotel, for about half a mile. Just one side of the street and a small square had escaped the general demolition. There was virtually no traffic, and the street was busy with all kinds of people, but my eyes were riveted to the Gypsy women. It was my first encounter with them, and I watched with pure amazement. There were large numbers of them moving along the pavement in groups, many dangling babies on their out-thrust hips. It was as though the street had become a stage and I had a part in an opera—*Carmen,* of course. They wore costume, rather than clothes, in the sense that although the colors were as varied as they were brilliant, the cut was uniform—a voluminous, swirling pleated skirt and a tight bodice over a blouse. And they were as uniform in their persons as in their dress. However different they were as individuals from one another, they all had a quality, part appearance, part manner, that was exclusively theirs. They moved with a vigor that made everyone else look tired and old, talking and laughing vivaciously among themselves. But what was most remarkable was the way they moved among the rest of us as though we did not exist.

Eventually, when I could take my eyes off the Gypsies, I walked up and down the old street. At the near end of this row of two-story brick buildings, set apart in a fenced enclosure, was an ancient Orthodox church. But the prize was in the middle of the row, obviously intended as a flamboyant centerpiece. It was a wonderful Baroque fantasy of stuccoed architecture called the Hotel Rareş (Ra-resh).* It was only twenty-two feet wide—I had to pace it out to believe how narrow it was—but it rose an extra story above the rest, and into this slim slice of facade every conceivable ornamental device and conceit had been crammed.

Each of the two upper floors had bay windows that projected out over the pavement. The two bays were joined together and extended above and below to make a single unit that was like half a vertical tube or capsule. This was decorated with insanely elaborate plasterwork, topped by monumental sculpture suitable to a Victorian mausoleum, above which a Botticellian Venus perched in her elaborate shell. Every windowpane—and I counted almost a hundred—was irregular in shape. A tiny but fantastically ornate balcony divided the two floors. Every variety of fruit and plant was plastered over this confectioner's reverie, in wreaths and garlands and bouquets. It was easy to imagine that at a propitious call from the gods, the whole thing would ascend into the heavens, like the gondola of a celestial balloon, with the chosen guests waving from the balcony, blissful and misty-eyed on their way to immortality.

No doubt the ground floor had once been equally ornate, but the entrance had been replaced by newer steel-framed doors and windows, advertising hot dogs, hamburgers, juices, and hot drinks. I stood opposite it for almost an hour, drawing it to the best of my ability. It was dated 1907, and I hoped that my father might have seen it before his father took him away to Brăila.

The synagogue was a disappointment. It was around the corner on a side street, and looked like a garage with a Star of David painted on one of the beige-colored doors. It was padlocked, seemingly deserted, with nobody in sight. Since it was the Sabbath, I assumed that it must have fallen into disuse.

I walked around the back of the row of old houses and found that point of view just as interesting. Alternate houses stretched back as much as a hundred feet, like the teeth of a comb, so that the rooms could get light from the side. Many rooms had their own access by external staircases and landings, and in most cases these had been encased by paneled wooden passages, richly built and decorated like furniture with their own little

---

*Peter Rareş was a hero of the great days of the kingdom of Bukovina, in the sixteenth century.

windows, so that the backs of the buildings were alive with these mysterious hidden runs. Sadly, it was all falling into terminal decay. The back of the hotel had actually fallen down, and quite recently too, it seemed, for the nicotine-stained paint on the doors leading into the vanished rooms was unweathered.

I had noticed an appealing restaurant near the post office, the Miorița, and went there for some lunch. It was clearly the luxury restaurant of Botoșani, with a few prosperous patrons eating in a cathedral hush, but I sat and ordered what turned out to be steak and kidneys. Close to my table was a young couple, talking a little more loudly than the rest, and in Italian. I listened unashamedly, and heard him say that she had given him rare moments of joy. They had ordered champagne, were holding hands, and drank alternately from their glasses and from each other's eyes.

Somehow, something the waitress said, either deliberately or accidentally, created a connection between me and the couple and we began to talk. In their happy state they were feeling generous to the world, and when they had asked me why I was there, they offered to help me. It was later that I learned the details of their story. She, Lucia, was Romanian, originally from a village near Botoșani, who had married an Italian textile executive and gone to raise a family in Florence. But her husband had betrayed her for another woman, and now she had returned to free herself of him. Her companion was a driver for that company, which also had a factory in Botoșani. They were lovers, but he would be leaving for Italy the next day.

Lucia said she knew a teacher who was an authority on the history of Botoșani and spoke both French and English. She would arrange for us to meet. Meanwhile, since her friend Vittorio had things to do, she would come with me to the market to change money. The rate I had been offered by the waitress was too low, she said. I ought to get at least thirteen hundred to the dollar. Feeling that I might be getting somewhere now, we walked to the market, but her information was wrong and I could get only eleven hundred, the same rate I had been getting all along.

However, we happened to run into her cousin, Florin, a good-looking, slightly bloated young man with Italianate features and an expansive manner, who insisted that we come up to his apartment for a drink. As we went, they asked—and this was all going on in pidgin English, Italian, and heaven-knows-what other idioms—where I was staying. Pretty quickly came the idea that I could stay in his apartment and save money, while paying him something that would be a great help to him. There was no bed, but I could be made comfortable on the floor. If it got me into contact with people, I was all for it, and agreed. We drank to the arrangement with a disgusting mixture of Nescafé and Coca-Cola, which they said was the fashionable drink of the moment, and went down to the street, where Lucia left me. She promised to fix me up with the teacher and told me to meet her at eleven the next morning at the Allegro, a café across the road from the Rareş Hotel.

Florin insisted on buying a beer. He was very warm—kissed me on the cheek, took my hand, and shook it. He had hot, moist palms. We walked to the Unirea together, where a different and very nice woman at the desk allowed me to get away without paying for that night. She even spoke English. Florin came up to my room, and then said he would return soon, when I had finished packing. He was going to fetch his daughter, and would be back.

"How soon?" I asked. "An hour?"

"Oh no, half an hour, maybe."

I packed and waited two hours, but he hadn't returned. It was late afternoon, and I decided to go to his apartment in case there had been a misunderstanding, but stopped downstairs to talk to the clerk, who, that day, was an attractive woman in her thirties, with dark hair and eyes and a sad but sympathetic manner. She spoke some English and it was easy to talk with her. She had come to Botoşani from Bucharest, she said, when she was eleven. It was before all the old buildings had been swept away by Ceauşescu.

She remembered how pretty it used to be. It was a Jewish city, she said, all the men in black with the curls, and in an almost exact repetition of Anatoly's phrases, she added how very clean it had been and that the Jews had "made it work." But people began flooding in from the villages to work in factories. The collectives were forcing them off the land. The old houses became slums, but people were glad of the opportunity to make a living. Then the demolition began. Ceauşescu pulled down all the old buildings to build those apartment blocks, and soon almost all the Jews had emigrated.

Now it was the opposite. The factories were shutting down, and the people were going back to the country. Life was very bad. She had been married for five years to a construction engineer, but he earned very little money. They had a tiny apartment, but "not what to put in it." And now she was pregnant.

Then she said: "This man you came with, you know he was drunk. When he comes down from your room, he goes back to the bar to get more beer."

I walked over to Florin's apartment, but there was no reply, so I returned to the Unirea, took back my room, and decided to forget the whole thing. Twenty minutes later, Florin arrived with a little girl, unable to understand my problem, determined to get me out of the Unirea and, when that failed, to get me over to his place for supper. He had a bunch of gladioli in his arms and said he was late because he had wanted to get flowers for his wife. If he was drunk he was holding it well, and the child was delightful, so I went with him, curious to see how this thing would play itself out.

There were usually people along the street trying to make a penny selling one thing or another. One woman had a bathroom scale you could weigh yourself on for a hundred lei. Another man had a collapsible card table and was selling lottery tickets, just as the veterans did in Paris after the war. Florin's daughter, a pretty thing of eight, had a winning ticket worth two hundred lei, and went to collect. Then she bought jelly beans with her winnings.

On the way home, Florin talked about his plan to bring a used Mercedes into Romania, and asked if I could help him when I went back to Germany. I said I doubted I would have time. He explained how profitable it would be and how badly he needed the money. In his apartment he poured some beer, put some potatoes on to cook, and then took his daughter to bed. When he returned, he was still talking about the car. Then he asked if I would let him sell me some lei, because he needed dollars. I said I didn't need any more, having just bought some, but he pleaded with me.

"Just ten dollars," he said.

"Well, what will you give me?"

"Six hundred to the dollar," he replied, or just over half the going rate.

I shook my head. This was getting ridiculous. He went into another room and brought out a black-bound Bible, asking me to admire it, saying how beautiful it was. I couldn't understand the motive. Was he going to swear an oath or sell it to me? He began again to talk about the car. Then he went back to the dollars, looking at me with puppy eyes. I could not get him off the subject. His only interest now was to find a way to make some money from me, and finally, acutely embarrassed to find what I hoped might be a friendship turn into such a sordid affair, I put a ten-dollar bill on the table, said he could have it, and left. I went back to the Rhapsodia for dinner and found I still had his Bible in my hand.

My friend was still behind the desk, and I told her I had found the synagogue locked. She said she had heard there was some kind of Jewish center or office in town, and found the address. It was at the other end of the Calea Națională. She also had a present for me. She had remembered to bring her English-language textbook with her. I could borrow it and try learning from it in reverse. I thanked her, and asked if she knew someone who could teach me Romanian. Yes, she said, she had a friend and would ask her that night. I asked what had happened to the Israelis. Her face showed a flicker of distaste. They were touring the countryside and would be back next day, she said. They were very difficult people. Nothing pleased them.

So I took my book into the restaurant. I had discovered another wine that I thought was even better than Murfatlar, as well as being cheaper. It was a golden wine, probably a chardonnay, called Cotnari Fetească. I ordered a bottle and sat down to eat and to consider my prospects in Botoşani.

There were always the city records, although I didn't know what they could tell me that I didn't already know. I knew where the town hall was, but it would be closed until Monday, and even then I would have to have someone with me to interpret. A twenty-dollar bill might be enough to overcome the resistance of a reluctant bureaucrat, but I simply wasn't doing well enough with the language to understand what was being said. Until then, all I could do was thrash around blindly in the hope of coming across someone, like Lucia's teacher, who could help. The day's experiences had made me very skeptical, but there was nothing to be lost in trying.

I was up early on Sunday, and went to the Calea Națională. It was too soon to expect Lucia—in fact, I hardly expected her at all—and the Allegro was deserted. I went looking for the Jewish Center and found an office door on the fourth floor of a newer building, but it was locked, as were all the other offices, of course, as was the synagogue.

To pass time I visited the Orthodox church. Some work was going on there. Scaffolding surrounded the doorway, and planks lay across the threshold. I walked in and saw scaffolding supporting a high platform all around the interior walls. Two men were working with lights in the cool gloom under the vaulting, apparently restoring ancient frescoes. I called out in English and French. The younger of the two replied that he spoke French and would be down in a minute.

He was a slim, handsome, and poetic-looking man, with a mass of dark wavy hair billowing above deep-set dreaming eyes. A mustache and clipped beard framed a generous mouth and a set of extremely bad teeth. I explained that I was an English writer visiting my father's birthplace, and he introduced himself as Ion Achiţenie (A-kee-*tsen*-ee-e), a painter from Bucharest. The other man was his father, an art professor, also from the capital, who was in charge of restoring the church during the vacation months.

We talked a little about his work. Some of it, he said, was not truly restoration. In places, nothing was left to indicate what might have been lost, and they were simply creating what they thought appropriate. I told him about a similar but larger church in Suceava that I had visited briefly, where Ceauşescu or his minions had ordered the frescoes to be coated with cement. I had watched students chipping it away, flake by flake. Ion and I established an easy relationship quite quickly, and he soon revealed his discontent with the situation. He was only doing the job, he said, to please his father, and cursed the day he had agreed. After months of struggling with bad conditions, not to mention the difficulties of working for one's father, he was desperate to be back with his wife and family and his painting. Although we were speaking quietly, his resentments echoed strangely in the ancient calm of this three-hundred-year-old building.

Making a joke of it, I told him the story of my experience with Florin and the problem I would have explaining to his cousin Lucia what had happened.

"If she turns up," I asked, "would you be willing to translate for me?"

He agreed to do it, and we went on talking for a while until it was time to go. Astonishingly, Lucia arrived at the same time I did, but I had the peculiar feeling that she was there only by chance—that our meeting was an accident. I brought her over to the church and put Florin's Bible in her hands, while Ion briefly told her my story.

She looked somewhat distraught at the news, but said only that she had phoned Dohoroi, where the teacher lived, and learned that he was on his way here now by bus. We could all meet later, at eleven-thirty. But first she was going to her last rendezvous with Vittorio. Then she left.

I thanked Ion and asked him what he made of the whole story, but he replied cryptically, and rather impatiently:

"That's life. If you want to achieve something, to create something worthwhile, you can't let these mercenary problems dominate."

His father had come down off the scaffolding, a tubby, genial man with a full gray beard and hot hands, like Florin's. I invited them both to have dinner with me at the Rhapsodia that night. The old man responded enthusiastically, and I went off to try the office and the synagogue again, but made no progress.

At eleven-thirty I was back at the Allegro. It was not much of a place, really, but in a town with so little happening, you could see its attraction. A wall had been broken through to join two small rooms. There were metal tables and chairs, a counter for a coffee machine in one corner, and there was rock 'n' roll. That was it. I sat down, ordered an espresso, and waited for Lucia.

It was a long wait, and painful on the ears. Two yards away, between me and the coffee machine, a man was shouting. He was strongly built, in the prime of life, Italian-looking, with a jaw like Mussolini's, and he was addressing his companion across the small table. He was glaring at him, grabbing his hand, poking him, waving his arms around, and literally screaming his words with anger, sarcasm, derision, contempt, the whole spectrum of violent emotion, yet the other man simply sat and listened as though he were in a normal conversation.

I tried to distract myself from this madness by making notes and watching people pass by. I observed that the receivers of the public phones were chained to the wall. A drunk, uttering elaborate courtesies, tried persistently to engage me in conversation. It occurred to me, as I sat there hot, deafened, and covered in flies, that Lucia and Vittorio were probably screwing lustily for the last time, oblivious to everything. Well, good luck to them, I thought, with considerable magnanimity.

After an hour I had had enough, and went out to stand in the sun and fresh air. Down a side street I caught sight, briefly, of Vittorio walking briskly away in the distance before he turned a corner. Shortly afterward Lucia, arm in arm with two other women, came down the street. Again I had the feeling that my appearance there was a complete surprise to her, but if so, she recovered rapidly. She said the *professore* had not arrived. She didn't know why. There was no reply from his home. Perhaps he was prevented from leaving, but we could both go to Dohoroi together, on the bus, that very afternoon. No problem. At three-thirty she would come to the Rhapsodia and get me. We repeated the details several times, to be sure. She sounded utterly convincing, as though she were looking forward to it.

I went back to the Rhapsodia lobby, which had become my headquarters, to work at the language. Lucia did not come, and by four it was obvious that she had bowed out of my life, if indeed she was ever in it. The desk clerk continued to be friendly, but she had come to the end of her resources. She would not be free, she said, to come to the archives with me, and knew nobody who could. Her friend was not free to teach me. She phoned the Unirea to see if we could find the woman I had talked with the previous day, but she worked only once a week, and nobody knew where she lived. I thought I would persuade Ion to come with me the next morning. I would again try the Jewish office and the synagogue. And if none of these avenues led anywhere, I would pack my bags and get out of here.

Dinner was not very successful. The father came wrapped in a raincoat, which he refused to take off. He drank a lot and was ebullient, but nothing made much sense. Ion talked, with some cynicism, about his life in Bucharest, reminding me that my problems were relatively of no account, but he did say he would come to the hotel the next morning to help me at the town hall.

My last night at the Unirea was strange and disturbing. Rushing through rapidly shifting dreams, I emerged into wakefulness at three in the morning, feeling very cold, with three words resounding in my mind, like a Hebrew incantation—*Shadam, Shitam, Maikem*—but they meant nothing to me. In the room above, people were laughing, arguing, jumping around. I heard two women giggling and protesting, and a man's voice making statements. The noise went on and on, subsiding and welling up again. I couldn't rouse myself enough to protest, nor could I sleep. I was depressed at the failure of my attempts to make something happen, feeling myself being drawn into a morass of futility. I felt I was wasting my time in Botoşani, and yet I hated to leave with so little achieved. The whole city seemed steeped in failure and resentment, and my own miserable thoughts circled around in my mind for a long time before I fell asleep.

After breakfast at the Rhapsodia—coffee, bread, butter, and *"gem"*—I sat in the lobby with my books. Ion did not come, and I was wondering whether

I could even bring myself to go and fetch him when a small woman in middle age came up to me, rather tentatively, and asked me, in French, whether I had plans to go anywhere that day. She was one of the Israelis, and she explained that a taxi was available to take her around the monasteries, but it cost too much for her alone. She was looking for someone to share the ride. I explained why I couldn't come and what I was trying to do.

"Oh, what a pity," she said. "Just yesterday we were going around the cemeteries with the Jewish community here. You could have come with us. You would have heard something, perhaps. But today they are all at the theater. We can go and ask them now if you like."

I was delighted at any opportunity. She introduced herself as Miriam, a librarian from Jerusalem, whose family had originated in Botoşani. We walked to the municipal theater together, where they were in the middle of some kind of presentation, and we waited a moment until we could speak with the leader of the community. He was an old man, short but upright, with a toothbrush mustache, in a brown striped suit with enormous padded shoulders. She explained my situation and he was remarkably unsympathetic, seeming to have no interest in the matter. He told her there was nothing he could do.

Somewhat taken aback, she said to me: "Well, at least we can go to the Starea Civilă."

"What's that?" I asked.

"It's the registry, the archive," she said, and we walked not to the huge concrete town hall where I would have taken Ion, but to the same nice little building where I had seen the marriage procession emerge two days earlier. I took it as a good omen. The registrar, a serious man of about forty-five, listened to Miriam with obvious respect and ushered us immediately into his office. Without any interruption or delay, his assistants produced the relevant register, a bound book for the years around 1897. He turned a number of pages, and there was the original record of my father's birth. It happened so quickly and correctly, I was taken by surprise at the emotion that welled up in me. I was extraordinarily affected. The handwritten page had for me something of the quality of, say, a piece of clothing that a loved person might have left behind. I wanted to touch it, run my fingers over it. Instead, I just looked.

Miriam translated what was written, and there was more than I already knew. She told me that Simha Sin Leizer had been thirty-six years old and his wife, Miniha, thirty-two. He was a man of property, she said, and his profession was roof building. Not much, perhaps, but enough that I could begin to construct some kind of a story about them. There was no more I wanted to do there now. I thanked the registrar, and we left.

I felt tremendously grateful to this nice woman, and explained how frustrated I had become.

"Oh," she exclaimed, "here they have the mentality of slaves. They are descended from slaves. But tell me. I have to change some money, and I was going to go to the bank, but maybe you know a better way. I am afraid to change money on the black market. In Timişoara I was cheated. They played a trick on me."

I said I would be glad to help her at the market, and we walked there together. The men I had changed with earlier were not to be found, and I didn't like the first two who presented themselves, but then a young man with glasses and a fresh complexion came up with some words of English. Miriam, whose English was as poor as his, joined in the conversation, and soon the deal was done, but we went on talking. He was named Traian (Try-*ahn*), after the emperor Trajan. He was a law student, he said, at the university of Iaşi (*Yahsh*) and changed money only to help supplement his stipend of ten dollars a month.

My plan was to travel to Iaşi that afternoon. Since Warsaw I had been leaving messages for Ginny with my cousin. In L'viv, at the George'a, I had finally contrived to make contact with her at a house in Slovakia where she had been staying for a while, walking and sketching. We had arranged to meet again at the Continental Hotel in Iaşi, in a couple of days' time, and then go on to Brăila together. Anxious to get more information about Iaşi, I asked Traian about places to stay, and he mentioned two hotels I already knew about. What chance was there, I asked, of finding someone with a room we could rent for a few days? Immediately he said yes, he did know someone. Just as quickly, I felt my confidence drain away. Another of these enthusiastic promises; another castle in the air that would collapse in damp disillusion. I almost didn't want to know. But he insisted that if I wanted the room, we would have to rush to the post office straightaway to make a call. He knew a chemical engineer with a small apartment.

His practical urgency carried some conviction. I said good-bye to Miriam, who still had business at the bank, and went with Traian, waiting for the scheme to collapse at every moment. He would not have the right change for the phone. The phone would be out of order. He would not be able to get through. The person, whoever he was, would not be there. The room would not be available. The building it was in would have fallen down.

No doubt I would have gone on to more sinister scenarios if he had not started talking on the phone. Then he smiled at me and handed me the receiver.

"Here, you can talk."

"Hello," I said.

A woman's voice replied: "Hello. I am Manuela."

It was like a movie script.

"I will meet you at the bus station," she said.

"But how will I know you?"

"Traian has already described you."

"Well, what do you look like?" I asked.

"I am very pretty," she said with a confident laugh. "Don't worry, I will find you."

Traian was looking very satisfied, but I had seen that expression on other faces, on Florin's face, and I was still ready for the plan to dissolve into nothing. However, I was going to Iași anyway, I was packed, so again, what was there to lose? He invited me to lunch with him at a "not so expensive place." We passed by the church, and I said good-bye to Ion. He made no reference to his offer of help. Evidently he had forgotten all about it, and I didn't bother to mention it. Things had turned out fine after all. I said my good-byes at the Rhapsodia, got my pack, and walked with Traian along that travesty of an avenue toward the bus station. He knew the bus schedule by heart, since he used it all the time.

Traian was from a peasant family that owned five acres outside Botoșani, and he was proud of having made his way out of there by his own efforts. Before the fall of Ceaușescu, he said, it would have been impossible. Until then only people with money and connections could get places at the university. Unfortunately, he now faced the prospect of graduating with no job to go to. We came to a stadium on the left of the road. On the pavement, workmen had started a fire with a heap of car tires to melt some tar, and the acrid black smoke was blowing in all directions.

We dived under the stadium into a small restaurant, where the smoke couldn't follow us. He recommended that I try *ciorbă* (*chor*-buh) *de burtă*, a creamy soup made with tripe that is a Romanian specialty. It was very good, and as I ate he told me about his interest in cooking. Did I know of any Romanian restaurants in America? He would like to be a chef, specializing in Romanian dishes. Did I think people in America would be interested? He asked every imaginable question about America and, like so many, dreamed of it as a paradise. Other Western countries did not qualify for this halo, perhaps because they were too familiar. I was the first "American" Traian had met, and nothing I said would convince him that I was not.

Traian took me to the bus station at two, with an hour to wait. Before leaving for work, he made sure I took the right bus by confiding me to a man from his own village, Mihai, who was also waiting. Mihai sat by my side, stolid and unyielding in his patient silence, with that jaunty Frank Sinatra hat on, and as time passed, an immense crowd gathered in front of me. There were many older women, in scarves, shawls, aprons, and boots. One of them slept near me, spread across her baskets. Her hands lay among the vegetables with fingers splayed, looking like freshly unearthed roots.

If all these people were waiting for the same bus, I knew there would be no chance for me, but Mihai's face remained passive and untroubled. Five minutes before three, most of them crowded into other buses, and when mine arrived, Mihai got me on it without difficulty. It was crowded at first. A rather coarse-looking kid sat next to me, but he got off at Tîrgu Frumos.

On the bus I had three hours to myself to contemplate the significance of what I had learned that day. Simha was a roof builder. That sounded much more prosaic and accessible than having to imagine him in a caftan and a large black hat trimmed with fox fur. He was "a man of property," meaning, I supposed, that he owned his house. It pleased me to think that he was a practical man who made things—very much after my own heart. I imagined him now as more pragmatic, particularly given the move to Brăila. After all, Brăila was a long way off, in a quite different environment, a commercial city on the Danube delta. Had the move been successful or disastrous? How would I ever know? The fact that my father had been able twice to visit England from Brăila struck me as a good sign. I planned to go there, to see what it was like, to get a sense of what he had grown up with. As for finding traces of the family down there, I was practically certain it would be impossible. After all, without a birthdate, in Botoşani I would have gotten nowhere. In Brăila I would have nothing—no births, no deaths, no marriages, and no address.

As we approached Iaşi, I prepared myself for the probability that there would be nobody to meet me at the other end. Traian's promises still seemed too good to be true. When we were almost there, it became clear that the bus was arriving half an hour early, and it made me sick to think that I would have to wait again for someone who wouldn't show up.

This time I had dared to put my pack in the luggage compartment, and as I stood by the bus to collect it, a woman next to me pleaded with me for help. She had too many bags. Would I help her carry them to the "*mashina*" parked nearby?

Great, I thought as I walked alongside her carrying her bundles. Who is going to recognize me now as the "lone American" off the bus?

Then a young woman stepped in front of me and asked, in Romanian, whether I was from Botoşani. Miraculously, it was Manuela. And, yes, she was very pretty.

# Chapter 24

She had raspberry lips, pearly teeth, a light complexion bursting with health, dark hair, and neat, regular features. She was tightly packed into a suit of thick gray flannel. It was a little heavy for her figure and must have been rather hot, but it seemed not to slow her down. She had a playful manner and a lot of self-confidence. I was very pleased to see her.

Locating Manuela's apartment was like bearing down on a military objective. It was identified by coordinates: floor number 5, of building number 11, in section G, of block number 913, at number 11 Strada Împăcării.* Admittedly, the street had a name, but the Strada Împăcării was a major artery running out of Iași, and its personality was anything but cozy or homelike. The address accurately described the sterility of her neighborhood. It was in the logical line of progression, from Suceava to Botoșani to Iași, more inhuman and on a bigger scale with each step.

Fortunately, I did not have to make my own way through the maze. Manuela and the two girlfriends who had come with her (in case Traian should unwittingly have delivered her up to an ax murderer) hired a taxi.

---

*The numbers have been changed.

After fifteen minutes of chaotic driving, we rattled across a long bridge over railway lines and got out on a broad, straight highway. Apartment blocks of bare concrete stretched on down the road as far as I could see through the hot haze of exhaust.

She said a vivacious good-bye to her friends, and the two of us walked across some dried ground where once there had been grass, into a block on our right. Before we entered the lobby, she warned me, quite fiercely I thought, that we must not talk on the staircase. Nor must I ever get into conversation with anyone I might meet coming or going. If I should pass someone on the stairs, I was to grunt meaninglessly and rush on. We walked up many flights of bare cement steps to the third floor.

Once we were inside she relaxed. She was very proud of her apartment. It had been difficult to get, and I think there had been some inevitable irregularity involved that made her vulnerable. If it were thought that she was subletting to a foreigner, she might lose it, and there were people in the building who might profit from reporting her. It was my first experience of the mild paranoia that seemed to flavor all life in Iaşi.

Manuela was a working graduate in her late twenties, whose job was analyzing steel samples, and her father was a much respected older engineer and Party member, who had certainly helped her with both her job and her apartment. As a result, she was able to rise to a standard of living that a poor undergraduate in America might just consider acceptable. Her home consisted of a small living room, an even smaller kitchen, and a tiny bathroom, and she had made the best of it with what was available. There were the standard convertible couch, a settee, shelves of board and brick, and a black-and-white TV. The bathroom functioned, a blessing not to be underestimated, even though hot water ran for only an hour or so in the morning and again at night. For me, as for her, it was luxury living. I got it at a price I could afford and which to her was a true windfall—all of six dollars a day.

She had taken time off from work to meet me, and could not stay long. However, her laboratory was not far away, and we walked out together. All the ground-floor premises of the apartment blocks had been intended to house shops, but scarcely any of them seemed to be functioning, and it was not easy to spot those that were. She showed me where I could buy a few essentials, such as bread, butter, eggs, milk, and so on. They were not always available, she said, but at least I would know where to try. I noticed, with relief, that she said these things without that air of complaint or resignation that I had found so prevalent in Romania.

Since the vegetable market was near her place of work, we went there too. Here at least there was a reasonable choice of fresh food. Most of the usual vegetables—potatoes, carrots, onions, eggplants, peppers, and tomatoes predominated—could be found on the stalls, and the square was bordered by small lock-up shops where, among other dairy products, were snowy mounds of a delicious goat cheese, called *telemea* but pronounced "tele-m-a-a," with a strong bleat on the end. Compared with any French market I knew, it was a listless and impoverished affair, but it would be a joy, especially for Ginny, to have fresh vegetables and a kitchen to cook in.

I had two days to occupy before Ginny arrived, and I spent them wandering around the city and exploring the surrounding hills. It was easy to get around in Iaşi. Transport was plentiful, if erratic, and tram lines ran everywhere. The trams themselves were in the last stages of dilapidation, and barely functional. For me this merely added to the sense of adventure, particularly as the fare was minuscule. But for the people of Iaşi, to whom the fare was a considerable amount, it must have been depressing. There were buses, also, that seemed to serve the edges of the city. They had been brought directly from Germany, where they had already run through their useful life, and still had the original German advertising painted on them. Passengers were no doubt relieved to know they could have their TVs, stereos, and VCRs repaired instantly at 8 Bruckenstrasse, if they could only discover where and in what town that was.

Iaşi had once been the capital of the Moldavian kingdom and is Romania's oldest university town. There are a few wonderful sights—some churches, and the National Theater—but I saved them up for Ginny's arrival. From my point of view, knowing that I would not be able to get to Bucharest, Iaşi was most useful as an opportunity to get some sense of city life in Romania.

The center was an awkward mix of old and new, but at least there was some sense of cultural continuity. Beyond the center, however, the outlook was dreary, and I walked around Manuela's neighborhood in a state of constant astonishment. In most European cities tremendous efforts have been made, during the past hundred years, to separate people from the various services that are otherwise likely to kill them or be offensive in some way—things like trains, holes in the ground, sewage, and refuse. Here there was no such sentimental mollycoddling. For example, to catch a tram to the railway station from Manuela's apartment, one turned left outside her block and eventually down a slope, through the rubble of unfinished building, to the level below the bridge. Here one stumbled across a succession of railway tracks, including the main line from Budapest to Moscow. Under the bridge itself, alongside the line, is a permanent flea market known as the Russian Market, but here were no samovars, icons, or balalaikas, only the most pathetic and useless-seeming things—defunct batteries, unstoppered bottles, worn slippers—which by their very nature evoke lives of desperation.

Winding around the streets of Iaşi, raised a few feet above ground, is a system of large and ugly pipes, partly covered with tattered insulation. My first guess was that they carried gas; then I thought sewage. Finally, I discovered that they delivered hot water from the power plants to the apartment blocks or, rather, not surprisingly, most of the time didn't.

Behind Manuela's block was a neighborhood of older, smaller blocks seeming quite habitable by comparison. On a quiet street with shade trees I passed a basketball hoop, its backboard crudely painted with all the American icons: NBA, Harlem, Chicago Bulls, and Los Angeles Lakers. Beyond that was a canal with dirt banks, charged with every kind of rubbish, including car batteries and tires, broken baskets, vegetable refuse, plastic, and scrap metal. Running along the other side of it, very obtrusive and ugly, was one of those thermal pipes, rusted and split in places, insulation hanging from it in shreds. A small footbridge crossed the canal, and here the city effectively ended. A path ran up a steep hillside and brought me to a place high above the city where there was a monastery and a cemetery, both very peaceful.

It could be quite bracing to be confronted with the realities of city life at every turn, but when the reality is mostly collapse and decay, it is physically and emotionally exhausting. My thoughts took me back again to life in London during the war, when buses often didn't run, buildings were hidden behind sandbags, hot water was rationed, the roads were sometimes a mess, and there were unexpected holes in the ground. At least then we knew the hardship had some end in view. In Iaşi, where a trip to the vegetable market can take you through the almost insupportable stench of anaerobic decay from mounds of abandoned garbage, there is no one to tell you that this is your finest hour.

Now that I had a place for Ginny and me to experience together, however briefly, some semblance of Romanian domestic life, I was all the more impatient for her to arrive. However, our good fortune brought with it a difficulty. She was to have found me at the Hotel Continental, where, sight unseen, I had once booked a room. Now I would have to find her, since she couldn't find me. At first this would seem to pose no problem at all, since it was simply a matter of leaving a message at the hotel. On Thursday morning I caught the usual tram—which had an appearance rather like two of those old, worn tobacco tins from the twenties joined together: dented, darkened, and with the paint rubbed off.

The hotel stood at the confluence of two main streets, overlooking a small open square. The first impression was good. It looked fairly imposing, and across the square was a paved café terrace, raised above the traffic and protected by a nice old carved stone balustrade. Sitting at small tables in the shade of colorful umbrellas were people who seemed to be actually enjoying themselves. It was a tantalizing glimpse of the life of relaxed enjoyment that the Romanian people would be so good at if only the cycle of corruption, delusion, and despair could be broken.

The hotel lobby was a disappointment—small, dark, and clinically uncomfortable. Worse, the staff appeared to consist of one rather disaffected woman, who knitted and answered phone calls only in Romanian. She let me know that she would be there just a short time. Then others would come. I could leave a message, but—she shrugged—who could tell what would happen to it? Most of the rest of my day was spent in the tram between the station, where I tried to intercept trains Ginny might be on, and the hotel, in case I had missed her. Long after nightfall I stood on the station platform watching the crowd disperse from the last train due in from the West. I trundled rather hopelessly back up the hill to the hotel. The original custodian was back, but the lobby was otherwise as deserted as it had been all day. I settled in to wait, rather dismally, only a little worried at the thought of the hundreds of miles of dark desolation that separated us and the nasty things that could happen in them. After all, she had no reason to be concerned if she was late or delayed. I would be comfortably ensconced in my hotel, wouldn't I?

From the adjacent parlor I heard the phone ring several times. Then it rang again, and something in the tone of the receptionist's voice made me walk over. She waved a dismissive hand at me, as if to say "No, no, it's not for you," while trying to mouth a word that made no sense to her. It sounded like *saké*. I knew she was trying to say Sharkey, Ginny's last name, and I seized the phone. She had missed the train in Cluj because of a time change and lost a day. I felt an enormous sense of relief, and gave her Manuela's phone number. The following night, I met her at the station.

Ginny's green eyes took in the tawdry scene with some wonderment. It was late evening again and dark as we skirted tracks and potholes, walking through blackness and occasional pools of lurid sodium light looking for a tram that never came. She remembered it afterward as having been an industrial scene, although there was actually no industry there, just degraded buildings. The entire journey through the nighttime squalor, including the bad-smelling lobby and the staircase where we maintained obligatory silence, amazed her. She said later it reminded her, perversely, of New York, a city she loves. Then we were in the apartment and spent a wonderful night relating our various discoveries. I told her what I could about my journey, and she talked about strange and wonderful hikes, how she had scaled a mountain once climbed by Marie Curie and Lenin, about the many fine people she had met in Slovakia, the days she had spent sketching in the Tatras, the family we should visit on our way back, and a thousand other things.

Manuela came to see us the next day to make sure we were comfortable in her nest. She took all the obstacles of Romanian life in her vigorous stride. She taught us how to make *mămăligă*, which is a kind of hominy or polenta that has sustained the Romanian peasantry for hundreds of years, and in her enthusiasm, she made it seem like a delicacy. She was eternally optimistic and in control of her life.

Her brother, Radu, was not so fortunate. I had met him on the afternoon of my arrival. He was a big man, three years younger than she, and a moving mountain of frustration. He had not applied himself so sternly to the acquisition of papers and qualifications and, as a result, was utterly demoralized and forced to live with his parents without work or money. Even so, he somehow managed to smoke Marlboros. He spoke no English, but Manuela translated for him and seemed to agree with everything he said, including his opinion that girls should stay out of politics and concentrate on being sweet and pretty.

According to Radu, it was still dangerous to speak out against the government, even in idle conversation in the café or on the tram. The police, he said, were the same people as before, and in a way it was worse now, because they felt their position to be threatened. He thought that the whole revolution had been a sham. He believed that the Communists had thrown Ceauşescu and his followers to the mob and then taken over in the name of democracy. Iliescu and the other new leaders were the same old wolves in sheeps' clothing.

The local police—he called them *sectorists*—had a room in each *sector*, or block, where they did their business and carried out interrogations as before. He described how he and three friends were taken in by them simply for standing together on the pavement, and how two of them were beaten up for protesting.

"They know how to hurt without leaving marks," he said. "Their bosses don't like it if they have to deal with complaints, but it's only an inconvenience. They have no trouble fabricating evidence to acquit themselves of blame."

He was desperate to get out of Romania, and saw me as his ticket to heaven (inviting more ironic reflections). The country, in his eyes, was rotten, and dominated by criminal entrepreneurs financed by money that had either been stashed away by the Communists before the revolution or stolen by Gypsies in the West. This last tale was so extraordinary that I asked about it several times. What did he mean? Oh yes, he said, it was well known that the Gypsies went to the Western countries and stole large amounts of goods and cars and used the proceeds to finance all these new businesses.

When I looked around Iaşi later, I saw the kinds of places he was referring to, shop premises that had been taken over to sell small luxury items from the West, like stereos, cameras, cassettes, cool clothes, whisky, and of course Marlboros. Almost invariably, the shop fronts were red and carried Marlboro ads. As for the Gypsy money story, I heard it from others, too, but I neither looked for nor was shown any evidence. To me it sounded utterly improbable, at least on the organized scale that Radu and others visualized it.

However, I understood how important it was to have somebody to blame, and this time it couldn't be the Jews. Iaşi was the scene of a terrible pogrom on June 29, 1941. Some twelve thousand Jews were massacred in the streets, under the auspices of the green-shirted Iron Guard. Naturally, after that, there were very few Jews left in Iaşi. So if it wasn't the Jews, it had to be the Gypsies?

.   .   .

From Iaşi we traveled on by train. At a station farther south, where we waited for a connection, a party of Gypsies had taken possession of the platforms. Not that we were ejected or threatened in any way. Our presence was simply ignored. We and the other passengers were of no account. Ginny and I were sitting with our backs to the station building, looking across two sets of tracks to another platform. On the far side of that platform a train stood ready to depart. It was an older Gypsy woman who first caught my attention. She stood on the far platform looking across to our right, shouting insults. She had her hands on her hips, with her head flung back, her body easily adopting the exaggerated stance of a stage actress, and she was letting rip at a middle-aged man with a big paunch, in a conical felt hat and tunic.

He was strutting up and down our platform, responding as best he could, although he was plainly drunk. The two were about fifty feet apart, and their raucous voices dominated the station. I couldn't understand a word, but I was sure they were denigrating each other's anatomies and personal habits. He pranced with his belly wobbling, while she cackled and howled and struck ever more dramatic poses. Nobody else said a word.

A younger woman sat on the step of one of the waiting carriages and watched the match, alert but seemingly unconcerned. My gaze was held mainly on a fourth person, a younger man, who was reclining on a bench on the far platform. As the howls of mirth and contempt swirled about him, he lay back against one armrest, his legs up on the seat, and smiled.

He was, I think, the most handsome man I have ever seen, in that particular Valentino/Sheikh of Arabee genre. Every aspect of his physical being was exceptional. His skin was not merely flawless, it also had the color, the luster, and the depth of the finest caramel. The hair was a shimmering mane of thick, wavy licorice-colored strands. The black eyes flashed. The nose was long, straight, and aristocratically molded; the mouth, full yet firm; the jawline, exquisite. In short, he was the model of the fairy-tale prince. Through quite ordinary clothing, by the merest suggestion, his body showed itself to be equal to his head, and without moving a muscle, he managed to convey an extraordinary degree of self-confidence and detachment.

Whatever his relationship to the squabbling elders, he was plainly so far above them in his thoughts that they might have been jesters brought on for his entertainment. The smile was at the same time tolerant and contemptuous, and I waited for him to say the few words that I was sure would shut them up, but he simply lay there unmoving, letting the charade continue.

Farcical as their role might be, the couple screaming at each other were at least members of the court. We, foreigners and Romanians alike, were nothing. We did not exist except as objects on the landscape. It was an uncanny experience, viewing them, as it were, through a one-way mirror. I found their complete indifference to the rest of us stunning, and slightly menacing, as though a family of tigers had wandered in from the jungle. It was Bruce Chatwin, I remembered, who claimed that in the Romany language the word for "settler" was the same as the word for "meat." I could believe it. Then, and later, I thought Gypsies looked at me in the same way that I might look at quail and rabbits around the house—of no particular interest unless I was hungry.

The truth is, I found their wild freedom of action appealing. The wonderful insouciance of the man on the bench was something that I, as a young man, would have given a great deal to possess. In fact, it was just that feeling that I sometimes discovered in myself on the three big journeys I have made in my life.

You could not hope for a more blatant example than the Gypsies of a minority regarding itself as a race apart. To that extent, they resemble the "mediaeval," inward-looking Jewish communities Sitwell observed, but there the similarity ends. A great chasm of difference divides them. On one side, I see the Gypsy, unashamed, loving, laughing, playing, running through all the tricks he knows to survive. On the other, I see the Jews, the Catholics, the Lutherans, all the guilty ones, struggling, through ritual and repression, to free themselves, while doing all the desperate little things they also must do to survive. Untouched by guilt, the Gypsy lives and dies fundamentally unchanged. Because of our guilt, and our daily duels with the devil, we the guilty ones can become anything or nothing, glorious or gross.

Perhaps my father, as a young man, watched the Gypsies as I did and said to himself, Why do I need to carry this burden through my life? I'll let it drop, be like them, and escape, as in a fairy story, only to discover, when he thought he was free of it, that the hump was still there, growing and twisting his actions into those old, familiar paths.

Would that be my story too? Was it possible that the tones and textures of a culture were so potent that they could have been transmitted to me by my father when he was himself in denial of them; and all in the first five years of my life? Or was the chant of the cantor somehow encoded in my chromosomes, resonating through my bone marrow, calling me to the synagogue through my blood? In the presence of these strutting, howling Gypsies my thoughts became untenable, even nonsensical. I was aware, quite suddenly, of the effort I had been making to worm my way into what I imagined to be a Jewish consciousness. It was a foolish, even offensive exercise. Regardless of my appearance, whatever that might suggest, I was no more Jewish than was Ginny. Nor did I need to be. From that point on, even as I delved deeper into the Jewishness of my father, I dropped the charade and became free of it.

Everyone needs some guilt to work with. I believe in the value of transforming and transcending guilt. And everyone needs a moral and ethical structure within which the work has to be carried out. Despite the unreligious upbringing my mother gave me, she handed down quite enough guilt and structure, inherited from her own sternly Lutheran upbringing. But she herself, I believe, ultimately failed in that higher test. Even in her later, more prosperous years, there was little joy in her life. For me, the issue is still in the balance, but now I see that one other ingredient is also needed, as a solvent, perhaps, to accomplish the task. It is what I have been pursuing, unwittingly, for half my life: It is the Gypsy in me.

# Chapter 25

We rolled into Brlila in the evening, after dark. Ginny had heard somewhere in her travels of a good hotel on the Piaha Traian, and we took a bus there. I felt a strong sense of comforting familiarity and relief when we got off the bus. It came from nothing more than the shape of the square, the houses around it, and the music that was drifting through the warm air from a corner café, reminding me of the soft Mediterranean nights of Provence. I visualized breezes blowing up the Danube from the Black Sea and imagined an iodine tang in the air.

We walked around the square twice before admitting that the hotel we were looking for no longer existed. I had been trying to ignore the hotel that all too obviously did exist. The Hotel Traian was the only eyesore on the square, a twelve-story concrete box that rudely interrupted the harmonious Victorian facades, but it was late and, over Ginny's objections, I insisted on going there. By then the music had stopped, the café had shut down. I lay in bed for a long time, repenting my error, kept awake by a defective water pump that was cycling on and off at eighteen-second intervals.

In the morning, determined to flee from the Traian, I discovered the Hotel

Pescăruş, a short walk away down a broad avenue named after Romania's favorite, and for all I knew only, poet, Mihai Eminescu. Eminescu had been haunting me through every town in Romania, just as Shevchenko dogged my footsteps in the Ukraine. I later discovered that there were many other poets worthy of a statue, including several from Brăila who, being Jews, had to write under Romanian-sounding pseudonyms. But Romania only recognizes Eminescu, who was famously anti-Semitic, and insists on presenting itself as a one-poet nation.

The facade of the Pescăruş was a taller and broader version of the Rareş in Botoşani, but less intricately wonderful to my eye. Inside, it was old and grubby, every inch of it needing renovation and every pipe needing to be reamed out. The linen was gray, the halls were smelly, and still it was a delight after the Traian. The proprietor was a wily fellow with an ingratiating manner, who would have me believe that he kept the hotel open as a service to posterity. When he offered to change money at an unfavorable rate, it was with the intimation that I would be doing my bit for old Brăila.

"They would have pulled it down. They still want to," he said, and hinted at plots, subterfuges, bribery, and corruption. I had to admit that its loss would be a tragedy. I was glad to play my part in saving it, but doubted that the rescue attempt could be kept up much longer if nobody took care of the plumbing.

In Brăila I thrashed around much as I had in Botoşani, with even less hope of success. I could not imagine where or how to start. I found the library, and I did my best to dig out newspapers, almanacs, even phone subscribers from the twenties and thirties. I learned much about the town, but nowhere did I find any mention of a Leizer family.

Brăila had been a great port. In the nineteenth century, it had been the major port in Europe for handling grain. This came as a surprise, though some bells rang faintly from my geography lessons, reminding me that the broad, fertile plains of Hungary and Romania were once the "breadbasket of Europe." All that wheat apparently used to be shipped out to the Black Sea from Brăila. In 1927, long after its heyday, Brăila was still handling 3 million tons, much of it destined for Britain. Then the USA and Canada began manipulating the market. Nineteen twenty-eight was a disaster for Brăila. Exports dropped to two hundred thousand tons, and in the following depression years trade never recovered.

It crossed my mind briefly that this had some significance for me, but I couldn't pin it down. Looking further back in the almanacs, I found telephone numbers for 1913. Among the full-page ads for champagne, and for McCormick of Chicago, were many Jewish names: Abramovic, Ackerman, Aresalom, Dreyfus, Eskenazy, Ehrenstein, Goldberg, Garfunkel, Lewy, Lubisch, Lowenstein, Mendel, and so on, but no Leizer. There was even an H. Simon living at 158 Griviței, but that was surely a coincidence. In those days, at the age of sixteen, my father could not have had his own telephone.

At the Traian Hotel, an English-speaking clerk suggested I try the regional museum and gave the name of the curator. She in turn passed me on to a Madame Vidis at the town archives, which were closer to the port and, for some reason, heavily guarded by armed soldiers. She appeared to be helpful, but without an address or any birth records to look up, she said she was helpless. She did, however, tell me that there was a synagogue in town, not far from the Pescăruș.

I had the same disappointing experience at first as I had had in Botoșani. The synagogue, on a side street called Petru Maior, was locked up behind a fence. True, it was a much more substantial building, painted in the same beige color, with a cupola, but it appeared just as deserted. I could find no sign that any of the adjacent buildings were in any way connected with it. I determined that this time I would find a way to make some contact with the Jewish community.

Meanwhile there were other things to do. Trying to get a sense of the maritime history of Brăila, we walked around the quaysides. Much of the port was obviously in disuse, but a small freighter was docked there, its deck loaded with hay bales. An armed soldier leaned indolently against the rail of the gangplank smoking a cigarette, and at that moment a crew member came ashore. From him we were able to learn that it was a Saudi Arabian ship and the hay was destined for Syria; it brought home to us how close to Asia and Arabia we had come.

At the corner of our avenue and the Piața Traian was a pretty nineteenth-century theater, where we watched a lively cabaret. The burlesque characters were so well acted that even without the language it was amusing. We took a bus to Tulcea, farther along down the Danube, cruised the delta on a small boat, and spent the night and the next morning with a marine biologist, who took us around the museum where all the species of the delta were displayed. There were other pleasures and indulgences to be enjoyed, but behind them all the melancholy was pervasive. Everyone projected it. Everything was running down. Wildlife on the delta was disappearing, fish stocks were vanishing, buildings were deteriorating, businesses faltering, roads crumbling, and faith in the future was a cynical joke.

On Sunday morning I sat on a bench in the Piaţa Traian, near the fountain. Two women with shopping bags came along and began pulling up the grass from the lawns and stuffing it into their bags, presumably to feed rabits or geese. A man came to clean his shoes with water from the fountain. A boy, appearing slightly deranged in a tight sweater, with bare feet and a fluffy new growth of hair on his bald head, hustled bulkily past me. Six small and ancient riding toys were lined up by the fountain—four kinds of horses with pedals, wheels, and legs, a car, and a brown bear. The ringmaster of this little menagerie was a corpulent man in long leather boots, a leather jacket and cap, and a camera slung from his neck. He swaggered a little in the manner of James Earl Jones and made a great performance out of photographing three giggling girls. The toys stood forlorn and unwanted. Everything appeared unreal, in suspense, as though I were watching scenes from a bygone age that had miraculously defied the wand of time and were lingering on until some absentminded wizard somewhere discovered his mistake.

I wandered around the streets, looking at the little stuccoed villas marooned in trash and weeds, where the phony princes and "Excellencies" of Bucharest once used to sport themselves in summer. Everything was a "might-have-been," nipped in the bud. It was difficult not to submit to the languor and fatalism, but that evening I made a new acquaintance, one of the few who seemed to have an optimistic, entrepreneurial approach to things. He told me immediately where the Jewish community office was, around a corner from Petru Maior, where I hadn't been.

I visited the office the next morning, on our last day. We had decided that we could not afford to spend more time in Brăila. A gray-haired woman with a matter-of-fact manner received me and understood my situation, although we had no easy shared language. She said the only person who could help me was a Mr. Obermann, who would be there later. It was not clear to me that he lived nearby, but as I waited and looked around, I saw his name on a brass plate outside a house opposite the synagogue, and rang the bell. After a moment a buzzer sounded, and I went in.

I faced a corridor and a flight of steps up to the next floor. I was impressed by how clean, polished, and preserved the woodwork, stair carpets, stair rods, and painted surfaces were, by contrast with everything I had experienced during the last months. There was nothing ostentatious or expensive about it. Just clean, neat, and in good repair. It was a minor revelation. An elderly woman with a strong, balanced presence stood at the top of the stairs. When we had established that French was the language of choice, she said she was Mr. Obermann's sister, Beatrice, and that he would be out shortly.

Her brother, Silo Obermann, was a man of medium height, slim, clean-shaven, with vigorous gray hair and intelligent eyes, which occasionally faded in confusion but then sharpened again dramatically as he recalled what he was seeking to remember. I learned later that he was seventy years old. His mouth frequently seemed on the verge of smiling, and he would have had great need for a sense of humor in his life, particularly in the forties, during the war, when he was drafted into a forced-labor battalion and had to build dikes and shovel snow with little food or clothing in subzero temperatures.

All these details came later. At first he listened to my story, told in French, and then led me around the corner to the office, where he brought out a great bound record book. He asked me when I thought the family had come to Brăila, and I guessed, without any basis, that it might have been 1910 or later. He began to leaf through the pages, and I could not at first understand what he hoped to find, but suddenly he said, "*Voilà*. There they are."

At first I said, "No. Not Lazar. Leizer!" Then I realized he must be referring to the same family. It recorded the birth of my uncle Simha (unknown to me, of course) in 1906, to Simha and Miniha Lazar. She was forty-one. He was forty-five. It was an exact fit. And they lived at Strada Rahovei, number 357. They had changed the spelling of their name to assimilate better. And even as I thought about it, I remembered from the very distant past that my mother had said something about an uncle in New York.

But the revelations were far from over. Silo took me out into the sunshine, at the corner of the street, and looking away to the avenue as though he were actually seeing someone, he said:

"I knew your father."

For a moment my heart sank. That would be impossible, I thought, but then I understood.

"You mean Simha. You knew Simha, my grandfather?"

"Yes, Simha. He was an important figure. He was the *procurist* at

Granimex, the man who buys the cereals for export. Granimex was one of the biggest companies, maybe *the* biggest. It belonged to the Halpern brothers. Yes, he was a big man in the business establishment, a most uncommon man."

Silo remembered him as being of medium height and fair. If I had not known of the red-haired, red-bearded Jews of Bukovina, I would have been thrown into doubt again, for my father was dark, but I knew the coloring was quite possible. He had stayed, said Silo, almost to the end, and emigrated to Israel just as the war began, when he was almost eighty.

I tried to find out more, but Silo had been very young, only a boy at the end of my grandfather's career. Even so, I asked just how strong their devotion to the forms of Judaism were. I told him my mother's account of the "kissing prohibition," and Silo sighed.

"Ah, yes," he said, "those Jewish laws," as if he regretted them himself. He said that for all he knew, Simha may have been devoutly Orthodox, but in Brăila the Jewish community was quite liberal. In all outward appearances they had assimilated to the general population. There were no black hats and gaberdines in Brăila, and Jews were not distinguishable from other citizens except by the features God gave them.

I was eager to take Ginny to visit Simha's house—if it still existed—where my father had lived as a boy, and Silo agreed that I could come back later and talk to him some more. Rahovei Street was one of the curved streets that lay just outside the center of town and was only a five-minute walk away. It was cobbled and, like the other streets, was badly degraded. We dodged past rubbish heaps, potholes, paving stones tilted by subsidence, and open manhole covers, but some trees still struggled to survive. The houses were single-storied, with flat roofs, and were separated from one another and the road by wrought-iron fences. At first sight, number 357 did not seem very imposing, colored as it was by the universal grime and dilapidation, but as I stood before it and tried to imagine it in its better days, I saw that it had a quite ornate facade. Corinthian pilasters framed the large windows of a room that filled the width of the house. A path ran back alongside the building, and it was possible to see that the house stretched a long way, far enough to accommodate many more rooms.

As we stood there, a man came out of the house and I explained that my "*tata*" had lived there. We could not converse, but I understood that he thought the house was a hundred years old and that it was a good house. It might even have been Simha who built it. At least he would have seen that it had a good roof.

I supposed that the family might have been there when my father was seven, or even earlier. I could picture him here, the same age that I was in Nazi Germany, playing with gentile friends, running up and down on these same cobblestones, perhaps with a hoop or a ball. It was not much, but in months to come, it became deeply satisfying to be able to place him in that street, in front of that house.

Silo Obermann told me in more detail later about the life of Jews in Brăila. Anti-Semitism has always been a fact of life in Romania. Though anti-Jewish laws were abolished in principle in the late nineteenth century, active discrimination persisted, and Romania's greatest statesmen and cultural figures were openly proud of their prejudices. Yet there was always ambivalence. King Carol conducted a notorious liaison with his Jewish mistress, Lupescu, and for a while went into exile because of it. But he was eventually brought back, with Lupescu, when political instability between the wars increased. It was difficult for Romanian business to function effectively without the Jews, and at the higher levels of management and banking, Jews were not troubled until fascism got into its stride.

In the thirties, threatened by the growing influence of the Green Shirts, a paramilitary movement akin to Hitler's Brown Shirts and Moseley's Black Shirts, Carol abandoned democracy altogether and imposed a dictatorship of his own. From then on, Jews became second-class citizens at best. They were excluded from higher education and from better jobs, and they began to leave in large numbers. Of the eleven thousand Jews in Brăila, six thousand emigrated before the real persecution began. By then, said Silo, all my family had left.

While there were terrible massacres of Jews in Bucharest and Iaşi, in Brăila there were no wholesale killings, only mistreatment. After the war, under the Communist regime, discrimination continued blatantly, relying on quite absurd excuses. Silo laughed at the recollection of a particularly humiliating device called *conjonctivite minoritaire*. This was a fictitious disease, which Jews were supposed to carry, that disqualified them from any career, such as the army, where they might contaminate their comrades. Before too long, most of the remaining Jews had gone.

He had one more thing, though, to add about my grandfather, now that he knew me better.

"He was very hard in business. A good man, and much respected in the community, but he drove a very hard bargain."

On reflection, that seemed only natural. In a shrinking market, only the fiercest players would be able to stay in the game. Perhaps one day it would be possible to find out more about Simha Lazar and how he had turned from a provincial roof builder to a major figure in the international grain trade. Meanwhile, I had seen and heard enough to make a real person of my father. During the ensuing months I turned the pieces of his life over in my mind, drawing on their significance and trying to fill in the blanks. Gradually, I began to feel that I knew him.

# Chapter 26

*T*he next morning we took the train to Transylvania, part of Ginny's intention being to do research on the Dracula legend for a writing project. Count Dracula, otherwise known as Vlad Ţepeş, or Vlad the Impaler, was born, it is said, in a building in Sighişoara that is now a restaurant. The journey took most of the day, and we were delighted, when we arrived, to find a stone village built on steep slopes that seemed not to have been disturbed for centuries. The small tourist office got us a room with a German-speaking family of ancient Saxon descent. There are still many in that region, and occasionally they celebrate their ancestry by dressing up in traditional costume—lederhosen and dirndl skirts—to dance and carouse with the rest of their tribe.

We went out that night to the Dracula Restaurant. It was well patronized, since the food was unusually good and consisted of pork cooked in more different ways than usual. Across the general hubbub, I saw three men sitting at a table against the far wall and behaving in what seemed to me to be a comically conspiratorial manner. Perhaps my imagination was excited by their appearance, which had a Disneyesque quality. One was a big, bluff man with gray hair who could have passed for a man of distinction, but only on a provincial repertory stage. Another was small, dark, and nervous, with a sly, impish grin. The third was a caricature of the absentminded professor, a burly, fubsy man in an overtight sweater, who peered out above his bushy beard through little, round spectacle lenses in wire frames. They would have made ideal antagonists for Tintin.

Although they spoke with exaggerated discretion, I could hear that they were British, and in the heat of my enjoyment, and not a little wine besides, I indulged myself by casting them as the rogues they appeared to be and inventing potted biographies for Ginny's amusement. The next day, when Ginny was away visiting Bran, driven by a taste for dark and awesome castles, I met the same trio on the gallery at the top of the old clock tower.

A little ashamed of myself, and unsure whether I had perhaps been talking too loudly the night before, I made myself as pleasant as I could and told them what I was up to. They had an interest in agriculture, apparently, and we discussed Romania's potential corn harvest, which was not promising. The small, foxy man, now wearing a gamekeeper's hat, spoke with a broad country dialect. The taller man wielded an Oxbridge accent, but sparingly. The other was silent. After a while, having revealed nothing about themselves, they made as if to leave.

"Are you on some kind of reconnaissance?" I asked, determined to draw something out of them.

"Oh, very much so," said the little fellow, with rather too much meaning, and thrust a small square of cardboard into my hand as he started down the steps.

"Our card," he said, with that sly grin of his.

The card read:

LORD HARLECH
BROGYNTYN
OSWESTRY
WALES

Could I have been so wrong about them? I wondered. Going down to the street a few moments later, I passed them at some distance on the cobbled square, and Mr. Fox raised his hat to me and winked. I speculated a long time on what their business might be. My letters to Brogyntyn were unanswered, and it was only much later I learned that Lord Harlech—the only

Harlech that any one of them could have been—was dead, killed in an accident the year before we met. Now I suffer from an even greater curiosity about what three confidence tricksters—for surely that's what they were— could have been doing in Sighişoara. The story makes a fitting footnote. For much of the journey I had struggled through language difficulties to understand, with partial success, what was going on around me. Here I met three men whose language I understood perfectly and who left me completely mystified.

Sighişoara's remarkable state of preservation gave the illusion of prosperity, and I was persuaded that there would be food in the shops. Having the use of a kitchen, I went out to buy some for the weekend, anticipating no problem. I thought eggs would be nice, and set off down the picturesque cobbled alleys, hoping for bread and butter, perhaps even milk as well. At the only shop nearby, I obtained sausage but nothing else. No points are scored for sausage in Romania. I scurried off to the town center, already sensing that I was late, and entered an *alimentara.* My request for eggs and butter was greeted with dismissive scorn, as though I had asked for coal and caviar. A customer, however, pointed down the street, made a left-turn gesture, and mentioned a red house. Heartened, I examined every shop on the left of the street. In the first, where there was a cold cabinet, several women laughed good-naturedly at me. At others I was brusquely banished. By this time I had noticed people coming toward me with heavily loaded shopping bags. Remembering how in other towns, when I had been carrying a bag, passersby often tried to glimpse its contents, I grasped the technique.

Like ants on a trail, they seemed to be bearing their booty from around a distant corner, and so, like any empty-handed ant, I raced against the current. But after five minutes the trail unaccountably fizzled out, with no shops anywhere in sight. Casting around aimlessly, as ants do, I finally went off down another narrow street and wound up where I had started. There, in deep shadow, I saw a shop I hadn't noticed before. Two girls in white were selling sausage. They said *"nu"* to eggs and butter, and added, I think, that such things were unheard of in Sighişoara. I was so impressed that I almost bought more sausage, but a man in the queue objected, saying that there were indeed eggs and butter to be had, and offering to show me where.

We walked the same way I'd gone before, and he pointed into a dark doorway. Inside was a woman weighing out plums and potatoes, and behind her, an hour after I had begun my search, I saw a tray of eggs. Butter, however, there was not. Cooking oil had not been available for a month. Bread was sold out. Milk I hadn't tasted since Germany. I could have had it in Poland, but not in coffee, which is the only way I want it. All instant coffee was called Ness and was always black and awful—the Black Ness Monster. Here and there you could find chicken from California. Why that and nothing else I don't know, but it seemed to confirm my worst thoughts about the chicken industry.

Ginny returned the next day, imbued with Gothic mystery, and we moved on to Sibiu, and to climb in the Făgăraş (Fuh-guh-*rahsh*) Mountains for a couple of days, before leaving the country through Arad to Hungary. Even in Romania, the improvement as we moved westward was noticeable. The towns were in better shape, the food a little more varied and plentiful, the people appearing to be better off. Our judgments were relative measures, of course. It was easy to forget the enormous chasm that still divided them from Western standards.

Our visit to the home of "the Impaler" had reminded me, for the first time in a long while, of the war in Bosnia. As we returned across Europe, the earlier, wilder thoughts from my solitary walk sprang back into my mind. In Hungary I saw English-language newspapers, with more news of the continuing human tragedy. The Serbs had mounted a great offensive on Sarajevo, which seemed likely to fall, although it was supposedly guaranteed by the United Nations. The suffering there was intense. The Clinton administration had resisted tremendous pressure to intervene. The Vance-Owen peace plan seemed more futile than ever. There was talk of air strikes, but NATO and the UN were at loggerheads. Evidence of atrocious massacres was mounting. The notion of a people's crusade to stop it all kept bothering me. I was really surprised. I thought I had gotten rid of it, but it would not leave me alone. I had come out of my wilderness with a vision, and I could not tell whether it was inspired or crazy.

I was well aware of the implications. If I pursued it, I would be accused of arrogance and naïveté on a stupefying scale. And if, despite the scoffing and jeering, I found a way to go through with it, I might in the end be responsible for leading people, myself included, to their death. I wanted to get home to my son. I had been given good news in Budapest about an invention that a Dutch company was developing for me, and I was eager to follow it up. A book of mine about to be published in New York was getting promising advance notices. I had many excellent reasons to forget about Bosnia and get on with my life, but I could not shake off the fear that if there was any chance, however slim, of affecting the issue, I would regret forever having let it slip. What did it matter, I said to myself, if the world took me for a vain and dangerous fool. And why shouldn't there be large numbers of people who felt as I did—that the politicians were powerless, and that this thing must be stopped before it contaminated us all. I thought of the quarter-million or more people who had read *Jupiter's Travels* and felt sure that they, at least, would know I was sincere.

After many days of this exhausting internal debate, I gave up fighting against my conviction and thought instead about how to follow it. By this time we were in Berlin. I had not said anything to Ginny, thinking it would frighten her, for my sake if not for her own, but I told her now. She was not openly critical, but I think she hoped I would come to my senses. For two days, from a friend's apartment in Charlottenburg, I phoned anyone who could help. As Ginny watched, with growing concern, I called friends and contacts in London, Paris, New York, San Francisco. To give them credit, they listened and none of them laughed. Manfred was willing to give it a try. He told me that in fact it had already been tried, though on a very much smaller scale, in August. He didn't know what had happened to the people involved, and assumed they must have abandoned the project. What they all wanted was to hear from somebody close to the action, who would say: "Yes, it will work."

Finally, I called Mickey Wallaczek, an Austrian friend who had driven supplies into Sarajevo at considerable risk, and told him of my idea. He was not dismissive, but the next day, after meditating on the matter, he assured me that the opposition would be too strong; things had gone too far and the forces for war and death were too committed. With a strange mixture of relief and despair, I finally let go. Later I had to explain the episode to myself. I recalled then that sixteen years earlier, coming back from the longest journey I had made or will ever make, I went through a similar period of evangelical enthusiasm, believing I had something important to tell the world.

Solitary travel has a peculiar power for those of us who are suited to it. Along with the discovery of one's own true nature and the opportunities to express it comes a corresponding freedom to think thoughts that might be judged odd, threatening, even reprehensible or lunatic, by one's familiar acquaintances. It is perfectly natural that prophets should come out of the wilderness bearing revelations, but all prophets are not created equal.

Some are giants, some are mediocre, some are of piddling stature, and some are nuts. The difficulty is that neither they nor those who receive their proclamations can really tell until much later.

Mine is not the pure asceticism of a single-handed yachtsman or a Saint-Exupéry. There is no lack of people in my journeys, and they are my principal interest. Nor am I a dispassionate voyeur peering into other people's lives. Strong connections are formed rapidly, and they nourish me. What distinguishes them from my relationships with friends and family at home is the absence of those expectations which I find burdensome and restrictive, demanding that I behave in certain predictable ways. These emotional transactions trade too heavily on guilt and obligation for my taste. When I travel alone, I experience a sense of freedom that occasionally comes close to ecstasy.

The physical freedom is an important element—the ability to stay or go as one pleases, to follow whatever the inner voice suggests, is a rare luxury in most lives, and there must be many who have never allowed themselves to experience that inner-directedness—the compass in the heart. More valuable to me even than that is the freedom to be whoever and whatever you feel yourself to be rather than having to conform to the patterns that others are accustomed to expect.

As Allen Ginsberg put it: "You can be anyone, this time around."

Of course, not everyone would find this cultural weightlessness agreeable. I seem to be more than usually uneasy with the identities that others pin on me. Perhaps what I lost when the war interrupted my childhood was my own sense of who I was, and so I don't care to have others tell me. At the age of eight, it is thought, we all lose something significant—what Robert Bly describes, by way of metaphor, as the "golden ball" in his book *Iron John*. Certainly his ruminations on fatherhood are right on the mark.

Fatherlessness is a plague that has ravaged much of European society for almost a century. My mother lost her father to disease, but had he survived that, there is every chance that the first great war would have claimed him, as it claimed so many millions of fathers on both sides.

I have no doubt that my mother's fatherlessness contributed to mine. Neither she nor her four sisters did very well with their husbands. Two were never married. Marta's husband ran away to Peru, and Mimi's husband seems to have dwindled away in her very ample shadow, for I never heard much about him. As for my uncle Fritz, the only man in the family, he is described as a pleasant but unreliable fellow with a weak heart, who died young. It is hardly surprising that in Germany's emasculated interwar society, much of Hitler's power derived from the mesmerizing effect he had on women.

My mother's inability to negotiate her marriage with my father would also have to owe something to that history, just as the eventual failure of my own marriage must, in some measure, be a continuation of the same story. And so it goes on. One single male child, myself, begets another single male child, my son, who, while not exactly fatherless, has for his dad a man who has tried, with limited success, to invent himself as a father, not having known one.

I would give a lot to discover how my father, Henry Simon, managed on his second attempt at marriage, but the trail has faded away. An advertisement in the personal columns of *The Times* produced no response, but then those once august columns have now shrunk to relative impotence. Somewhere, I suppose, I have two authentically Jewish half sisters, who could tell me a great deal, but it is unlikely now that I shall find them.

Released from my obsession with Bosnia, I returned to California with Ginny and during the following months began gradually to put my father's life together. The significance of the collapse in Brăila's grain trade in 1928 became clear. That was the year the grain brokers in the City of London went bust, the year that my father lost his job. I thought he must have used his family connections in Brăila to get that job in the first place, when Britain was importing the cereals that his father was exporting. Possibly those early trips to England were made on grain ships that traveled through the Mediterranean. He might even have made stops along the way—at Alexandria, perhaps, or Marseilles, such marvelous windows on the world at that time. And finally to have arrived in London, a city so very different from what it is today, when it was the hub of a great empire, still functioning as a relentless machine of law, order, and effective business. How impressive that must have seemed to him, knowing how corrupt and arbitrary were the powers that governed his life in Romania. No wonder he took to the bowler hat and umbrella like a duck to water.

Soon it occurred to me that perhaps he had never really made that break with his past, never really detached himself from his family. Maybe he had hidden from them the fact that he was married to a "goy." Then he would have had to hide from my mother the fact that he was still in touch with his family. I could imagine all the convolutions of deception so easily. Out of the past, another hidden memory disclosed itself, of my mother telling me that he used to go to Paris for weekends alone. Did I actually remember the words "dirty weekends," or was that something I added out of my own pornographic schoolboy vocabulary? I do remember that he came home once with a strangely delicious sweet called "halva," all the way from Paris. And once he took me to the circus at the Crystal Palace before it burned down. It was a fantasy of glass, red plush, and indoor trees. But he didn't take my mother.

I read about his death in the newspaper in 1962. Oddly enough, it was *my* newspaper. I was the features editor of a national daily newspaper, and in the proof of the first edition, on the front page, was a "squib," a single-paragraph story, that was bound to be dropped later, when more important news took its place. The headline read BBC MAN FOUND DEAD.

We had his name slightly wrong, of course, and his age, too, but there was no doubt it was him. The BBC connection was known to me.

"Good Lord," I said. "My father's dead."

I wouldn't have known that I had said it, but a young cartoonist called Mike Molloy, standing nearby, remembered it very well much later—as one of the stranger things he had observed in his long career.

Sometime after that, his executors sent me a check for a hundred pounds. It seemed like a very impersonal token, and not enough to make a difference. A hairbrush or a pair of cuff links would have been better. Who *did* get the cuff links, I wondered? After all, his other children were both girls. I must have learned about the girls from the nice elderly man who came up from the country to see me. He was a friend of my father's at the BBC. I think his main reason for seeking me out was to counter the unfortunate effect of the one hundred pounds. He wanted me to know that my father was better than that, but he didn't provide much evidence beyond saying: "He was a good man."

With some faint stirring of curiosity, I asked him if it would be a good idea to meet these half sisters of mine.

"Later, perhaps," he said. "Yes, later."

He didn't sound very convincing, and I needed little excuse to drop the idea. It embarrassed me, and I forgot all about it. The only other piece of information that stuck with me from that short encounter was that it was not at the BBC's London offices that my father had worked but at the establishment in Cheltenham. At the time, I didn't know that Cheltenham was generally understood to be a euphemism for Military Intelligence.

Today, when I see him standing, rather reserved, at the back of that sepia-toned party of happy tennis players, I feel a flood of sympathy for him. Sepia suits him. There is so much feeling concealed in those old photographs, and I have searched them long and carefully, hoping for tears or blood, or honey and ashes. I have looked long at my old passport picture, too, attempting to know that five-year-old boy I once was, who looked back at me with bruised bewilderment, until the tears came to my own eyes. I cried for him, but some of those tears were for my son, too.

Obviously, my father was a man of ability, with a gift for languages, who longed to fit into a society that could accept him and use what he had to offer. No doubt after the flagrant anti-Semitism that was commonplace in Romania, he wanted to appear as neutral as possible in England. Did he adopt my mother as a disguise? Hardly, for he neither took her out nor shared his business life with her.

Her strong, rebellious spirit must have intoxicated him, being so much what he perhaps aspired to, until he discovered that he could not control it and that it clashed painfully with instincts buried in him that he could not eradicate, old Jewish precepts on the role of the wife and mother in the family. If I was made the victim of his mistake, I am in a very large and good company. And if, as a result, I have made my own versions of the same mistake, well, that is after all the way of the world. I cannot know how well he learned from his experience, but he had at least one friend anxious to tell me that he was a good man. I am willing now to believe it.

His role in Military Intelligence, I am sure, was not remarkable. It began, I believe, in the war, when his ability to monitor broadcasts in Romanian and other languages of the Axis powers must have been useful. Probably, he went on doing the same kind of work during the Cold War. Routine work, no doubt.

His appetite for chicken liver pâté and other rich food probably undid him. One of the few small complaints my mother did pass on retrospectively was that he kept butter for himself at home but wouldn't allow any for me. She mentioned it as an example of his meanness, but ironically, he probably did my constitution a favor. He had a stroke not long before he died, which, his friend told me, had left him partially paralyzed. He was evidently unwilling to be a burden to his family and to the society he admired so deeply. He took control of his life for the last time—attached a hose to the exhaust pipe of his car, and died in his garage at the age of sixty-five. It was that act which brought him briefly onto the front page of my newspaper one fateful afternoon in 1962.

For many years, that dramatic act was what came first to my mind when I thought of him, but now that I have found a way to bring him, however ethereally, to life again, his suicide recedes in importance. I remember, suddenly, that he used a lotion on his hair called Bay Rum—the sweetly pungent scent of it is in my nostrils as I write—and, yes, he wore a hair net in bed, to hold his hair in place. In the only photograph I have of him, his decorum alongside the others is marked. Outward appearance must have been crucial to him, I think. Not to have command of his actions and his appearance would surely have made him feel terribly insecure, and a bad stroke could have been too much to bear. I wonder what he thought of in that garage; I wonder if he thought of me.

# Epilogue

If today I could drop from the sky to any point along the trajectory of my journey from Russia to Romania, I think I would choose a place where there are geese on green grass. It is that image which returns most frequently to my mind, and floating in with it are visions of great space, innocence, and simplicity. It could be in the hills of Bukovina or anywhere north of there, but most probably I am thinking of Rohatyn.

Occasionally, I hear from Leda and Michael. They have had to spend their summer holiday working to harvest crops in Poland in order to get by. Their life is extremely hard and I do not envy them, yet I am powerfully attracted to the possibilities suggested by their circumstances. It is the peasant in me that is drawn to the land and the Gypsy in me that believes the grass is greener, but the strongest pull comes from the fantastic notion that there, where Western time stood still, is a chance to live the last fifty years all over again and do it better.

I daresay my idea of investing the former Yugoslavia with a nonviolent army was extravagant and unworkable. It was certainly far too late. But in a general sense, a transfusion of people from West to East would be a healthy phenomenon. The business opportunities, risky though they seem, are all too obvious to our big corporations and financial buccaneers. It is upsetting to think of the vacuum being filled so completely by large, alien commercial interests. Enterprising individuals with only modest amounts of money could do rather well there, and counter the tendency for foreign exploitation. Many of us thrive in adversity, and perhaps the ideas and experience we would bring with us might help counter the terrible trend to ethnic puritanism. It is too late now to recover the lives lost in Bosnia, or even to re-create the mixed communities that once lived in peace there, but it is certain that there can be no peaceful future in these enclaves of ethnic purity, whether there or anywhere else.

I cannot deny my father's wisdom in choosing to leave Romania when he did. I wish that if he were that age today he could consider going back, but Jews are no more welcome now than they ever were, it seems. Even as I write, while Hindus are building a temple on the outskirts of London, the Polish president's religious adviser is spewing out absurd anti-Semitic messages. Whenever opportunistic politicians like Milosevic or Karadzic are in trouble, they will resort to the same old stratagems, whipping up hatred with charges that will seem all the more credible when the enemy is a foreign devil.

Michael tells me that he has bought a piece of green grassland and that he now considers it mine and my son's. Leda tells me that her indefatigable uncle Viktor is growing vegetables on it, and they are doing well. Both Michael and Leda are very eager to see my son, to have me bring him there. Part of me wonders why, but I am also delighted, and a little nervous. Will he see anything of what I saw over there? And in the larger sense, will my discovery of my father help him discover his?

Perhaps this book will be published in Ukrainian. Then I will use my *kupón* royalties to buy a fine white goose to put out on my green grass, and one day we will all go there to celebrate, with my goose and Viktor's vegetables. I hope— and not just for Ginny's sake—that the vegetables are organic.

## ABOUT THE AUTHOR

Raised in a blockaded England during World War II, TED SIMON grew up with a powerful urge to explore the world and abandoned a career in science to become a journalist. He wrote about his four-year journey around the world by motorcycle in the book *Jupiter's Travels,* which has been published in six languages and was an international bestseller. His other books are *Riding Home, Grand Prix Year,* and *The River Stops Here.*